D0903420

PORN

Also by the author:

Sex and Gender: On the Development of
    Masculinity and Femininity
Splitting: A Case of Female Masculinity
The Transsexual Experiment: Sex and Gender,
    vol. 3
Perversion: The Erotic Form of Hatred
Sexual Excitement: Dynamics of Erotic Life
Observing the Erotic Imagination
Presentations of Gender
Cognitive Science and Psychoanalysis (with
    K. M. Colby)
Intimate Communications: Erotics and the Study
    of Culture (with G. Herdt)
Pain and Passion

ROBERT J. STOLLER, M.D.

PORN

MYTHS FOR THE
TWENTIETH CENTURY

HQ
472
.U6
S86
1991

Yale University Press
New Haven and London

Kbs

INDIANA-
PURDUE
LIBRARY
MAR 8 1993
FORT WAYNE

WITHDRAWN

Published with assistance from the foundation established in memory of Philip Hamilton
McMillan of the Class of 1894, Yale College.

Copyright © 1991 by Yale University. All rights reserved.

This book may not be reproduced, in whole or in part, including illustrations, in any form
(beyond that copying permitted by Sections 107 and 108 of the U.S. Copyright Law and except
by reviewers for the public press), without written permission from the publishers.

Designed by Nancy Ovedovitz. Set in Times Roman type by The Composing Room of
Michigan, Inc. Printed in the United States of America by Vail-Ballou Press, Binghamton,
New York.

Library of Congress Cataloging-in-Publication Data

Stoller, Robert J.
    Porn : myths for the twentieth century / Robert J. Stoller.
        p.   cm.
    Includes bibliographical references and index.
    ISBN 0-300-05092-5
    1. Pornography—United States.   2. Sex oriented businesses—United States.
    3. Sex in motion pictures.   I. Title.
HQ472.U6S86   1991
363.4'7'0973—dc20   91-13623
                                                                            CIP

The paper in this book meets the guidelines for permanence and durability of the Committee on
Production Guidelines for Book Longevity of the Council on Library Resources.

10   9   8   7   6   5   4   3   2   1

5-24-93

CONTENTS

CONTENTS

· · · · · ·
PREFACE
· · · · · ·

You have in your hands a fragment from an ongoing piece of urban ethnography,* an adventure with pornography. It is in itself a piece of a larger study on the origins and dynamics of erotic excitement that, though proceeding for thirty years, has been without conscious plan. This study is not linear: one phase does not lead to the next to the next to the next, each completed before I move along. Instead, a dim awareness might sit, percolating, warming, but to the side until I am ready to appreciate it.

And so it was with the interest that only recently emerged sufficiently to be reported in this study of the industry that produces adult heterosexual pornography. My main reason for wanting to get familiar with the people thus engaged was my belief that, to be successful, they must intuitively understand the dynamics of the erotic lives of their audience. I had my theories about such dynamics, but these ideas were derived from only a few people who, though carefully observed—primarily in psychoanalytic treatment—might not represent the world at large. Complex fantasies (beliefs, daydreams, commitments, relationships, myths, preoccupations) held en masse (that is, "culture") can be discovered, confirmed, dissected, and transformed into their components by inquiring into what the people who make pornography are thinking of, feel, imagine they are doing, why, and to and for whom as they ply their trade. The

---

*It may not really be ethnography; certainly I am not an ethnographer. But I have fun playing at it and trying to change the dimensions of ethnography without having to pay that discipline's price in training, scholarship, physical hardship, responsibility, and dedication.

first purpose of this book, then, is to contemplate further a theory of erotic excitement.

The second has to do with ethnography; more with how ethnography and psychoanalysis can strengthen each other; even more with changing ethnography into a stronger research discipline (see Herdt and Stoller 1990).

Though I am a psychoanalyst, the observations reported here do not come out of analytic treatment. Psychoanalyst colleagues will miss the excitement that can—may—come as we hear from people's depths. So I bring no big news to you about the people who make porn. Nonetheless, as a way to extend the findings of ethnography—obvious enough and easy to apply—I recommend my method. It is a simple technique for studying almost any naturalistic phenomenon in a culture, a journalism run through an analyst's mind, without deadlines or the need to cater to a wide audience.

Among the advantages are that a psychoanalyst may be (1) trained and steeped in a special skepticism about informants' stories and alert to motivations not always credited by nonanalysts; (2) clinically skilled in interviewing; and (3) interested in people's capacity to use and misuse their psychopathology. Contrariwise, the analyst may be burdened by (1) theory that can predict anything and explain everything (including failures of prediction); (2) a tendency to dismiss nonpsychoanalytically produced data and ideas; (3) unfamiliarity with ethnographic method and ideas, especially regarding culture as not just the psychodynamics of the individual writ large; and (4) a sometimes weakened awareness that all stories, including the analyst's, are relative: just one more version.

The idea that the people who create pornography embody the communications systems that make up a culture's avowed erotic desires had begun to surface years before, on my interviewing, for a medical students' lecture course on psychopathology, a woman representing the category Hysterical (now called Histrionic) Personality (Stoller 1985a). The so-willing woman found for me was not a patient—not someone admitting to both stress and the need for help—but a professional erotic dancer and centerfold celebrity. I interviewed her with the students and talked to her a few other times (but because she was not a patient, I never met her after that). Had she wanted to talk longer, she would have raised from subliminal to full consciousness my ideas about studying a culture's fantasies by means of the private fantasies of those hired to represent the fantasies.

Presenting at meetings case material illustrated with pornography or advertisements for it, I was heading toward my present state. In the midst of that work, I shared my ideas with a colleague. Months later, he mentioned that he had met someone connected to someone connected to the X-rated industry.

Perhaps some someone could arrange to help me. Which led to my talking with Bill, a pornographer, whom you will meet shortly. Since then, Bill has introduced me to some of his friends and colleagues, a few of whom will also present themselves to you.

I need the reader's permission to avoid discussing important questions I would have to tackle if this book were titled *Pornography*. The more colloquial *Porn* has different connotations. It focuses on consumers who are overtly more or less heterosexual men—to a lesser extent also women—and on the industry that supplies the product. (I know almost nothing yet about gay pornography.) Women's pornography, like women's erotic styles in general, is something else and is not accurately covered by the word *porn*. I know little yet about its production, know only one thing really: that it *is* pornography. (Note the vocabulary difference between those making pornographic films and me: they use the businesslike term *X-Rated Industry,* I use *porn*. Mine gets closer to the complexities, I think.)

I recommend to the reader the book *Hard Core* (Williams 1989) for its careful study of the history of the making of heterosexual pornographic films. This lively, thoughtful work, with its extensive review of the literature of the subject and its fine sense of psychodynamics, could well serve as a text for which my informants' conversations are the illustrations.

At any rate, I shall not here: review the literature on research in pornography, attend closely and unpolemically to the political issues raised by feminist and conservative commentators regarding pornography's effects on society, discuss the moral questions pornography's presence raises, evaluate the legal problems pornography raises, or promote a plan of social action. Instead, I shall try only to display who does what, how, when, where, why, and therefore to whom in porn.

ACKNOWLEDGMENTS

I want to express my thanks:

to Ms. Gladys Topkis for her ever-patient, ever-constant, ever-disciplined editorial wisdom;

to Ms. Laura Dooley for her good eye and good taste in guiding my words on this manifestly tasteless subject;

to Dr. Otto Kernberg for knowing and advising me on how to keep this book's structure taut and on target;

and to my secretary, Mrs. Flora Degen, for her unending kindness, good humor, and sanity as I confront her with the need to tame a feral manuscript.

PART ONE

A KIND OF ETHNOGRAPHY

Chapter 1 **INTRODUCTION TO A KIND**

OF ETHNOGRAPHY

The theories and findings of some studies of human behavior have been weakened by two convictions held by the researchers. One is that informants' subjectivity—experienced, for instance, as feelings, fantasies, and sense of self—is a red herring in the research. The other is that the use of the researcher's subjectivity, in the form of full awareness or in a subliminal state such as empathy, guarantees error and must either be removed from one's methodology or have its traces erased from the record.

Few psychoanalysts would agree. To us it is obvious that if you want to know why people do something, it can help to ask them; that the statements people give us (whether we are ethnographers, psychoanalysts, behaviorists, pollsters, employees, spouses, torturers, neighbors, teachers, waiters, or scientists) depend on how they perceive us, how we perceive them, the time of day, the setting, our choice of words and inflections and hairstyle, the way we dress, their age and ours, whether we or they are standing or sitting—anything; that if you rely on (not simply use) informants, you had better know well who they are, and if I am your reader, you had better let me know precisely who your informant was, including what the relationship was between the two of you in regard to such factors as your personalities, how you established your relationship, whether you the researcher are paying (and if so, how much and in what form), what else you want to get from your informants* and the informants

*An informant in this study reminded me that "informant" is not only the ethnographer's term but the policeman's.

from you, how the informants are perceived by their own people and which people say what (in other words, the same sort of information you would like—and do not get—when electing a senator, applying for a loan, interviewing for a job, reading a reporter's story in the morning paper); that translators do not just translate but also interpret, gloss, reverse meanings because of their own psychic state, forget, drop out words or sentences; that the psychologies—psychoanalysis, psychology, sociology, history, economics, political science, anthropology, and so on—are racist; that to study a culture, a practice, a preference, an act, and not use the subjectivity of individuals, is to deny yourself essential data.

So much for the process of observing. The same holds for the reports of observations. It is obvious that one's observations are not the same as reality (whatever that is) but are only one's private versions of reality; that the person observing the observer—such as a reader—needs also to know about the observer in the hope that biases can be understood; that what we publicly present of our data is shaped by our personalities and by who we imagine our audience to be; that it is less shameful to admit than to ignore prejudices, for with the admission, the reader at least has a way to judge what we say; that we cannot fully trust the reports of a prejudiced investigator, or of an investigator not prejudiced, or of those who are religious or not religious, Marxist or capitalist, Democrat or Republican, black or white, male or female, old or young, psychoanalyzed or not, straight or gay, drunk or sober, pessimist or optimist, smart or dumb, honest or deceitful. Data are conditional; a fact is not a fact without being a fantasy.

Laboratory instruments are calibrated before use, but we know that we can never calibrate the personality of the reporter (for example, ethnographer, psychoanalyst). Neither our opinions of who we are nor the opinions of our friends, enemies, or relatives will finally indicate the correct way to hear or read us. Though it is as yet unacceptable, perhaps we should some day demand of those who write reports on human encounters and claim to be scientists (or even just honest reporters) that they reveal who they were during the moments when the data mentioned were formed.

Perhaps you will enjoy the following report from the *Los Angeles Times* (1987) as much as I do:

> Testifying on behalf of the writer of a book that accuses a respected Army physician of the murder of his wife and children, author William F. Buckley Jr. on Wednesday described writers as "investigative artists" who may woo their subjects into revealing their worst secrets.
>
> "I wouldn't lie about my own beliefs," Buckley said, but the columnist and talk

show host said it was "elementary technique" for a writer to conceal his own opinions to keep an interviewee talking.

"If you were writing about somebody who was a renowned philanderer and he said, 'Don't you think my wife is impossible?' You might say, 'Yes, she is rather hard to get along with,' simply for the purpose of lubricating the discussion," Buckley suggested. [In these circumstances, one might, for greater safety, use a condom.]

"The priorities are to encourage the person you're writing about to tell you everything, and if that takes going down to a bar and having a beer with him, you go down to the bar and have a beer with him. . . . It's part of the ordeal of being a writer." . . .

Buckley's testimony, in which he appeared as an expert witness on McGinniss' behalf, erupted at points into a verbal jousting match with MacDonald's attorney over a writer's obligation to his subjects and the meaning of a lie.

He resisted attempts by lawyer Gary Bostwick, representing MacDonald, to ascertain whether an author is entitled to lie to a subject in order to win his cooperation, insisting that the definition of a lie is "not that easy."

But Buckley, founder of the conservative magazine National Review and host of a PBS television program, "Firing Line," insisted that a writer has no obligation to tell his interview subject when he disagrees with him.

"A writer is an artist, and he wants to encourage the subject to reveal himself," Buckley said. "I shouldn't think an author ought to take on the job of passing moral judgment on a subject."

Buckley spoke strongly in support of a writer's "absolute, total discretion . . . subject to libel" in portraying an interview subject, arguing that threats against such discretion "would destroy the profession."

"I don't think that people would ever read, or would have any appetite for reading, books that were merely mechanical applications of formulae that were arrived at before the books were ever written," he said. (See also Malcolm 1990.)

I note here my surprise that there are anthropologists, sociologists, psychologists, and hard-nosed psychiatrists who defend the purist conviction that subjective data are not simply unscientific but—worse—ruin one's view of the objective world, as if the objective world is not made up of people in their full, ripe subjectivity. If these researchers really believed it is unnecessary to understand individuals' subjectivity, then they would never go to the theater, enjoy poetry, look at a painting, or read anything but sine and cosine tables, pornography, tide charts, stock exchange quotations, or the reports of classical behaviorists. Everything that most stirs these researchers in their private world they would erase from their published work. In itself, that may be an ethnographic finding worth investigating.

When touching above on racism, I was thinking, for instance, of the ethnographers who find their own private life crucial for understanding themselves—as, for instance, diaries can reveal—but hold that the inner life of the people they inspect is not as essential for understanding them.

Well, maybe some ethnographers are not racist. (Not likely.) But most ethnographies are. There shines through the writing so little respect for the complexity of informants (in contrast to, say, the researcher's friends in a poker game); for the complexity of the topic being studied—myths, for example (as compared to what has been absorbed about, say, Knute Rockne's role in sports history); for the culture at large (as compared to the meaning of a movie star's becoming president). This defect must contribute to the thinness of the thickest ethnographies.

The trouble with thickness—complexity—for me is that there is no end. The more informants, the more information; the more questions; the more modifications; the more exceptions; the more stories, all different. Few forests, mostly trees.

Since everyone is racist, the accusation has more value if one can also distinguish the non-racist elements, such as a researcher's racism as he or she lives the fieldwork versus the desire to overcome it (or to hide it); the racism (a.k.a. pride) subjects direct at us; the ebb and flow of racist responses as researcher and subject interact; and—important if political propaganda is to be reduced—admitting that what really counts is not the presence of racist impulses but their exact form—how strong, with what manifestations, under what circumstances, and for what purposes.

There are times when we need objectivity—ignoring our awareness of "I" or "you"—for discovery. But at other times, it will ruin the chances for discovery. Certain objects of scientific study—say, quarks—do not care much about our opinions of them.* But humans do, though treated like quarks. I look out on Westwood Village, the shopping area by the UCLA campus. Suppose we wanted to know why people were there. Would we start only by observing bus-stop signs or how soft drinks are displayed in markets? A clever sociologist could probably learn something that way, but are there not also other ways to get at people's motives, feelings, fantasies, passions?

Or if I want to examine how yams are harvested in the Trobriands, I may not need to know what the harvesters are thinking and feeling. But if I would know why they raise more than they can ever eat, I should, among other things, ask them. And if I am really sophisticated, I shall remember that their first response may be shaped by who they perceive me to be (friend or stranger, for example) and that later responses may reveal complex, even contradictory motives, all present at different levels of awareness inside the same surface behavior. Racism is the refusal to get into another's mind.

Here is Evans-Pritchard's classic complaint against the Nuer (1968:12–13).

---

*Even that, some say, is not true (Braginski et al. 1981:547).

I: Who are you?

Cuol: A man.

I: What is your name?

Cuol: Do you want to know my *name*?

I: Yes.

Cuol: You want to know *my* name?

I: Yes, you have come to visit me in my tent and I would like to know who you
    are.

Cuol: All right. I am Cuol. What is your name?

I: My name is Pritchard.

Cuol: What is your father's name?

I: My father's name is also Pritchard.

Cuol: No, that cannot be true. You cannot have the same name as your father.

I: It is the name of my lineage. What is the name of your lineage?

Cuol: Do you want to know the name of my lineage?

I: Yes.

Cuol: What will you do with it if I tell you? Will you take it to your country?

I: I don't want to do anything with it. I just want to know it since I am living at
    your camp.

Cuol: Oh well, we are Lou.

I: I did not ask the name of your tribe. I know that. I am asking you the name of
    your lineage.

Cuol: Why do you want to know the name of my lineage?

I: I don't want to know it.

Cuol: Then why do you ask me for it? Give me some tobacco.

I defy the most patient ethnologist to make headway against this kind of opposi-
    tion. One is just driven crazy by it.

(No wonder Evans-Pritchard withdrew from subjectivity into Structuralism.)

The question of the relationship of subjectivity to the study of human behavior certainly need not be restricted to anthropology. The pendulum that has
swung away from psychoanalysis—the microscopic study of subjectivity—
was carrying psychology, sociology, and psychiatry as well. And so these days,
from a mixture of good and bad motives, influential scholars in these disci-
plines reject subjectivity either as part of their methodology or as a subject for
study.

It seems impossible, but I have heard that there are anthropologists who
think affects are culture-bound or that people from widely different cultures can
communicate with each other only at cognitive or superficial, nonempathic
levels. (For reviews, see Bennett 1946; Devereux 1980; La Barre 1978; LeVine

1973; Turner 1975, 1978.) I do not believe it and did not find it in the brief ethnographic moment of intimate communications that Professor Gilbert Herdt allowed me to share with him and his Sambia friends in Papua New Guinea (Herdt and Stoller 1990).

For instance, when a man wept, we did not think he was laughing; when a woman spoke with cold rage about the husband who won her by kidnapping and ravaging her, we did not think, as she talked of this, that she was feeling romance; when a translator turned, in disgust and sarcasm, from a man he felt was unmanly, we did not think this was homosexual excitement; when an informant moved, with resistance, toward silence, we did not hear exuberant free associating; when a man struggled whether to tell us a secret, we did not think he was hungry; when a woman took a stick to another who had fouled up a ceremonial feast, we did not think she was suffering a phobic state; when a two-year-old grabbed his mother's breast for suckling and she did not notice, we did not think she was creating an excessively close symbiosis; when a girl shyly hid her face, we did not find her lustful; when a man of demolished reputation—a "rubbish" man—knotted his face in pain, we did not read that as hostility. But if a long-married couple exchanged a glance, we might know no more about what they felt or were communicating to each other than when the same happens at home. For, of course, there are, in a relationship or a culture, idiosyncrasies and subtleties that confuse the outside observer.

Then, at the opposite extreme to those who believe that there is nothing universal in affects are those who believe only in the universal structure of the mind; they see affects as a function of the mind's cognitive structure. Though they know that, say, the behavior of anger varies, they believe that the variance has no ultimate significance; for what one really studies is the structural man-ifestations of Mind, not minds. I cannot grasp that. Let me show why, with an example taken from findings on sexual excitement: fetishism.

Chinese men of a past era took it for granted—"it was natural"—that bound feet aroused one; that is, everyone. (And "everyone," of course, refers to men only. Women's excitement did not count.) Those who shared the conviction, both men and their fetishized women, probably had as profuse, subtle, and complex criteria for what makes a fabulously formed crushed foot as we do for women's breasts (Ellis 1936, 2:21–22). And *we* all "know" that, "naturally,". everywhere, women's breasts (of certain configurations, mass, levitation, color, number, and location) are exciting.

> In Rome, Dufour remarks, "Matrons having appropriated the use of the shoe (*soccus*) prostitutes were not allowed to use it, and were obliged to have their feet always naked in sandals or slippers (*crepida* and *solea*), which they fastened over the instep with gilt bands. Tibullus delights to describe his mistress's little foot, compressed by

the band that imprisoned it: *Ansaque compressos colligat arcta pedes*. Nudity of the foot in woman was a sign of prostitution, and their brilliant whiteness acted afar as a pimp to attract looks and desires" (Dufour, *Histoire de la Prostitution*, vol. II, ch. xviii).

This feeling seems to have survived in a more or less vague and unconscious form in mediaeval Europe. "In the tenth century," according to Dufour (*Histoire de la Prostitution*, vol. VI, p. 11), "shoes *à la poulaine*, with a claw or beak, pursued for more than four centuries by the anathemas of popes and the invectives of preachers, were always regarded by mediaeval casuists as the most abominable emblems of immodesty. At a first glance it is not easy to see why these shoes—terminating in a lion's claw, an eagle's beak, the prow of a ship, or other metal appendage—should be so scandalous. The excommunication inflicted on this kind of footgear preceded the impudent invention of some libertine, who wore *poulaines* in the shape of the phallus, a custom adopted also by women. This kind of *poulaine* was denounced as *mandite de Dieu* (Ducange's Glossary, at the word *Poulainia*) and prohibited by royal ordinances (see letter of Charles V., 17 October, 1367, regarding the garments of the women of Montpellier). Great lords and ladies continued, however, to wear *poulaines*." In Louis XI.'s court they were still worn a quarter of an ell in length.

Spain, ever tenacious of ancient ideas, appears to have preserved longer than other countries the ancient classic traditions in regard to the foot as a focus of modesty and an object of sexual attraction. In Spanish religious pictures it was always necessary that the Virgin's feet should be concealed, the clergy ordaining that her robe should be long and flowing, so that the feet might be covered with decent folds. Pacheco, the master and father-in-law of Velazquez, writes in 1649 in his *Arte de la Pintura:* "What can be more foreign from the respect which we owe to the purity of Our Lady the Virgin than to paint her sitting down with one of her knees placed over the other, and often with her sacred feet uncovered and naked. Let thanks be given to the Holy Inquisition which commands that this liberty should be corrected!" It was Pacheco's duty in Seville to see that these commands were obeyed. At the court of Philip IV. at this time the princesses never showed their feet, as we may see in the pictures of Velazquez. When a local manufacturer desired to present that monarch's second bride, Mariana of Austria, with some silk stockings the offer was indignantly rejected by the Court Chamberlain: "The Queen of Spain has no legs!" . . . Max Dessoir mentions ("Psychologie der Vita Sexualis," *Zeitschrift für Psychiatrie*, 1894, p. 954) that in Spanish pornographic photographs women always have their shoes on, and he considers this an indication of perversity. I have seen the statement (attributed to Gautier's *Voyage en Espagne*, where, however, it does not occur) that Spanish prostitutes uncover their feet in sign of assent, and Madame d'Aulnoy stated that in her time to show her lover her feet was a Spanish woman's final favor. (Ellis 1936, 2:25–26)

I knew that Kalutwo, a Sambia man, was sad and that Fay, who wanted to be a pornqueen, was sad; perceiving that alerted me to what might next transpire between us. But I needed much more information to know why each became sad and the nature of that sadness. Knowing the language, jargon, and culture gets one started; knowing the sad person helps; knowing the circumstances in which the sadness arose helps; knowing of the possibility that a conscious affect, like sadness, may contain or hide other affects also helps. It is unlikely that there are ethnographers who would not recognize sadness in another person; will they not also see that that sadness may not be outside their ethnography but might be a part of it? Not that empathy is necessary for all ethnography; there are still many areas of cross-cultural research in which personal meaning may not add to the research: aspects of kinship, social structure, ecology, myth, and so on. (In the same way, an unempathic psychiatrist may work creatively on the biochemistry of schizophrenia or mechanisms of conditioning.) And some problems can speak only through quantitative methods.

Here are two reports—one objective, one subjective—on the same event. Both inform, yet they do not overlap.

> Farther to the French right, Davout was to attack frontally a group of field works on which the Russian left centre was formed; and the extreme right of the French army was composed of the weak corps of Poniatowski. The whole line was not more than about 2 m. long, giving an average of over 20 men per yard. When the Russians closed on their centre they were even more densely massed and their reserves were subjected to an effective fire from the French field guns. At 6 A.M. on September 7 the French attack began. By 8 A.M. the Russian centre was driven in, and though a furious counter-attack enabled Prince Bagration's troops to win back their original line, fresh French troops under Davout and Ney drove them back again. (*Encyclopedia Britannica* 1929, s.v. "Borodino")

> "Look out!" rang out a frightened cry from a soldier, and like a bird, with swift, whirring wings alighting on the earth, a grenade dropped with a dull thud a couple of paces from Prince Andrey, near the major's horse. The horse, with no question of whether it were right or wrong to show fear, snorted, reared, almost throwing the major, and galloped away. The horse's terror infected the men. "Lie down!" shouted the adjutant, throwing himself on the ground. Prince Andrey stood in uncertainty. The shell was smoking and rotating like a top between him and the recumbent adjutant, near a bush of wormwood in the rut between the meadow and the field. "Can this be death?" Prince Andrey wondered, with an utterly new, wistful feeling, looking at the grass, at the wormwood and at the thread of smoke coiling from the rotating top. "I can't die, I don't want to die, I love life, I love this grass and earth and air." (Tolstoy n.d.:757)

You understand: empathy helps. A greatly anticipated feast day turned partly sour because two Sambia women clashed in preparing the meal. Herdt, Moondi (a teenage bachelor), and I watched this blundering at the fire pit, the two whites mildly amused (racist: all humor has hostility at its core). But something quite different was building in Moondi, though we did not observe it because we were watching the mess. He suddenly broke, ran forward, stood in the rain on the mound of heaped-up debris the women had scattered, and there—alone—froze, transfixed for minutes. It seemed strange to me but much less so to

Herdt, who clarified: Moondi was sulking. And sulking is a complex, compound affect, heavy with manipulations—culture-bound. My empathy was diminished because of my not knowing what Sambia sulking looks like and not recognizing why this situation was one in which Moondi would sulk. Suddenly Moondi exploded with anger (I had no problem recognizing *that* affect), yelled at the women for their stupidity, stomped off, and then stood back silently in despair.

How could an ethnographer not be tempted to study such a display, so fascinating to us? And if you are interested, how will you go about studying it? Do you learn less from Moondi's reactions than from watching the feast rules unfold? Sambia culture is not just in those rules, or reflected in the ceremonies, or in the sweet potato gardens; it is also in Moondi. (That is why I study Bill and his pornographing: the erotic history of the West as well as its history of the development, maintenance, and pathology of masculinity and femininity, are buried, alive, in them.)

Moondi's sulk is a biopsy of Sambia culture. Why was he sulking; how did he learn to do it that way; what is the history of sulking; who was he trying to influence; did it have anything to do with his masculinity; would he have put on the same show if men, not women, had blundered; what did he hope to accomplish by this intensely self-centered and yet terribly public exhibition; what could we learn from his sulk about feasts that go right and go wrong, eating customs, styles of communicating, the universality of certain defense mechanisms, the concept of self, mother-infant relations and techniques of childrearing, relations between Sambia men and women, all men and women in the world, and the invention of art from the muck of reality; what, in his melodrama, does Moondi express about his parents and siblings, his childhood, the culturally permitted expressions of righteousness, and the forms in which anger is allowed modulation? Or—to drop all objectivity—how could an ethnographer who is at bottom a student of human psychology not be curious when seeing this stylized behavior?

To complete our little investigation, the next day we asked Moondi what he was doing: what it had meant to him and what he was trying to communicate. Must one legislate such data out of ethnography? Watching him sulk might be traditional ethnography, but asking him about its personal meanings apparently is not.

The issue is empathy, the observer's capacity to sample—resonate to—another's interior (a less full and for research a more usable identification than sympathy). Our object was the Sambia, the last people in the Eastern Highlands to be contacted and pacified. One could hardly find a people more different from ourselves and who remained so different until so recently. War and hunting formed the bedrock of masculine culture. A stone-age technology prevailed until the late 1960s. But many social changes have occurred since then, and at an increasingly rapid pace since the mid-1970s. The old has mixed with the new, though traditional culture still organizes everyday life in many fundamental ways. Yet, in spite of the contrast between Sambia culture and our own, I felt no primal difficulty in communicating across the two cultures.

More than that—and this is an assertion others will have to challenge—we found Sambia who were potentially as self-reflective and as psychologically minded as the direct inheritors of Freud's discoveries. (The same of course holds in the porn industry.) I shall not make a serious attempt to explain that finding; you might better ask if it needs more explaining in a tribal society than the same capacity does in our own. These people, who are so outward-directed—how to hunt, how to war, how to placate malevolent spirits, how to observe and cheat on taboos, how to garden, how to maneuver in the jungle: skills not enhanced by one's desire to know oneself, to get to the root of one's motivations, to reduce self-deception—were far more than just Herdt's informants. Though they never heard of such a thing, they were able easily, for years with Herdt and then for days with me, a stranger, to search themselves for answers to questions about meaning. And as over the years the probing became deeper and more psychodynamic, some of them had no trouble moving enthusiastically and with curiosity into realms of the mind they not only had never recognized in themselves or others but for which their culture has no concepts, no intimations. I can get the same results with the subjects of my erotic studies in Los Angeles, as long as I do not refuse to empathize with them, do not treat them as monsters, am able to loosen the natural arrogance of my erotic prejudices, forgo the dimwitted pleasure of letting theory satisfy ignorance.

What would the ethnographers who do not believe in universal affects say to my conviction that there are people in every culture with the (usually inhibited) capacity—even hunger—to know themselves?

Let us think more on the belief that our understanding of culture improves if we are allowed into individuals' minds. I look on any moment of a person's mental life as being composed of multiple scripts working at varying levels of awareness. (I use *script* in its usual meaning: a tale complete with characters delineated to play their assigned parts.) I believe that any instant of conscious experience is a compacted knot—microdot—of these scripts, almost all of which are active and yet out of consciousness, each playing its part to make the algebraic sum that we experience as the instant's conscious awareness. That makes the study of subjectivity terribly complex, for, there being a lifetime of scripts in any moment, then no matter how one tries to find all the reasons for a piece of behavior, only some can be recovered. (I can only hope that not too many of those found are simply my inventions.)

In a personal encounter—including those of psychoanalysts and of ethnographers, of course—each participant's mass of scripts meets the other's. It is almost a miracle, then, that on occasion, people actually understand each other. Usually it takes strangers time to sort out and decipher enough of each's storylines for the initial romance and paranoia to cool. Example. I am now in the Trobriand Islands, where I am a stranger, not as with our Sambia friends. (Think of all the scripts implied even in this last skinny sentence.) I want to take a photograph.

There am I, the same eye and the same camera that, when poking at the Sambia, happily excite them to pose. But this young Trobriand man, preparing, with everyone else in the village, for a yam festival, curses me and turns his back: lots of scripts (and you need not know the language to understand what he says). Is he "just" angry (that set of scripts), looking for money (another set), frightened (another), all of the above, or none of the above? What does he think I am doing? Am I stealing his soul or otherwise supernaturally invading him? Is he, in thinking whatever he does, responding to his own fantasies only, or is he also responding to some of mine (who I think he is, who I think I am, what I plan to do with the pictures)?

At what level of awareness does he recognize that I am treating him as a fetish, a tourist's object, to be taken home and shown to friends? He would be right if he realized I did so with him, and I would think the same were he to take my picture. But is that all there is to it; is it nothing more than disregard for him as a person? Could there not simultaneously be other scripts: nonhostile curiosity, admiration, respect, affection (complicated, as I write about this now, by an "I-am-now-magnanimous" playlet)?

When he treated me this way, I was immediately irritated for having been misunderstood. Later I recognized that there was actually a picosecond before "immediately" when I was first uneasy—the soft form of fearful—and then hurt, a pleasanter, more righteous affect than fear. The next transformation, to irritation, completed the cure of my fear, now putting him in jeopardy. I stared a hole in his back; he turned toward me. Perhaps inside him I had become a new form of his father (or uncle: mother's brother there takes on much of the oedipal power fathers do for us). At any rate, he—now to me a boy—looked embarrassed, then shy. He cast his eyes down and away, turned aside, and began talking with someone else. Stories: deceptions; myths; manipulations; a colonialist melodrama.

Another example. My wife and I come on a *singsing* near Kundiawa, in the

Central Highlands of Papua New Guinea; there could not be a richer or more colorful spectacle. Everything wild and wonderful in Highlands culture, drawn from the customs of unknown past generations, roars around us. Our greatest expectations are surpassed; it is a grand day for touristic scripts. Then we learn that this fantastic and yet traditional pageant—spontaneous, genuine, joyous, savage—is for the consecration of a new Roman Catholic church. Our scripts shift.

In the boiling center of the approaching dancing mob is a completely different headdress, golden and austere amid the hundreds of flaming bird-of-paradise arrays. It is a bishop's miter. The bishop, we are relieved to see, is black: local man makes good. Happy, refreshing script.

A few days later, at the Madang airport, waiting out another canceled plane, we talk with an American priest. He confirms our impression that the bishop was having a grand time. And it was so different from Detroit, where the bishop was born and has lived all his life. Even touristic ethnography is a complex art.

When these issues of subjectivity are ignored, we are unsure what to make of an observer's account. Are not ethnographic and psychoanalytic data often described with the same low level of reliability as is the news in today's paper? Which apparent facts are really just opinions? Which stories are incomplete? Which convictions should be reconverted to questions? Let us return to erotics for another example that should make us cautious in answering this question. How closely does ethnography match reality? Even Malinowski, who in his ethnographic monographs comes close, and in his diaries even closer, did not quite make real what his Trobrianders thought and felt erotically.

Though the present sexual freedom of many communities in Western society would make a Trobriander blush, there was a time—and Malinowski marked it well—when Trobrianders were notorious in our world for their promiscuity. Without having the facts, one sensibly assumes that promiscuity is motivated by lust; who would have doubted that fifty or sixty years ago? Likewise, in our day, who would question that teenage ghetto black girls, so sexually active, would be driven, in such a risky business—in their teens, so many have babies—by erotic need? Yet, Rainwater (1970:302) says:

> Only rarely in our field data do adolescent girls indicate an autonomous interest in coitus, even when they have engaged in intercourse with more than one boyfriend. In Ladner's sample, only half the girls who had had sexual intercourse indicated that they derived any particular enjoyment from it, and only two of the 15 girls said they had orgasm during intercourse and enjoyed specific sexual gratification. In short, these girls seem to have a basically passive attitude toward coitus, and it means more to them for their developing identities than for the pleasures of the act itself. [I'd be surprised if this were not true for wealthy white girls, too. My guess is that few

women in Western society lose their virginity—how odd this phrase, with its emphasis on loss, sounds—in a sweep of erotic passion.]

It is probable that the Pruitt-Igoe girls [those Rainwater studied] have sexual
relationships primarily because they are pressured by their boyfriends and because if
they do not eventually cooperate they have to accept a definition of themselves as
immature. In this they share more than may be apparent with middle-class girls, who
often maintain that they engage in necking and petting because it is expected rather
than because they actually enjoy the behavior. However, one has the impression that
middle-class girls more rapidly find heavy petting pleasurable and learn to look
forward to its repetition, perhaps because it represents a compromise between the
potential moral costs of sexual relations and the cost in perpetuated childhood status
of not engaging in any kind of sexual activity. The lower-class girl is presented with
an all-or-nothing situation in which to have the status of maturity she must run greater
moral risks.

So let us be warned by Rainwater's findings and retreat from certainty regarding
the sexual excitement of Trobrianders.

Now to further this little exercise, let us call forth as our informant George, a
white expatriate who has lived for some years on one of the Trobriand Islands.
Gentled by whisky and cigars, he answers my questions. (You are by now, I
hope, suspicious about informants: why is George willing to talk to me, what
does he make of my questions, what is his relationship with me, how much
whisky did he drink, and who paid for it? Just be sure that you are as suspicious
of everyone's informants, even those who do not free their associations with
alcohol.) A balding, time-splayed beachcomber type who hides his keen and
perceptive intelligence, George is not the sleek, muscled youth with whom
Trobriand girls consort. Yet he has widely sampled the women. (He says. Has
he? How reliable are informants about their erotic lives; are there—of course
there are—cultural differences; individual differences? Does alcohol [how
much] increase candor in general; selectively? Does it lead to exaggeration;
when; with whom? What about the cigar: to what extent does he smoke it for the
nicotine and to what extent for expanding his sense of being a man?)

George does not share Malinowski's sentiment that the girls are promiscuous
from erotic desire. Though he grants that there is plenty of fornication, for him
this reputation is not a function of lust. In fact, he says, no Trobriand woman
has orgasms. I question. He amends: "With me." He goes on, with regret and
poignancy that smack of truth: despite their beautiful and available breasts,
none gets turned on by his fondling. In contrast, he says, in the Highlands he
has never met a woman who was not orgasmic and whose breasts were not
erotically sensitive. And this even though the Highlands women are, he says,
prudish and Trobrianders are not.

Malinowski's (1929:488) turn:

Yakalusa, a daughter of a chief of Kasana'i, was accused of spontaneously approaching men, talking to them, and inviting them to have intercourse with her. A similar reputation attached to several girls in Omarakana. Again there are clear cases on record of nymphomaniacs, who could not be satisfied with moderate sexual intercourse and required a number of men every night. There was a girl of Kitava who actually made the round of the whole island in search of erotic diversion. While I was staying in Sinaketa she was also a visitor there and gossip was very active though not specially antagonistic. It was said that she would go out into the jungle with a group of boys and withdraw with one after another, spending days and nights in this occupation.

Malinowski refers to this as "sexual greed and lechery . . . inability to master desire." George would disagree; Rainwater would suggest we do as he did— improve the validity of the data with careful interviewing; Masters and Johnson would tell us to connect apparatus and go look.

If we presume that George is reporting his experiences accurately (a dangerous piece of methodology), we owe him our respect, if not envy, for investigating directly rather than by hearsay. But then Malinowski counters (1929:337– 339):

Above all, the natives despise the European position and consider it unpractical and improper. The natives, of course, know it, because white men frequently cohabit with native women, some even being married to them. But, as they say: "The man overlies heavily the woman; he presses her heavily downwards, she cannot respond." [Do they really talk like natives in a Tarzan movie? What data might be lost in translation?]

Altogether the natives are certain that white men do not know how to carry out intercourse effectively. As a matter of fact, it is one of the special accomplishments of native cook-boys and servants who have been for some time in the employ of white traders, planters, or officials, to imitate the copulatory methods of their masters. In the Trobriands, Gomaya was perhaps the best actor in this respect. He still remembered a famous Greek buccaneer (Nicholas Minister was the name he went by among other beachcombers), who had lived in the islands even before the establishment of the government station. Gomaya's performance consisted in the imitation of a very clumsy reclining position, and in the execution of a few sketchy and flabby movements. In this the brevity and lack of vigour of the European performance were caricatured. Indeed, to the native idea, the white man achieves orgasm far too quickly; and there seems to be no doubt that the Melanesian takes a much longer time and employs a much greater amount of mechanical energy to reach the same result. This, together with the handicap of the unfamiliar position, probably accounts for the complaints of white men that native girls are not responsive. Many a white informant has spoken to me about perhaps the only word in the native language which he ever learned, *kubilabala* ("move on horizontally"), repeated to him with some intensity during the sexual act. This verb defines the horizontal motion during sexual intercourse, which should be mutual.

The point here is decidedly not that either George or Malinowski is right but rather that *we still do not know*. That awareness, if we care enough, can spur us to find ways to get better answers. Malinowski uses the word *orgasm* to describe the women's experience; for example, "As the act proceeds and the movements become more energetic, the man, I was told, waits until the woman is ready for orgasm" (1929:339). It is certainly unlikely, in such a clear sentence, that he is on the wrong track. For greater surety, however, we would still like to know who told him, exactly what was said, why his informant told him, and what the informant was thinking.

This next anecdote shows how one can miss the point even when the right words are used in a sentence. Herdt and I are talking with Penjukwi, a young Sambia woman (Herdt and Stoller 1990). She says that she has orgasms when nursing her babies. Herdt is surprised; he has never heard this said before. I, knowing that it happens with some women, am interested to learn more. So we keep questioning her. After many minutes, my vaguely puzzled feeling—my only clue that there is more to be learned—changes to a sense that there is something wrong with what the words mean. Then we understand: Penjukwi is using the same word for ejecting fluid from a breast and for orgasm. (Other informants later confirmed this usage, which had never emerged until then.)

Our understanding is still clouded, however, until we understand facts about Sambia culture that Sambians take for granted: the tremendous meaning of semen and its relation to milk. Herdt had discovered, years earlier, that at the center of Sambia life is a semen cult, practiced by the males but kept secret from the females. The men believe that all humans start as females, external anatomic features notwithstanding, and that boys acquire the maleness necessary for war and hunting only by constantly drinking semen from their first initiation (around age seven to ten) until puberty. Though this knowledge is supposedly a dread secret of the males, it is open knowledge among males and females that mother's milk and pandanus sap are alike in their effects and necessary for health and strength. Where we might unconsciously equate breast with penis and milk with semen, they do so explicitly, placing those equations at the center of their culture. And so for them both experiences are covered by the same word.

When, earlier in our questioning, Penjukwi had said that nursing was very pleasurable, producing orgasms, I had no doubt at first that, with the Sambia as with us, the pleasure she described could only be erotic. The clinician, however, learns to keep listening.

I do not believe that this sort of semantic problem is buried in Malinowski's use of the word *orgasm*, but what we found with Penjukwi alerts us that words that seem clear when first used and translated can give faulty impressions.

To get back to George, Malinowski, and our search for informed uncertainty: If Malinowski had had intercourse with the women and reported that they had orgasms, that would be helpful. Our next step might then be to check whether Trobriand women use the modern Western device of simulating orgasms. And when George reports that his partners are not aroused, for the sake of completeness we want to know that they do not—as Victorian ladies sometimes did—hide their orgasms.

George has set up a nice experimental design. The same stimulus—George—has allegedly produced a different response in two groups, and so we suspect that the two groups are different: Trobrianders never have orgasms with him; Highlanders always do. The problem with his pilot study is that we do not really know yet that his amatory skills are applied equally to both groups: is he, for instance, different, unbeknown to himself, because by his standards the Trobriand women are more beautiful or more promiscuous or more outspoken or more demanding or less dazzled by a middle-aged white man? Or could it be that Highlander women have cultural beliefs about types like George that are different from Trobrianders'?

Or maybe his whole story is fairy dust, concocted from moonlight and tradewinds. Or maybe I made it up. Certainly in the past explorers and naturalists misinterpreted, distorted, and even invented new findings. Remember the unicorn.

I do not want the reader to lose sight of my point here. How, when, and where people have orgasms is not a weighty ethnographic issue. What is important, I assert, is the methodology of gathering trustworthy information. The problem, then, is this: Can we psychoanalysts demonstrate that the study of subjectivity—the defining quality of human existence—is important? And can the ethnographer both use and study subjectivity, not treating it as a contaminant in the work?

Cross-checking one's findings by means of different data-collecting techniques is a measure of science. I have simulated that standard by talking with people who make porn to see if built into their work are the dynamics of excitement that I think we find in those who consume porn. In that way social dynamics test intrapsychic dynamics.

Simulate is the right word, for this first effort of mine is far from a controlled study: informants' responses need cross-checking, though we can be sure that for certain behaviors, including fantasizing, we can never have a complete picture. Occam needs Rashomon.

That, as some ethnographers know, holds for ethnography. The researcher hard to fool at home is the target, when paddling in alien waters, of shills, mountebanks, leg-pullers, and other interested parties. The problem is compounded since the ethnographer translates, edits, paraphrases, rewrites, and slants informants' discourse. What the audience receives (and further distorts by interpretation) is suspect. Perhaps the problem of accurate report is insoluble (Colby and Stoller 1988); at any rate, I have tried to ease it by using extensive transcripts, though by being edited, they could fool you.

Even if we knew the criteria for the best informant, we might have trouble finding that person; we can be thrillingly sure we have him or her and yet be wrong. Maybe it takes profound familiarity with a culture—a rare event in ethnography—just to evaluate such a helper. Informants, being just like you and me, have their own fish to fry. They were not born to serve us.

I cannot resolve a perhaps fatal flaw in this polemic: who is to say which version of a story is right? There is always another informant whose story can change our judgment of what is true, and there is always another observer— maybe yet unborn—whose new perspective will overthrow today's truths. Worse, the same informant can give different versions as later circumstances or moods arise. For every friend I can mobilize to say that the psychoanalyst has a sharp vision, there are ten who scorn that claim.

Analyst colleagues will say that my transcripts reveal glimpses of the deeper processes at work in these informants but nothing like what data unearthed in psychoanalytic treatment would reveal. I agree but do not feel that analytic interpretations in treatment are necessarily reliable.

The best one can do is convince one's audience: when we are convinced, we are satisfied, a process that is by no means the same as a scientific proof. And that smug feeling may have little to do with reality, no matter how much we agree.

Let me amplify this. The dumb luck that connected me to Bill was compounded in that not only was he well placed in the industry, well informed, and articulate but his warmth and cooperation were energized by his hope that I, a professor, could bring his story to a new audience: we could scratch each other's backs. So he recommended informants to me in a manner that brought them to the first interviews with a softening of the suspicions people of a subculture often bring to an establishment figure. As a result, many of his friends have continued, in or out of treatment, to talk with me.*

During these years of studying porn, I have made forays into the world of sadomasochism, both institutionalized and private. It was different, however,

---

*Not all. A few he asked never called me; a couple who called never kept the appointments; a few who came in once or twice did not keep further appointments.

with the B&D (Bondage and Discipline) people. Lieutenant Pierson, of the West Hollywood Sheriff's Department, called the owners of three B&D clubs and asked if he could bring me around. All said yes, having been tapped before by sociologists, psychologists, TV interviewers, or newspaper and magazine journalists. They were far from media virgins, their interviewing skills well honed, their arguments tightly formed, their speeches canned.* They were pretty impervious to the unexpected question. That was no great problem for me, since I believe that one can spend fruitful hours (especially when one is a man-from-Mars and thus unfamiliar with the fundamentals of the trade) hearing these commercials.

But when the official B&D statements had been pronounced, these informants, different from Bill and his colleagues, were closed down by suspicion. (I can usually hear it coming on the phone, sometimes even before we've met.) They had no idea who I was other than that, though working at the university, I had come via the sheriff's department, both attributes that do not necessarily recommend one to a business on the razor's edge of the law. (They may have also presumed I was dirty-old-man-ing them.) So, the house versions told and tours conducted, I found myself unable to move to what must be the next level of investigation: one-to-one interviews conducted with the same confidentiality and in the same style I would use for a patient. In this situation, clinical skill increases the flow of information, especially when one guarantees not only confidentiality but a capacity to listen. (I have dealt with these weaknesses by talking for the past few years with—not treating—an S&M colleague and a heterosexual S&M couple and by treating an S&M woman, but these happy expedients are not the same as intimate communication with someone in the B&D business.)

So I take ethnography reports with a grain of salt and wonder, along with Professor Herdt, whether ethnographers' training is adequate if they are not clinically skilled. (Herdt [Herdt and Stoller 1990] calls the not-yet-created discipline for remedying this "clinical ethnography.")

Another element that I could not imagine were I an alien ethnographer is perhaps at work. The owners of the three clubs—two men and a woman—all maintain the official stance of being dominants (though in erotic behavior they might take a fling at submission). So, in dealing with me, they were, I felt, nervously, smilingly, firmly but subtly subordinating me, despite my comfort in being subordinate as their guest and because of my expressed naïveté regarding

---

*Though this was also true at first with Bill's colleagues, my meeting them through Bill and their willingness therefore to talk with me on my turf let me be more clinically supple than was possible in the living room of a B&D establishment.

both the business and the erotic aspects of their work. My every move, from arrival to departure, every spot where I was put in a room, every placement of the people I talked with, was controlled (not so different from what patients think they must put up with on coming to me). And, though I was treated politely, I was not allowed to talk informally and privately with anyone. The owners, like Structuralists, insisted on the official versions of the myths uncontaminated by the garbage of individuals' subjectivity.

By contrast, in studying the manufacture of pornography, I was fortunate. Rather than arriving at my informants' threshold under the auspices of the Los Angeles County Sheriff's Department, I had the luck to have my informants come voluntarily to my office—that space capsule—with me under suspicion of nothing worse than being, perhaps, an academic: foolish, erotically suppressed.

The protection of the academic ambience has its price: my observations are the reports of the informants, not the behavior reported on. That is also true when, in treating patients, we do not observe them in their real world. To increase objectivity, we give up the ethnographer's advantage in participant-observation.

A few words here on the space suit—how to be in and yet not in a situation. Like the emergency room doctor, police officer, playwright, prostitute, politician, reporter, judge, moviegoer, historian, artist, teacher, philosopher, bank loan officer, military commander, consul general, charity fundraiser, and comedian, I, when practicing psychoanalysis and when talking with nonpatient informants, need to be cool while they and their reality are hot. And those who are hot—in the soup—need us (love and hate us for being) cool, lest we respond as uncontrolledly as they. I would not dare to do this work if I were not protected by my square profession—professor-analyst-psychiatrist—square clothes and demeanor, square-looking office, square life history and private life, and enjoyment of all that squareness.

In studying pornography, this stance lets me put aside private reactions— such as moral outrage, disgust, excitement, and political enthusiasms—that would prevent me from hearing my informants.

Which brings us to Bill and his colleagues in porn.

Chapter 2   **FETISH MACHINERY**

I hope you will see in the transcripts that follow how the fetishizing process manifested in porn emerges from fetishizing processes that are psychodynamically active in the makers of porn. It is, of course, easier to do a job right when one brings natural abilities to it: the happy melding of neurosis with inherent drives. Bill, our pornographer-performer, is a man full of energy, continually concentrated on his work, with high capacity for repeated orgasms, accompanied by the ability to delay orgasm indefinitely. His enthusiasms are in the service of a rebelliousness aimed originally at his mother, he feels, but turned onto society since his teens. This deflected anger supports him professionally and interpersonally, facilitating his choice of working at what he considers an antisocial task and his sympathizing with the "siblings"—the performers—in their struggles with the parents—the producers, the owners, and the straight society that opposes porn.

His effectiveness in getting out the product is enhanced by decisions, made in childhood and adolescence, not to be trapped in a love that commits one by intimacy, by openness—that is, by needs that make one vulnerable to others. So, though he is an unendingly dependable erotic performer, he does not perform from erotic desire and does not turn to others for erotic pleasure. He is an erotic machine. He will, then, be wanted as a performer, script writer, and director as long as porn makes money by producing materials that do not portray loving, intimate erotism. He is a jovial, relaxed, modest, frank, unstuffy—that is, American—version of Doctors Frankenstein and Moreau. And his creatures, different from theirs, are expected to portray fun, though he does so by parodying terror-inflicting characters. Porn, as Bill does it, is meant to be silly. So he is thrilled when straight society gets angry, for that proves to him that the enemy—the moral crusaders—are idiots for taking the idiocy of porn seriously.

In addition to Bill, I have talked with others in the industry: male and female performers, a former woman performer then public relations executive now would-be talk show hostess; a bibliographer-critic of porn; a woman journalist in and of porn; a gay publisher; a publisher of S&M porn; a scriptwriter; an S&M illustrator; husbands, a wife-performer, boyfriends, a female friend of a woman-performer. (Since I finished writing this book, I have continued to meet and talk with new informants, men and women, as well as with all the informants reported herein, except Happy.) All of these interviews—nontreatment and treatment—have illuminated this study of porn, but the book would be far too long if I reported each of them. You probably need no reminder that my view of porn is distorted by the sorts of people chance has thus far brought me: too few informants, too few male performers, no female directors or producers, only one performer who has dropped out, a woman who got out just before starting, and so on. But when these blanks are filled in, will the resulting view be accurate? Can there even be an accurate view?

Though I have spent a lot of time with men in the porn business, they have been primarily creators of the material; I have talked with only five men who were performers, and four of them were also writers-directors-producers. There may be a cultural-psychodynamic factor in this paucity, for Bill referred a half-dozen other men to me, only one of whom called. By contrast, most of the women made appointments, and only one who did so failed to come in.

The informants told me three kinds of stories. The first is the canned interview, the official exhibition polished for and by newspaper, radio, and TV interviews (Bill, Kay, and Nina). The second is the story told so often to oneself and one's acquaintances that it has become one's myth (for instance, Bill and Jim). The third is the unrehearsed, nonperformance *cri du coeur* (for instance, Happy). Some informants used a mix of these techniques (for instance, Bill and Ron).

The more people I talk with, the more I know I need to know more. Though certain features then appear in the fog, I get an increasing sense of the complexity of the subculture. So my skepticism regarding most ethnographers' reports is not a theoretic stance but comes from detailed experience—and I even speak the same language and live in the same city as my informants. Yet there is, you may agree, an advantage in this complexity. Talking with more and more informants and more and more with each, I not only learn more facts about porn. Because almost all these informants know one another and all are linked to at least one other, the interweaving of personalities and stories makes the individual parts become the dynamic system I have called "porn."

Bill first decided to introduce me to a young woman starting in his industry. She would exemplify the they-are-born-that-way erotic "hotness" he says is necessary for a pornqueen (but not for male performers). I was familiar with that quality as a pathognomonic feature of a not-yet-named subcategory of those who fit the larger diagnosis of "hysterical" (or "histrionic") personality. (See, for instance, Stoller 1985a, with its description of a woman who used that quality manically as a centerfold, and Stoller 1979 for an extended study of a woman also with chronic erotic tenseness who was not driven to professional exhibitionism.) Women of this subcategory think and feel erotically day and night and have consciously done so since early childhood—three, four, five, six. They are profoundly exhibitionistic: always feeling that they are being watched, always preparing themselves for being watched, and therefore always alert to their physical appearance (so proving that they are right: they really are looked at all the time).

To get this done well, they may spend hours on—are highly focused on—cosmetics, fashions, sexy underwear, erotically provocative movements, performing (more even than just practicing) before mirrors, fantasizing being in or engaged in the professions of exhibitionism, such as acting, dancing, singing, and modeling. They are not only always "on stage" but, in being so, transmit their (not necessarily genital) excitement about being watched. This then stimulates the necessary reciprocal fantasies in the audience, which is composed of men who will want the woman and of women who will admire or envy her. This unending performance creates an aura—a miasma, when the overtones are darker—of erotism. Such a woman grabs her culture's definitions of femininity and drives them to extremes. Still, most of us know that though they are notoriously preoccupied with the erotic—the only egg in their basket—their erotic lives are chaos.

These women of hysterical personality (which, I suspect, includes, beyond pornqueens, other exotics, such as some nude models and dancers and the sex queens of the non-porn movie world) are even more charged with this insatiable excitement than are their sisters-in-diagnosis. (It is insatiable because it is at bottom not erotic—only its surface appearances are—and it therefore cannot be satisfied by erotic acts.)

Organic or psychologic theories can account for such intensity. A brain abnormality—for example, an anatomically well-placed tumor or electrode—can spark fierce erotic behavior, though I doubt that it would produce the raging hysteria seen in these women unless the patient was already a hysteric. That theory supports Bill's idea that pornqueens are born this way and some of the folklore of the fun-loving sex experts of the 1960s: all women are not only unendingly erotic but, given a fair shake, unendingly orgasmic (a feminist version of the worst horror stories told by Inquisitors and other male philosophers down the millennia as they tried to fathom the Mystery in women's Hell-inspired erotism). This theory is at present untestable. So if I disagree with it as a general explanation for womankind, I can do so only from bias, not fact. I do not doubt, however, that some women and men are more biologically endowed for the erotic arts than others.

Barring the rare midbrain tickle, however, I prefer looking for necessary antecedents in infancy and childhood, which then focuses my gaze on what I try to imagine happens inside the infant-child and what can be reported and observed as the members of the family interact.

If we analysts put our hypotheses vaguely enough, we cannot be wrong. So if I say that I expect to find in the pornqueen type a woman who was relatively abandoned by her mother (underprotected, underloved, underattended, undernoticed) and overstimulated by a father who was both erotically attracted to his daughter and repelled by her because of his hatred of himself projected onto her, then I have described, depending on the degree to which these factors are present, a lot of families that do not produce pornqueens. We need more precise descriptions in the hope that we can fit, with conviction, the theory with the woman's actual state.

At any rate, Bill knew he would have no trouble finding a natural and that, being a natural, she would gladly come in and display herself for the sake of science. As you will see, the first natural he encountered among those just entering the industry around the time he and I met was a girl who, though well heated erotically, was so pithed by Thorazine that she was not suitable. Then he met another and judged her a future "pornpersonality," as he put it. But, though she passed the heat test, she failed others equally important. She did not fill her exhibitionism (in contrast to her genitals) with lust but was instead ravaged by shame: she was unutterably shy. So by the time I met her she was of more interest to me in my business than to Bill in his; her story will not be told here.

The transcripts have been edited as follows: Chunks of our conversations have been removed when touching on issues not pertinent to this book. Parts have been removed or changed in order to preserve confidentiality. Most of my comments, which served to encourage, keep people moving, raise questions, express my puzzlement, or describe my functions in studying erotic or gender behavior, have been removed. Hemming and hawing, natural language that is incomprehensible when written, and comparable impediments to free flow of reading (as different from listening) have been cleaned up. In a few instances two or three interviews have been collapsed into one.

All participants have reviewed this material from its raw form as transcripts through proof and have been free throughout to make modifications as they wished, including the right to stop publication of anything about themselves.

To make better sense of the transcripts, you need introductions. Bill first. We met because I asked a colleague if he knew anyone in the porn business. Months later, an attorney called; he was connected to the industry and would be visiting Los Angeles. On the way, however, he became ill and so contacted Bill to talk with me.

Opium to an addict it was, telling Bill someone at a university wanted to hear him talk about his work. Since his goal in life is immortality—fame forever, whatever the cost—he saw me as an opportunity. He was right.

Bill carries himself in an optimistic, buoyant, relaxed, open-faced, physically healthy way. He looks and acts younger than his age. He enjoys—visibly—every moment of the interviews and even breezily discusses traumatic experiences of childhood and adolescence. Some of what he says has been worked over before: he is a storyteller with everyone. But as the hours pass, especially when he talks of his childhood, he sometimes settles into a quieter mood. He can talk indefinitely without coaching or questions. In fact, everything I say is an interruption. He enjoys showing off his mind—his story—but is not exhibitionistic about his person. I find him frank, generous, honest yet sophisticated in how he uses his innocence, and greatly amused by himself, implying success in undoing early traumas. His willingness to die for his cause—"fuck society"—makes him a menace when he denies that AIDS threatens him and his colleagues.

The money that pays for producing porn, it is rumored, is cash. In our nimble civilization that suggests a laundering process. Bill avoids feeling that he is a part of this business by staying clear of the chain of operation that leads from the top—where, far from porn, the cash is generated—down to him (the three monkeys of Nikko). The physiology of our culture connects all of us to immoral and criminal enterprises (though I do not think we are thereby inherently worse than other cultures, only richer). So Bill, as good a rationalizer as the rest of us, does not find his unsavory business worse than, say, that of bankers who launder cash, students who trash teachers, union members who vote for leaders they know are crooked, stock manipulators, makers of cheeses produced in filthy factories, asbestos manufacturers and their company doctors, children who push drugs, supporters of boxing fights, sellers of tickets to paradise, advertising copy writers, "amateur" and professional athletes, book and art critics, art gallery owners, traffic ticket fixers, tax cheats, watermelon growers, bribers and blackmailers, drunk drivers, bought and sold politicians and judges, municipal bus drivers, water robbers, highway builders, fertilizer and bugkiller manufacturers, restaurant owners who charge more than two times retail for wines, and creators of beautiful but tasteless tomatoes.

Bill enjoys presenting himself as being attached to no one and needing no one but his girlfriend; he is, I believe, correct in that assessment. As he talks, you will learn enough about his parents that you may decide, as I have, that his self-sufficiency and rebelliousness grow from techniques he used for dealing with them.

He makes no effort to seem a star, porno or otherwise. This modesty mirrors his happily expressed belief that he is not and does not need to be a star. He strikes me as being what he says he is. This gives him an endearing quality he confesses to having. His rebellion against society is not in his appearance, mannerisms, or presentation of self but in his work, which is his only interest (besides playing football and rooting for the Detroit Lions and New York Yankees), day and night. His worldliness makes him wise about his profession and yet has an innocence about it—a holy-fool quality, energized by submerged belligerence—that, in his business, could be fatal: good-humored denial of danger hides from him an outcome that would not surprise him.

A further orientation as you read the transcripts. If these were playwrights' scripts, you would be carried by art. If the artist's style was verisimilitude, you would feel the action to be genuine though you were led to that conclusion by contrivance; precise rendition of speech would ruin the work. But my purposes are different. If I monkey around very much with what my informants said, you cannot trust my report. (Compare Capote.) In my game one is obliged to use what real people really said, end up with a version my informant and I vouch for, and still keep the reader's interest and sense of the argument supported by the data. An artless art.

I wish it were possible to publish for you to hear, at this point, an audiotape of a few minutes of Bill and me (and everyone herein) talking; it would greatly enlarge your sense of us. But there are the problems of confidentiality and publication costs.

I have debated whether to keep up a running commentary, interjected into the transcripts, of my opinions. This could include what is occurring; or what I felt and thought at the moment; or what is the significance of the moment for a larger view, such as: First Amendment, ethnographic method, psychoanalytic theory. I shall almost never do so, despite the value in informing you. The disadvantage, as I see it, is that with the added knowledge you are no longer there in the room with us, the invisible observer, free to judge without the impediments my comments, however enlightening, might provide.

You and I may feel, for instance, that a speaker—informant or I—is being defensive. I shall not insert that gloss, even if I judge that not all readers will think of it without my comment.

Another example. When Bill remembers the night his father died, were it not for what I write now, I would not raise the question whether this is a genuine memory (whatever that is) or one manufactured by him as the years passed. Bill loves rhetoric: hyperbole, shock-phrases. He wants to seem outrageous. For me to be a truth squad, shooting at him with brackets, might deflect the reader from his style of presentation to my post hoc harassing.

And I shall not send up warning flags to remind you that the facts I give you are only the words that we spoke. The assertions made—by Bill, for instance—do not necessarily contain facts—the truth, the whole truth, and nothing but the truth—but only hearsay. Let the hearsays speak for themselves; and you, ethnographing with me, lay one person's story against another's and another's. For you know that these are simply informants' versions—which may or may not be their truth. But certainly the informants' versions are not the versions the people they describe would give (Stoller 1988). Just beware lest you always end with the same convictions with which you started.

Chapter 3 **BILL, A PORNOGRAPHER**

Bill Margold* suggests ideas for, writes, directs, and acts in porn flicks. As you will see, Bill is profoundly self-centered and an endless talker. Depending on the form and degree of your antisocial elements, you will find his attempts at humor appropriate, tasteless, or —worse—unfunny. Whatever—he can bring you closer to the way porn is created than most anyone you will ever meet. And that, for an ethnographic study, is a gift. In addition, his description of his childhood suggests how its traumas and frustrations feed into his occupation; few in the business allow such entrée into their motives.

He enthusiastically sets forth. This is our first meeting, six years ago.

B: You [Dr. Stoller] have the opportunity to be a tourist in a very strange land. It's the most misunderstood industry in the world. The last time I was approached to do something like this [to be interviewed], the man wound up analogizing us to having the same kind of death wish that bullfighters, skydivers, and racecar drivers have, which is probably true, because I'm in an antisocial, highly immoral, against-the-grain, ultra-rebellious form of entertainment. We're the last rebels in society. At least we're better than the stupid terrorists who go around blowing up people. No one ever died from an overdose of pornography.

If you want any background on my part, I'm a college graduate. I got into

*Bill has insisted that no facts here be disguised (though he and I have deleted some details less pertinent to our work). First, he wants the world to know who he is and what he has accomplished, and second, he says that everyone mentioned in these transcripts has already been described in his published writings. In places, nonetheless, I have refused to use even a performer's pseudonym if I think the material would harm someone's reputation.

the Industry years ago, to write stories about it. I wanted to live out my fantasies. In a sense, I'm going through my adolescence at this point. You have to have a totally exhibitionistic, narcissistic flair to survive in the Adult Industry, because you're competing against yourself. It's very difficult under the pressure of the lights and the camera and the action.

We're pieces of meat. I have referred to my cohorts as pieces of meat, and they don't like being called pieces of meat, but we are indeed pieces of meat. Because without the appendage, we are of no value whatsoever. Without the ability to manipulate that appendage up, in, out, and off on cue, we're of no value whatsoever. There are about fifty male performers in the world. And about twenty of those work regularly. The other ones are just nickel-and-dime-type people: stagger in and stagger out. I am not a star. I am not a John Holmes, I'm not a John Leslie, I am not a Jamie Gillis, or an Eric Edwards, or a Herschel Savage, or Paul Thomas, or Joey Silvera. And that's about (oh, maybe Harry Reems), that's about it for the stars in our Industry, the male stars.

S: What makes a star?

B: Longevity. A bit of the macho ethic. They have to look pretty good. We can't have weak-looking, unhealthy, unpalatable people on screen. I have survived because I look ordinary. I have this incredible ability to look different to each person who meets me. I can deliver the "everyman" to them on a silver platter. But I never pursued the stardom aspect of it. It takes, basically, testing yourself more than I want to be tested. Under the gun I have survived, I have not failed to function since I began performing years ago. I can get up, get in, get out, get off on cue, I can give you a cum shot, which is known as the money shot, the male orgasm, on cue, ten seconds, "pop." I can do that while I'm carrying on a conversation, without real metabolic change half the time, which makes me almost automatistic, like a robot. Which is not that much fun to be with when I'm working, because I'm concentrating on other things than the sex, which, under the pressure, is secondary. The achievement of controlling yourself and then getting off when you're supposed to, that's the ultimate satisfaction. It results in light-headedness and giddiness, and you laugh a lot. A lot of times in my films when I get off on cue and have done my job well, I'll cackle fiendishly. That's my salute to myself. I'm delighted with myself.

This is the "playpen for the damned." [This, and lines like it, are pre-pared phrases, Bill quoting himself.] We are, like I say, one of the last sets of rebels in America, or in the world. I get a big kick out of that. But the stars are the ones who have done four-five hundred films, a thousand films. Holmes has been in about four thousand different situations. I don't want to be bothered doing that. I'm trying to carve my own niche in the Industry. I'm known as the bad boy, because I usually wind up doing things that are foul on screen.

My whole reason for being in the Industry is to satisfy the desire of the men in the world who basically don't much care for women and want to see the men in my Industry getting even with the women they couldn't have when they were growing up. I *strongly* believe this, and the Industry hates me for saying it. But I really believe that even the most satisfied Casanova-Don Juan-satyr has always wanted somebody he couldn't get, and because of that he starts to harbor a revenge. So we come on a woman's face or somewhat brutalize her sexually: we're getting even for their [the men viewers'] lost dreams. I believe this.

I've been told this by people in audiences after I've done horrible things on screen to women. I'm not hurting them. It's only an act, but it looks real—because I can scare people—I have a booming voice and I can become very intimidating. That gets the audience excited. I've heard audiences cheer me when I do something foul on screen. When I've strangled a person or sodomized a person, or brutalized a person, the audience is cheering my action, and then when I've fulfilled my warped desire, the audience applauds. I am not that way in real life. I don't have the time to beat somebody up in bed. I don't have the inclination or the time. It takes a lot of work to be brutal; it takes a whole lot of work. It's much more fun just to roll and hug like a couple of bears and have sex and enjoy yourself. I enjoy sex. I don't want to be bothered in bed putting on a gigantic show, and fist-fucking, and all that kind of stuff, which really doesn't interest me. It's very difficult for me to fist-fuck anyway now, because my hands have been smashed up from playing football. [Cracks his knuckles wildly.]

S: What's all that cracking?

B: Football. I've had almost every finger broken on both hands.

S: You're not still playing?

B: I am. I've always played for fun. See, I developed late in everything. I didn't even know how to play football until I was sixteen years old, because I was a bit of a toad. If you remember a movie called "American Graffiti"— the Charlie Martin Smith character—I was that character in high school. I was a nerd before nerds were known.

In the 1950s I was very straight, very dull, a totally introverted person. And then in college, when I discovered myself, I began to realize I enjoyed power. So I began to have fun. I came out of my shell just enough, started to learn about sex but really wasn't that interested because it just wasn't worth it. I didn't see any great thrill; masturbation was more satisfactory, didn't cost a goddamn thing. I had no money to go out on dates anyway. So I lived in that fantasy long enough until I finally met a girl I could fall in love with, or at least fall in lust with, and she said I was good at what I did. So I began to develop. My adolescent period really began when I was twenty-eight and I'm still in it. I'm still delighted with sex where most people my age [forty-four in 1991] are bored with it by this time. I'm still frolicking around in it. As I say, "a playpen for the damned."

And now I get paid for it, which is not really the main point, because I don't care about money. I am essentially antimercenary. I like money to survive on, but it's not the main reason I exist. I exist for glory, immortality, and because what I'm doing now and what I will continue to do until I can no longer function is perpetuate my image. People recognize me. I am desperately in need of that. I suffer from an inferiority complex. So I validate my purpose for being by doing this. I don't mind seeing my name on an outhouse wall as long as they spell it right.

When I graduated from college, I thought I wanted to be a movie reviewer. I didn't know what I was going to do next. I had been in Los Angeles' Central Juvenile Hall when I was a kid. I was an incorrigible. When I was in Juvenile Hall, being an incorrigible was a Class A crime. It kept me out of the Marines and the Navy. I tried, when I graduated from Hamilton High School, sixteen years old, to go into the Marines. They refused to take me because of my incorrigibility record. A year later, the Navy decided not to take me. At that point, 1961, you couldn't get a real job until you were eighteen. It's a strange society that would not let you work anywhere. I had to work on a golf course. I survived that way until I was eighteen. Then I got a series of jobs and decided to go to college.

I began supporting myself selling dog food door-to-door, which was fun—pure ground beef, hard-boiled eggs, cottage cheese, alfalfa, wheat germ, soybean.

Then, after graduating from college and working on a newspaper as a film reviewer, having been in Juvenile Hall, I decided to go back there and work. So I worked as a Probation Officer for a few years and in a sense repaid that part of my debt. But I got fired because I don't like rules and you had to follow rules. I overidentified with the children. I became one of them. I banded with them against the counselors. There was a series of oppressions that went on in Juvenile Hall, and I wasn't going to turn the place into a jail. It should never be a jail; it should basically be a rehabilitation situation to send the kid out somewhere else.

When I was working in Juvenile Hall, a fourteen-year-old kid came in and told me that he was getting laid and getting paid in Hollywood. I became incredibly indignant and went to Hollywood to investigate. The very industry I'm in now. I was going there to blow the whistle. I figured if I wrote a story revealing the Industry for using children, that I would be a great journalist, Pulitzer Prize, and be a wonderful human being. So I went there. They took one look at me. I was very, very, very straight. I looked like a toad. I walked in there and they figured, "This guy's a cop." So they didn't invite me back. I was going to expose the X-rated Industry because there were underage children in the Industry.

S: He was screwing some girl for the movies?

B: And he made twenty-five dollars. I didn't think that was right. So I went to the place he sent me to, to expose them.

S: Were you pretending that you were going to work?

B: Oh, yeah. I would have written this big exposé, been patted on the head and won a prize, probably wound up dead in the gutter. They of course never called me, and I put it out of my mind. So I continued at Juvenile Hall.

But I knew the handwriting was on the wall: I was doomed there because I'd broken every rule possible. I had a big Civil Service hearing, and the kids cried. They said keep me around, because I loved them. No kid in the years I was there ever raised his hand to me in hostility. I had a perfect rapport with the kids. It was the counselors who hated my guts, because I broke all the rules and I sided with the kids against the counselors. It was all right. I'd worn out my welcome and was probably living on borrowed time. I was writing; I went to work on an underground adult newspaper, and in early 1972 I got a call from a man named Reb who owned a modeling agency called Sunset International. He called me all kinds of names and said I had not put his [porno] ad in the newspaper. I went down to defend the owner of the paper and walked into a small office and was confronted by a 220-pound Hell's Angel type. Now even at my maximum weight, I'm not about to tackle my weight in Hell's Angels. I'm not a physical person; I don't have the time to beat somebody up. I can outtalk them, but my hands break easy and I don't want to be bothered hitting somebody.

So I said, "Tell you what I'm going to do," realizing that here he was, the Lenny of *Of Mice and Men*, "I'll write a story about you," and he mulled that over for a while like the ogre in *Jack and the Beanstalk*, and said, "Okay, what the hell." So I wrote a real nice story about him—"Reb's Rent-A-Chick Service." I came back to the agency with the story, and I told him [the paper's owner], "I want to do a story on this business." At this point I was no longer going to expose it. I figured I would write a story about what it's like to be in the X-rated Industry. I had no idea what I was going to do, I didn't have any idea I was going to do anything sexually. I figured I'd just go onto a movie set and write a story. So he said, "All right. I'll see what I can do for you."

A couple of months passed. I got fired from the paper because the guy was trying to absorb my ego: he wouldn't let me put my name in the paper any more and I got very unhappy about that. I got a call from Reb. He said, "Come on down. You're going to be in a movie called *The Goddaughter*." I walked in, they read me for a role, I was terrified. I couldn't act. First of all, I didn't even know how to act. They made me take my clothes off and looked at me. I was chattering. I was freezing and my cock was the size of a sleeping worm. I didn't think I was going to do any sex anyway. I said to them, "I'll write a story about you" (I was on another newspaper) "if you just let me be around. I don't care about being paid, because I'll get paid by the people who are putting out the newspaper." And they of course figured: how could they lose? One hundred and thirty-six hours later, which is what it took to make the film, I had been in the movie.

The main reason I got into the movie was to get killed. I'd always wanted to die in a film, because I played cowboys and Indians all my life, and I am essentially still very much a child. So I figured it would be fun to die on camera and then get to go see myself on the screen. I had no idea I was going to do sex. So I got killed, and they thought that was real nice. I got stabbed and shot and fell into a pool of blood and wiggled around on the floor. And the director was screaming at me to stop moving and I wouldn't stop moving. I refused to die when I was supposed to.

But then it seemed the people began to disappear on the set, and they weren't coming back. They would get tired—136 hours is a long time to work in about five days—people were staying up, God knows, 20 hours at a time, and people were worn out. So they said would I mind taking more of a part in the film. And I said as long as I don't have to say anything, that's okay, because I'd been given the role of Dummy anyway where I had no lines. But I was told to do this: get on a couch and start playing around with some girls. Now this was simulated action at this point.

So I got on the couch and began playing with them, and they shot the scene. Then they noticed I had forgotten to take my pants off, but the scene was already in the can. So they were really howling at me by this time, and I was all ashamed, I was terrified, I was in way over my head. Then another character disappeared from the movie, and they said, "Let's put Dummy in bed with the lead." And I said, "What are you talking about putting Dummy in bed? I don't want to get in bed with her." Here's this really mean woman. (She's dead, she overdosed a couple of years ago.) I got in bed with her and she said, "Now you don't touch me here; you don't touch me here; you don't touch me here." And I said, "What am I supposed to do?" She said, "I'll just do everything I want to you." It's still simulated at this point.

So we rolled around for a while. And then she said a few things to me. And I said a few things to her. And I'm just terrified. If you ever see the movie, which, thank God, most people won't, because the movie was locked up in the jail somewhere and has never been seen since it played once, and I'll get to that experience in a second. What happened is I really didn't like what I was doing to her, and I didn't know I could mistreat her or start acting up. But by the second time I had to work with her in the same movie, just before I go off to die, by that time I said, "No, to hell with it." So I began pushing her all over the bed and became more of a macho than a Dummy. And she really got into it, and we had a nice time. Then when it was all over, they applauded and they came up and said, "That was really good, why don't you do a little more stuff like that?" And I said, "No, I don't think so." It's still simulated, but she responded to me. So I became more interested than I should.

They began to notice that I had a few things other men don't. I have about a 10½-inch dick. That's what they say: I'm not really in love with my own cock, but they say it's big. At one point it was the second biggest in the Industry and now it's maybe the third, and I guess they get all excited about this. I don't really give a shit, you know, it does what it has to do. One of the nicknames for it is "The Hose," because I have my own practice, that I learned about six months after this movie, of getting myself up. I don't let people touch me until I'm ready to work. My left hand has been my best friend since I was thirteen years old. It knows what goes on. So it's going to help me. I don't want to be nibbled on; I don't want to be petted; I don't want to be made love to.

Because the cock at that moment belongs to the screen, not to the woman I'm with. So it does the job it's supposed to do. It becomes basically a piece of meat that does what it has to do. I treat it almost as a separate entity. I've even been photographed on camera, in films, talking to it and discussing things with it. It has its own personality, which is a lot of fun. Well, six or eight months later I'd done my first hard-core film, *The California Connection* (released on video as *The Erotic Adventures of Peter Galore*). Hard core: get up, get in, get out, get off. Penetration. I had realized that what I wanted to do was the immortality situation: the money meant nothing, but I wanted to see myself on the screen, 35 millimeter, go into a movie theater and see myself. And speaking of that, *The Goddaughter* came out at the Pussycat Theater, and of course, I ran down to see it.

I was sitting in the audience. The movie starts up, and it ends. I'm not on the screen. I'm sitting there: "Oh, my God, I'm on the cutting room floor." I was about to fall on the ground crying when all of a sudden the movie starts up again in the middle—the reels had been shown completely out of order—and there are all my scenes. The movie had made no sense of who this character was who wanders through, has these strange sex scenes, and gets killed. But there I was, bigger than life in a terrible performance, because I did have a few lines which I managed to swallow and sound like a mouse when I delivered them. I was awful. It was a *terrible* performance.

S: Does the audience even care that the reels are out of order?

B: Oh, no. Many times I've sat in a theater and watched the entire film emulsify on the screen, and the audience doesn't move. I think they're dead. [Laugh.] They're lobotomized. All they want to do is see tits and asses and holes and poles. I wanted to do hard core, but not for the sex, obviously. I went to San Francisco, and that's a story unto itself. Because in those days, 1972—the early days of hard core—they drove me around for two hours trying to get me lost so I didn't know where I was going.

   To break the law, which is what we do, by the way. We are prostitutes, we are paid, we do break the law because we are performing sexual acts for money. I am not glorifying what I do. It is illegal, but to me it is massaging the law. We don't force anybody into it. I don't drag a woman off the street and force her to suck my dick. Because if I forced her to suck my dick, my dick would be down her throat after she bit it off. You don't force somebody to blow you, let's put it that way. Linda Lovelace said somebody put a gun to her head in *Deep Throat*. I told her publicly (via TV hookup—"The 3:30 Show" in October 1984) that the only gun put to her head was the gun of poverty, and she turned it on this Industry and began firing hypocritical bullets at it. The woman lied. I don't blame her for turning on the Industry, but she should at least have her facts right. I have seen the dog loop with Linda Lovelace, *Doggierama*.

S: What does that mean?

B: Well, Linda Lovelace and this embarrassed looking Doberman-German shepherd that she screwed many, many years ago. That dog did not want to do that. That dog looked worried, very concerned about what he was getting into, and was not happy when it was all over.

S: Let me interrupt you again. What do you mean by "dog loop"?

B: She worked with a dog.

S: But "loop" means?

B: Ten-minute film. A loop is a ten-minute film based on I guess the symbolism of the loop of film that it goes around, it fills up one loop. First she screws poor Eric Edwards, who is one of the legends in the business, and then in comes the embarrassed dog that she takes on. And the dog is truly not happy about his performance. Rex the Wonder Dog it was called. The dog got more money than Eric Edwards got, as legend has it. If you ever want to see the damn thing, my friend has this piece of junk. It's awful. Not really interesting, bad performance on all parts. Well, I went to San Francisco.

S: This is the driving-you-around? You didn't know where you were?

B: But I knew exactly where I was because I had been to San Francisco previously. I knew all the streets. So finally when *they* got lost, I had to tell them where we were going. [Laugh.] Then they began to realize that I was different. They were used to stupid people in the Industry. But I could start discussing things on any level that I wanted. So I went up and did the hard core for a book called *Sexual Stamina*. I shot for seven hours. I had five cum shots.

It was funny, because I didn't know I wasn't supposed to continue to go off. So every time I felt like going off, I would. I'd pull out, go off in somebody's face, go off on a back, go off, whatever I felt like doing. When it was all over they said, "You didn't need to do *that* much." I said, "Well, no one told me not to." [Laugh.] I'm very naive in that situation. I like to give more because I figure I'm having so much fun doing it that to me it's not a job. I don't look at it like work. No one is going to believe I did it in one day. Knocking off five cum shots in seven hours. I think I had eighteen orgasms in thirty-five hours once, which was an interesting experience but, you know, I no longer do that kind of stuff. I can still give you two in five minutes if I have to, that's one of my stocks in trade.

I proved that a couple of times. In *Olympic Fever* we knocked off the first blow job, and I said, "That wasn't good enough, let's do another." So everybody looks around and says, "What are you talking about, you can't get another cum shot." And I said, "Oh, yeah?"—bam!—bigger, better, almost choked her, fantastic stuff. And I felt that was real nice. They were all happy. The director called me up three months later, when they were editing the film, and he said, "You son-of-a-bitch." And I said, "That's right." That's what I deal in, you know. I'm not going to do anything ordinary. I'm not in them for the sex, I'm not in them for the money, I'm in them for glory, and I want to keep on upstaging everybody else I'm with.

I have been in the Industry for sixteen years, and I have seen the Industry go from the playpen to Wall Street. To Century City. It's become big business. Out of the gutter to Century City. The innocent fun of years ago has unfortunately become business. It has become work. What's really funny about it now is that the kids in the Industry charge overtime. To me that's ludicrous. You don't charge overtime when you're robbing the bank. So why charge it when you're having sex? When they are performing something that is essentially illegal they charge overtime. They get out those goddamn adding machines and start computing their overtime. I say, "How in the hell can you do this?" And they say, "Oh, well, fifty dollars extra an hour. It adds up, it adds up." You hear the goddamn dollar signs go off in their heads. I hate greedy people, I really hate them.

I'm now a consultant to people who are starting out in the Industry. I advise them, "Don't be greedy because you will eventually earn what you deserve," which could amount to $500, $1,000, $1,500, $2,000 a day cash, which is not bad. But don't come in and demand $1,000 a day until you've earned the right to get it, because you're only as good as the person who's jacking off because of you. If the world is not jacking off over your image, you're not a sex star. I don't think people rush home to jack off over me, but at least I have been told I entertain them. I have played a diversity of roles. I've probably been involved at this point in about 300 projects in various situations: acting, writing, directing, completely formulating projects. So about 250, in which I've probably played about 60 different characters.

I have a lot of fun doing this. The pressure is there. I have directed X-rated films or X-rated videos. I have come up to someone and told them it's time to go to their sex scene. They've looked at me as if I was taking them to be beheaded at the guillotine, as if this was the time for the firing squad.

S: Men *and* women?

B: The women don't worry. The women essentially—and I'm not denigrating them—don't really have to do very much. They have to lay there, or they have to perform the acts of oral sex. Some of the women are so worried now about the various and sundry diseases, which I don't live in fear of—I figure if you're healthy, you're not going to catch anything—that they stuff all kinds of sponges in themselves or they put these antibacterial lozenges inside their vaginas which freeze the poor man's cock, which is not fair. They have very little regard in those cases for the men that they're working with. It's sort of sad. The old days—and I'm talking like a veteran, which I am—they seemed to care more. Now essentially the women are going through the motions. They're basically nothing more than carnal cash registers. That's very sad. They're not into it as much as they were. That's not to say all of them are like that. There are still the exceptions. We're casting one of my latest projects with what I believe are a number of exceptions.

S: Tell me about that. You mentioned on the phone this girl that you've just discovered.

B: Oh, yes. I'm ambivalent about her. I thought about bringing her today, but I figured she would just sit here and you would not be impressed by a woman who had been Thorazined to the point where her brain has been fried. I don't know what I'm going to do with her. She is, from the neck down, like a pea out of a pod, truly, almost in the state of still forming her sexuality. A flawless body, just absolutely perfect. From the neck up, she has a very nice face, a nice head of hair and great teeth, but unfortunately her brain is operating at a sixth-grade level. She was in numerous homes for boys and girls and these homes have a habit of dispensing drugs for most anything, gratuitously.

I warn people about this business. When a girl enters my office, I put them through a grueling interview, nothing physical, all mental. I try to destroy them and drive them out of my industry and out of my office because I don't want their conscience on mine. I don't want them to do something now for the money that will haunt them ten years from now. I'm terrified of that. I am not that big-hearted, not that magnanimous. I don't want Jacob Marley's ghost coming back to get this Scrooge. The whole series of them clanking around after me. I don't need that. The kids that I've allowed into the Industry: those are the ones who convinced me, coming into my office and putting up with my interviews, that they wanted to be famous, they wanted to be a star, that the main reason they were there was to perpetuate their image. That they could survive. A great sex star is born, she's not made. They have to come into my office [that is, of their own accord] and they have to be born hot. [Ron, whom you meet in chapter 10, feels that child sexual abuse creates a lot of the heat.] The flame has to be there. I can fan the flame, I can turn it into a forest fire.

S: What's the difference whether they're hot or not? They're not feeling anything while they're doing it. [Wrong. Some do sometimes. Bill knows this.]

B: But they have to make the audience believe. I don't care if they feel it; they have to make the audience *believe* that they feel it.

S: You're looking to see if they're hot to *perform*.

B: Exactly. But the heat has to be something that they believe. They have to believe themselves to be sexual animals, whether they bring that across to the person they're working with or not. They have to have carnal confidence in themselves. That's what I look for. And sex stars are rare, very, very rare, because a lot of them just don't want to be doing this. They hate what they're doing. Sex stars hate it. A lot of them despise what they're doing for a living. Absolutely do despise it.

S: They do it because?

B: Because I think they feel they're trapped.

S: Wait a minute, this isn't agreeing—

B: I know, but these aren't the ones I discovered. The ones I discovered are content with their lives. But there are other ones that I've not discovered, that I come upon, who are miserable. I have a girl in the Industry now who I love and adore as a big sister. I can see that she's tearing apart inside. I think she's going to commit suicide because she hates what she's doing. She goes through the motions.

S: Why does she do it?

B: Money. Absolute total money. Greedy. I fired her off my last movie, and then she convinced me she wanted to come back and do it. So I wound up giving her two hundred dollars extra, but I said, "This is hurting me more than it's hurting you, I can't stand what I'm doing to you." She said, "It's all right, I'll survive." But she really hates what she's doing. She despises it, and the guys [the male performers] come up to me and tell me they're not having any fun with her. It's not really their job to have fun, but at least it's nice if she does something to help them along. Some guys need to be made love to. I'm not like that.

 The girl is basically an extension of my left hand. It sounds horrible and dehumanizing, but I don't want to be bothered having to worry if the girl knows what she's doing because many of them don't have any idea. I have a lot of dead nerve endings in my lower back from football injuries. When I was in my real prime as a porn performer, I was known as "Leather Dick" because I had no feeling in my cock. It would get up and stay hard and you could hang baby elephants from it and nothing would happen. When I first got into the Industry I used to wash my cock off after every time I worked, with alcohol or aftershave lotion, which eventually wound up killing a couple of layers of skin. So between that and the nerve endings, people could chew on my cock with razor blades and I wouldn't know what the hell was going on.

S: Then what makes you come?

B: Mental. I come when I want to come. I'm a machine. It's not much fun.

S: Even when you're with a girlfriend?

B: No [not much fun]. It's still mental, it really is. The physical thing is sort of fun. I try and subordinate the physical or subordinate the mental when I'm with a girl that I'm having a real sexual situation with. But if I don't want to come I ain't going to come. I used to be able to go on and on. I'd wear out people. I don't bother doing that any more. It's just not worth it to me. I don't work as much as I used to. So my dick has become more fragile. It's become not as leathery now, but because I still abuse the cock as I used to abuse it, I can wear holes in it real fast.

S: I'm not clear what you mean.

B: Well, I get myself up and my cock is big. And in order to get it interested in what it is doing, I have to pull enough blood down in the son of a bitch to get it hard. My cock hard is a lot bigger than most other men's. So I have to keep on pulling on it to keep the thing interested in what it's doing.

S: You mean literally? As you're getting ready to work with the girl in the movie—

B: I get myself up. I don't let her touch me.

S: You don't get up on camera, you're already up?

B: I'm up. I don't want to waste time. God forbid.

S: The girl doesn't get you up?

B: No.

S: That's true all the time?

B: For me.

S: Whether you're working or you're not working?

B: Well, I've now taken it into my real life, too. I don't mind letting girls in my real life play around with me down there, but if nothing's happening, I get myself up. Then they're very happy. Because I just don't want to be bothered. A lot of girls don't know how to perform oral sex. They get down and start nibbling around like I'm chicken food, and I don't really want to be bothered having them [he makes a slurping sound] because it's not enough pressure for me. I need a lot of physical pressure. It's difficult for a girl to understand, because they think they're going to hurt me. You can't hurt my cock . . . well, maybe now, because I don't work a lot. But back in the old days, you could beat the thing to death, and I wouldn't feel anything.

S: You say something inside your head, then . . . is that what happens [to cause an orgasm]?

B: Yeah, a trigger [for example, a signal from the film director]. 10, 9, 8, 7, 6—

S: And if it's with a girl—

B: It's when they want me to go off. It's when they feel they need to have me come. My favorite position is doggie style. I don't like missionary. I like doggie style, because I like pounding into somebody. I can screw doggie style forever. Women love the feel of internal ejaculation. So they start mewling "Come, come, come." So all right. I can come with almost no emotional response. I'm not going to get all panting and puffing and excited.

S: Do you feel orgasm?

B: Yeah, that I do. I definitely can knock down playing cards with a cum shot if I wanted to. I'm not worried about that, and it is rather large. I have copious cum shots, which is nice, because the audience loves that: blast a person in the eye, blind them. They [audience] get all excited. They hop up and down, which is okay with me. But usually my first cum shot is nowhere near as good as my second one. That's why I like back-to-back, because the first one sort of gets me interested in the second one which is about to come. So with that one I give more. That one feels better physically to me. It's like I'm cleaning out things.

Many people have a misconception of the horrible things we do. We don't do anything bad. Nobody forces anybody to do this. This is not indentured servitude; it's not slavery. The women come in, they volunteer to do this, they get paid well, they get paid usually more than the man gets, although occasionally a man will get paid more. Our industry is essentially a Garden of Eden surrounded by the [poisonous] Love Canal so if you're willing to swim through the Love Canal, you'll find the Garden of Eden. It's familial. The kids all sort of take care of themselves and watch out for each other. There are a lot of very close friendships in the Industry, because we're all banded together insulated from the rest of the world who doesn't know what the fuck we're doing. Quite frankly, they don't much care for us.

A lot of the people that I grew up with have very little use for me because of what I do. I don't have a whole lot of friends. I don't have a lot of time for a lot of friends. I am extremely egocentric and must be the center of attention at all times. I am very unhappy when people are not paying attention to me. That's another reason that I'm in this industry: here they have no choice.

S: If ever there was a natural genius for this work, you sound like it. First of all you're biologically endowed the way most men are not, not just the size but the capacity, and this leather cock, and all that. And second, your need to be the center of attention. And you're intelligent. What a marvelous combination.

B: The intelligence factor is a paradox, because a lot of the people in the Industry are not. Because I'm intelligent, I pose a threat to the Industry. They hate that. I can outthink them. I can outcreate a lot of them. They don't want to be bothered by me. They wish I would go away. I'm not going anywhere, because this is my home. I have established myself in the Industry, and they can't get rid of me.

S: What dangers are there for you?

B: In what respect?

S: I don't know. Mafia.

B: Well, they say the Mafia exists in our business. I tend to believe that like any good moneymaking entertainment, we are controlled by powers we don't know anything about. But I have never been approached by anybody with a handful of tomato paste, let's put it that way.

S: I don't know what that means.

B: Mafia, Italian. The Black Hand. There is probably syndicate control of the distribution end of the Industry.

S: Let me see if I understand: they don't give a damn about the performance; they're not going to be involved in that because that's not where the money is. That's [making the movie only] what you know about.

B: Exactly.

S: Once the thing is in the can—

B: That's not my concern.

S: And is being distributed, that's where the money comes along and you wouldn't hear about that. There would be no reason why they would—

B: Nor do I want to be involved with them. They're not going to bother with me. Of course, I wouldn't mind having that kind of protection, you know. It would be nice to be affiliated with that kind of background.

S: To be protected by. But to be the subject of their attention might not be so good.

B: Well, I'm sure they know I exist. I've had tangential dealings with people who have tangential dealings with people who have tangential dealings. I just don't want to know the names or be involved with the faces. I'm in the creative end. I'm not in the financial end. I'm not interested in the financial. I don't want to be bothered by it. People approach me to get into the financial end, and I wave my hands saying, "No, pardon me, I'm not interested." They'll give me money to produce. I don't want to get involved in that. They want me to put together the whole package, then negotiate the deal of taking the finished entity to the distributor. The business is inherently unscrupulous because of its nefarious dealings with its own anti-morality: Why should I trust these people I'm dealing with? Why do I want to bother dealing with somebody else's money? Let them deal with it and find out that these people aren't the nicest people in the world. There *are* some nice people [in the Industry]. I simply want to be left alone to create. I have always said that.

[I talk with an ex-minor-performer, ex-semi-producer, Alex. He has been out of the Industry for several years and is glad to have retired intact. He has heard of but does not know Bill, having worked on the East Coast. Remember: what he speaks, as is usually the case with informants anywhere, is hearsay, however declamatory the rhetoric.]

A: Mr. Zip once offered me a promotion, what he does: a producer, a nominal producer. I said, "What's involved in this?" He said, "You go to the guys who have the money, and you get the money, and you take it out, and you hire people with that money, and you're responsible for paying them, which means that if somebody gets arrested, it's likely to be you." I said, "Then what happens? Do your employers pay for my criminal defense? What then occurs?" He said, "Up to a point. We'll try and get you bailed out, but after that, you're on your own." And I said, "I'm sure I could do this job and your employers would be happy with me, but I'm not sure I would be happy with them." He said, "My employers are always happy with the people they hire. If they're not, they kill them." I said, "I think I know as much about your employers as I care to know. In fact, I think I know *more* about them than I care to, and I would prefer not to discuss this again." We never did.

S: Let me ask you now about the bad ones: are they the producers or the money men?

A: Backers. And distributors. I know something about it. The people who put conventional [non-pornography] magazines on the newsstand and in your drugstore are mostly Mafia front companies. That and the vending machine business. Cigarettes, candy, concession businesses of that kind, mobile catering businesses that go around to construction sites, these are traditional organized crime businesses for one very good reason. They do a tremendous volume of cash in small amounts. Organized crime always has lots of cash that it needs to launder from its other businesses: drugs, prostitution, things like that. The accumulation of surplus cash is a headache in all cash businesses.

What would you do if you found yourself with $200,000 in $20 bills that you could not take to the bank? What would you do with all those $20 bills? $200,000 in $20 bills would fill this bookcase. It takes up a lot of room. What do you do with all those goddamn twenties? Can you go out and buy a house with $20 bills? Not unless you want to be visited by the Internal Revenue Service. You can't even go out and buy a car that way. Any cash transaction over $10,000 with any financial institution is automatically reported to the federal government. So what are you going to do with all that money? You've got to figure out a business that takes in a lot of $20 bills, into which you could stream the $20 bills from your other business in a way not obvious. If the business is collecting $10 here and $20 there, it's difficult for any auditor to trace the source of all that money: that's the great advantage of these little cash businesses.

That is why organized crime is always interested in little cash businesses. This porn video is a perfect opportunity for them; it's done with anonymous consumers through hole-in-the-wall outlets all over the country. The collection system for the money from shops is full of holes, so shaky and uneven and complicated and convoluted that it's impossible for investigators to trace the money that comes through them back to its source. So a business of this kind is attractive to organized crime.

The real money is made in income streaming. They're making their money laundering through the distribution side. People who make pornographic films complain endlessly that they never see the actual money that comes in off of them. They never know how much money is really being made, because the accounting is fanciful. The market is manipulated to satisfy the needs of the money laundering part of the Industry.

So that's how organized crime gets into this. That's why they're big in magazine distribution and periodical distribution: nickels and dimes from newsstands all over the country, not the sort of thing that federal investigators can run down very easily. I think they started out in the distribution end of it, and it turned out to be so successful that they decided to move into production. Logical. There was a shortage of product. They couldn't turn over these things on the newsstands fast enough to stream all that extra cash in, mostly, I think, from cocaine. You know, the tremendous bloating of the underground economy that's been produced by the growth of the drug culture in this country is really one of the things that's destabilizing the whole economy. It's like Colombia: just more cash than the economy can absorb. So they're always looking for new places to bury that money.

That's one reason why there's so much porn being made: they need to put stuff on the shelves so they can show income. Guys who are thinking about where they're going to hide ten billion illegal dollars from Colombia cocaine are not very concerned with what happens to porn performers in Los Angeles. If they don't care what happens to those ten-year-old kids smoking crack on the street corner, they sure as hell don't care about a bunch of porn performers. They're probably morally on fairly safe ground: at least these [porn] people are consenting adults. The other victims of this scam [for example, child addicts] are considerably less consenting.

I'll tell you something you might as well know about my point of view: I'm unsentimental about crooks. I don't like them. I don't have anything good to say about them. I have sympathy for a black street hustler who never had much chance to do anything else in his life, but I don't have sympathy for a guy who lives in a nice suburb and sits at a desk all day long figuring out some way to chisel $100,000 here and $100,000 there and doesn't give a fuck about who gets killed in the process. Don't have much sympathy for guys like that, who think they're smarter than everybody else and who believe that if anyone else were offered the same opportunity, they would do the same thing. The basic philosophical underpinning of being a crook is that everyone else is a crook; "they just weren't smart enough to figure this out on their own."

In some sense, everyone is a bag man for somebody in the chain of command. (That's one reason I got out a few years ago.) They don't meet with Al Capone [laugh], you know what I mean? They meet with an underling. But the people who set up these deals *want* the people below them to know that it would be dangerous to take the suitcase and run with it. They have an *interest* in having the people that they invest in understand the nature of the investment: when you [crook] invest in cash, you have no legal recourse should they decide to rip you off. So you have to make it very clear to them that you will use nonlegal recourse should they attempt this. (It's not the kind of business that you can be in if you're not that kind of person.) In that sense, the vending machine business and the garbage hauling business are like that, too. In any of those cash businesses, you've got to be prepared to collect with a baseball bat, because cash contracts are hard to enforce.

S: A guy I know in the business [Bill] would never deny that he knows broadly [what goes on], and he says he wants to stay away from them. On the other hand, the employees way down: the performers.

A: They know they ain't working for the Girl Scouts; even the performers know that. They know they're working for some bad people.

On a day-to-day basis it's not like Vito comes around in his suit with the wide lapels and his black shirt with a white tie to collect the money from the cash box every week. It's not like that. But somebody you don't know, somebody you've never seen and have no idea he's involved in this business, is in fact a partner. The person you see who you think is your boss may not be your boss at all.

B: But they're jealous of what I create a lot of times. Because they are so egotistical themselves. They are so imbued with their own self-worth, which doesn't really exist. Prime example: a few years ago we made the first all-black [performers] video. The video differentiates from film in that a video is shot on video tape, cannot go into the theaters. It then comes out on cassette and goes into your television set and you watch it at home. Well, before we made the first black video, the man in charge, who is financing it, said, "You can't do this." He was a pompous ass who challenged us to do it. He said, "You won't be able to finish this project." He said it was too complicated and had too many things going on in the script. [For the record:

Hot Chocolate, written by Lem Elijah and directed by Drea (ex-wife)—W.M.]

There were about eight sex scenes in the movie, some good character delineations, some scene set changes—location situations—where you went from room to room to room, and we had yet to do a complicated video. We'd done some simple stuff before but nothing really complicated with a real story. It takes time to set up the lights. Sometimes two to three hours' set-up time to shoot a five-minute sequence. He thought we couldn't do it. We did it in twenty-three hours total shooting time. We did it, and history has proven us right. I came back to him with scripts for three more video projects, figuring that now I've proven I can accomplish this, he would accept it. He looked at the scripts and said, "No, we're not doing these, I didn't think them up." So I basically swallowed my pride and left, but since then I've hated his guts tremendously.

I have the scripts. Nobody has really attempted to do them, but they will. I've done a lot of projects. When somebody approaches me now, it depends on the amount of money they want to spend, because a video can be made for between $12,000 and $50,000. A theatrical venture is about $80,000 to $150,000. "Theatrical" means goes to theater, 35 millimeter. It can also be shot 16 millimeter, but usually you shoot 35 because it gives you a much better print, 35 is how Hollywood shoots their movies. Sixteen means you'd have to blow it up to show it in the 35 theater. And there's a grainy look to the production. You can shoot 16 properly taking an extra day or two to properly light and use proper ratios and apertures and all that kind of technical trash, which I don't know about.

Video has to be compartmentalized down and has to be formulated. It has to be set up like dominoes. If one domino is out of place, video falls completely apart because you go from scene to scene to scene to scene, and you manipulate all your people. I just set up a three-day video shoot where we knocked off twenty-one sex scenes for three one-day videos, and I incorporated the sex scenes to make them fit into their respective projects. This was an amazing accomplishment on my part. They gave me a $400 bonus, which was sort of nice. Now they want me to do three more of them. I had fun. I was moving entire herds of cattle in one room, moving the other herd of cattle out. I don't think anybody knew what they were shooting, but it all fell together. It was hilarious. I wrote all three scripts and kept working the people so no one would have to have two cum shots in a row. People just going in and out of there: "What movie is this for? . . . Okay." Only I knew the magic. It was fun. It was a big kick for me doing that. It was the first time I'd ever done it. Again they told me I couldn't do it. Whenever somebody tells me I can't do something, I prove to them that I can. I enjoyed myself. I'm not sure I want to do it every week, because I wasn't even in it.

Well, I was. I was in one where I did a narration. I basically tied it together interviewing this girl who then reflects back on her adventures, and I jacked off at the end. And then I played football in another one. I managed to write a football scene into the movie where they shot these people going out and having a lunch break where they played football. And they do voice-over talking about coming home and screwing their wives, and the team they're playing consisted of me and two grips.

The Industry began with tiny 8-millimeter loops and then went to 16-millimeter features to 35-millimeter features to the theatrical industry, which was really fantastic. In the mid-70s there were like 1,500 X-rated theaters in the United States. There may be 300 now, because of the video influx. We've become commonplace, too. We've become passé in our own time. The world has accepted us, which is probably the worst they could do. We're no longer different, we're no longer unique, we're no longer extraordinary.

S: If you were passé, then something else would be supplying the sexual needs.

B: I don't think so. I think people are turning back into themselves. I think that swinging has become somewhat passé also. People can take us home now in videotape form and discover that, quite frankly, we're very dull. A lot of the movies we make are boring, really badly done, badly shot. You can't hear them, you can't see them, and after a while watching people fuck gets to be a real drag. I believe in a number of things when I direct: I like to have my sex scenes begin, middle, and end. I like to have petting; I like to have kissing if I can get away with it; I like to have people get out of their clothes on camera; I like to have an entire sex scene. So if you're going to jack-off over this, you're going to have the beginning, middle, and end. I don't want to have these fragmented pieces of shit on the screen where you're watching two people screwing and all of a sudden go to another room and you can't even tell who's screwing who. That doesn't help the mental situation. Sex is in the mind.

I met this couple. They found out who I was [porno performer], and they wanted to get together. And I said, "We don't have to rush this. You can wait." And they said, "Can we get together Saturday night?" And I said, "Yes." And I said, "You know, we don't have to do anything when I meet you. We can just talk." "Okay, okay, we'll just talk." I said, "Good." I'm not forcing myself on anybody. So we finally did meet. It was nice. They rented a room, and I screwed the wife and she was very happy. We had a nice experience.

S: Are there any criteria for a woman to appeal to you?

B: No.

S: You don't care what they look like?

B: No.

S: Or their personality?

B: Well, they have to want me. Then I perform. Because it doesn't require any kind of aesthetics, physical or mental arousement on my part, to perform. I am a piece of meat. I provide pleasure, which amounts to anywhere between 8 and 10½ inches, depending on my interest. If I'm more interested, apparently I get bigger. I don't *know* any of these things, because I've never really taken a close look at my dick at its maximum length. You gain an inch at the moment of ejaculation, you do swell and you do get harder and longer; that's physiological. So you pick up tremendous size. I've almost split people open. They start howling, well, you know, it's just natural, what can I do? I've had people who won't work with me. I'm not as big as Holmes. I'm just big enough, you know. I was at one time in the top three in the business. I have no idea where I am now, I have no idea where I rank. I don't even care, I never even flaunted the big-dick thing. It was something that I just happened to have. I work on it, and sometimes it grows to enormous lengths because I manage to *really* pull on it and bring a lot of blood in there and sometimes—

S: It's not a matter of psychological—

B: No, it's all a matter of physical abuse. Truly physical abuse.

S: And that holds also when you're with woman X, Y, or Z? Your size depends not on her at all—

B: It depends on her powers of manual manipulation—

S: That's mechanical. It doesn't depend on her, the person?

B: No. Manual manipulation. [But he's said he doesn't need women to touch him.]

S: What she looks like, how she expresses her personality, how excited she was?

B: No, the woman was essentially ordinary. What I find in these relationships is that the woman is going through the motions for the husband's pleasure. Throughout the whole thing, the husband just sat at one end and let her blow him while she was fucking me and I was fucking her, but he never really got into much of this. He just watched his wife get pronged: she was a small woman. She was pretty good, though. She really had a good time. I made her very happy. The room cost them a hundred dollars. I volunteered to pay for half the room but they said, "Oh, no, no, no." And when it was all over with, they said they would get in touch. They probably won't, because I very rarely have ever seen anybody again.

S: What defines it being "all over"?

B: After I ejaculate, after she's satisfied and that's it.

S: By "satisfied" you mean after she comes?

B: Oh, yeah, well, she went off. She was quite happy that way already. By the time I had screwed her, she was starting to get tired.

S: So what ends it?

B: Well, they derived tremendous satisfaction from having me get off. Both of them were delighted when I decided to go off.

S: And what decided you to go off at that point?

B: We did missionary first, which I don't like because I have bad wrists. So I switched into doggie style, which gives me my piledriving ability, but after a while my knee began to hurt me to the point that I made the announcement that I could not continue to piledrive into this woman much longer, and she said, "Well then go off, please, go off." And I said, "All right, I'll be happy to," and that was it. My knee was really bothering me.

S: Suppose you didn't go off? What would it do to you?

B: Nothing. I have proven that I don't have to. That really upsets some people. I don't need to go off. I can pile-drive forever, and if I don't go off, what the hell do I care? I just pull out.

S: You don't need an orgasm?

B: [Laugh.] Why? I've had thousands of them in my life. One more ain't going to make much difference. I'm not starving for an orgasm. I don't need it: I've proven what I can do. My whole life is not geared to getting off.

S: And in the movie?

B: Oh, in the movie it's professional, absolutely. That's mandatory.

S: But you've said there are times when you do it to yourself, don't you?

B: I don't know any more. [Laugh.] Oh, sure, when I was jacking off as a kid; when I was first screwing.

S: When did it stop that you needed orgasms, or wanted them, or enjoyed them?

B: I still do enjoy them. I still enjoy them. I enjoy them masturbatorily, I enjoy them in film more than in private life, because in film, if I can choreograph them and give them to an audience on cue, it brings tremendous adulation.

S: You're talking about an enjoyment which is the sense of the audience and the satisfaction with a good job?

B: Right. Sexual gratification, I still enjoy it. The greatest physical orgasm I've ever had in my life was a masturbatory one in a movie against a mirror, not for the fact that I did it on cue, but because I'd held off for about eight hours. It was the single most bone-rattling, toe-curling, hair-standing-up-on-end orgasm of my career. I must have come for a minute. It was *all encompassing* and an incredible cum shot. The irony of it is, you'll probably never see it. I don't know where that film went. It may come out some day on video, because theatrically it probably disappeared. I'm a character in love with myself in a mirror, and it's the ultimate narcissistic play. I really got into it, because here I was in a roomful of mirrors watching myself 120 dimensions deep. It was just fantastic. That is the single greatest orgasm of my life. And that was sexually satisfying. Christ, I couldn't stand up. You know, I was drained. I was shaking on the ground, flopping around like a flounder.

S: Does anything—I've got to get this accurate—

B: Turn me on?

S: Yeah, turn you on. But I wanted to get it accurate, because you told me what turns you on is your hand. But I don't mean in that sense. What others . . . let's say that you're part of the human race, shall we pretend that for a moment?

B: What a detestable thought. [Laugh.]

S: Yeah, I know that. Let's pretend that you are not this alien in human disguise. So then I ask you—

B: What turns me on more than anything else and always has is hugging and kissing. I love to hug and kiss people.

S: It turns you on and gives you an erection?

B: Um-hmmm.

S: And that's not just mechanical?

B: No.

S: And what do you do about that?

B: In what respect?

S: Then do you want an orgasm from that, or is it—

B: No, not necessarily. I don't approach sex as an orgasm-getting experience. I approach sex as: giving more than I get. I love to show people what I've learned. I learned the exhibitionism in the Industry. I was not an exhibitionist before I got into the Industry. I was naive. When I was younger, I did not waste time pursuing the orgasm to get off. I would make sure to satisfy them first. The guys would brag about how they'd screw these girls. To me it felt like they were using them. I didn't want to be ordinary. I didn't want to use anybody. So I figured if I gave them pleasure, I was going to be different. I hate the idea of being like anybody else.

S: I've noted that. When you gave them pleasure, was that erotically exciting for you or just altruistic?

B: Altruistic.

S: It didn't change the degree of your excitement?

B: No. But they liked it, and that thrilled me.

S: But not erotically?

B: No, it just made me very happy.

S: It seems as if you're saying now that there's no fantasy, that it's mechanical.

B: If I feel I need an orgasm, if I feel some kind of sexual tension, if I feel some type of pressure [snaps fingers], I jack off.

S: With any picture or story in mind?*

B: No.

S: Just purely cock?

B: Yeah. It's mine. [Laugh.] What the hell. You know, my toy. I haven't needed to have a tremendous sex drive. I've done what I had to in front of the camera. I was just talking about it with a guy: he said my orgasm is excellent on camera, which makes me happy. My normal anatomical female interest is bone-rail-thin, essentially titless, tomboy.

S: I'm not clear. You say that the physical appearance of women has never made any difference.

B: Oh, no, no, no, no.

S: Now you tell me that it does with breasts.

B: I always like to look at thin women. I don't like fat people, because they can only get fatter. I just don't like fat people. I think that has to do with my mother, who was round. Maybe it doesn't have to do with my mother. Maybe it just has to do with the fact I don't like unattractiveness. I'm intolerant of things that are wrong. This is a very bad way to be, but I just don't like flaws in the human body, particularly when I know that in most cases, unless it's glandular, that flaw can go away. I will tolerate a handicap if it's a handicap that is beyond the person's control, but if it's not beyond their control, I will not tolerate it. I am very critical. If there is something wrong that you can take care of, take care of it. But from the first I always liked women thin.

S: That was not erotic?

B: No, it was more of a comfortable image for me to handle. I liked bone-rail-thin women. I like anything that did not remind me of a maternal situation. You know, you'll never meet my mother [died in 1980—W.M.]. I guess the root of all evil comes from Mommy and the root of all good, too.

    She was a fascinating woman. Everybody else just loved her. You would have been fascinated by the woman, very bright, very sharp. She had the

---

*The story is, I believe: "I shall not have, do not need, a story"—that is, another person.

ability to charm anybody except me. And I would tell people about her and the problems I had with her. Then they'd meet her, and they would tell me I was wrong. That used to be amazing. I had social workers tell me that I didn't know what I was talking about, and I said, "That's great, she's a marvelous person."

S: You're all alone [at the time of this interview; for several years now he has lived with the porn star Viper—the official name he gave her].

B: Yeah. But not lonely. There's a big difference. It's not a sense of abandonment, because I've never felt abandoned. It's very difficult to understand, because we get into these things and I think: where did all this antisocial hostility and being unable to fit in come from? I don't know, except that I also know that my mother was in some ways as much of a rebel as I was. She was as outspoken as I am now, she was as quick to go to a fight as I am: verbal, never physical. There was a wire-terrier mentality about the woman that I used to enjoy. We weren't bad together when we weren't fighting. That's the problem: we were always fighting because I always wanted things. She spoiled me rotten and told me she loved me and then put me in boarding school. That made no sense to me. I was brighter than anybody else. I had to settle for friends that I could control, and I didn't like that.

S: Do you remember ever feeling hurt by this or were you already leather?

B: Oh, yeah, I was hurt. Sitting in the Santa Monica jail in 1956 on the verge of going to Central Juvenile Hall. That is the night that I grew up, essentially. I sat there and I cried for three, four, five, six hours. I cried until I was raw. And then I stopped crying that day. I remember the date (June 30, 1956) perfectly. I saw a movie, walked home, and was taken off the street by two Juvenile Hall probation officers because my mother couldn't control me. I used to say "no" to her; that's how she couldn't control me. I was put in Juvenile Hall, and I stopped crying. I said to myself, "Why am I crying? No one's listening." The cops were really good, they were very bright. They did not pay attention to my crying. Had they paid attention to me, it might have ruined me. That was the best thing they ever did . . . they just let me cry in a room. I cried and cried, because I always used to get what I wanted when I cried. This was the first time no one came to me.

So they took me down to Juvenile Hall in a car. I remember the ride. In Juvenile Hall I found out the one great lesson of my life: everything you get—you earn. The ladder: you start at number thirty and work your way to the top. And man alive, that gave me everything I ever wanted to learn about human psychology. I found out that you earn not by kissing ass but by performing and proving that you're better than somebody else. I never kissed anybody's ass. That was what I was taught by these wonderful human beings down there who said you've got to prove that you can climb that ladder. And I said to myself, "Well, I'm going to get to the goddamn top." And the day I left there I was at the top. And then I went to Vista Del Mar [a resident treatment center for children] and the home was very nice and comfortable for four years. Then when I got out of high school I was on my own.

S: This is correct: you were abandoned?

B: No. My mother put me in Juvenile Hall and then came to see me to take me out, and I said, "No, I don't want to leave, I like it here." And boy, then she went nuts. Oh, she cried, and I said, "It serves you right." I was bitter, but I had listened to other kids in Juvenile Hall who had been put in there, who didn't have parents or who were on their own and had led a lot worse life than I had. And I figured I had had a pretty good time. I was healthy. They called me "Professor" because I could answer all the questions. I thought that was fun. I loved Juvenile Hall. That's why I went back to work there. I went back to work there, and even then I was thwarted in my what-appeared-to-be good intentions. I went down there to get the job, and I did not have a sociology degree. They said, "Why do you want to do this?" and I said, "Because I was there. I think I can help these kids." They said they thought I could do a better job in the field. I said, "No, no, I want to go to the Hall."

I had to wait three months to get to the Hall. They would have hired me immediately to go into the field, but the field's worthless. You can't do anything for the kids in the field. It's in the Hall, where the kids come in traumatized, that you work. I had a great few years in the Hall. I really did, but unfortunately, as I do even in my own industry now, I identify with the kids rather than the adults. I will always be one of the kids. I told the producers that, and they went crazy. I said, "I am not one of you. I'm one of the kids. I'm not on your side, I'm on their side." And they went, "Oh, you can't be; you make money." I said, "No, that's not the most important thing. I just want to create, and I want to be left alone." That's the whole thing.

S: Your father—

B: He died when I was four.

S: When you were four. That's why the whole story that you just told me—

B: Goes haywire—

S: Doesn't have him as a character. Because he was dead.

B: He was a very powerful man. Had he lived, he would have been famous. I would have gone to Harvard. I'd be a lawyer. I have an ability to talk. God knows I don't long for it, but it's interesting. I had a taste of that lifestyle when I went to a very posh military school in Los Angeles. I didn't like it. I didn't fit in for some reason. This was years before Juvenile Hall.

My first nude experience took place there (Black Foxe). They forced me to swim. Even at six years old, I was real fast, I was like a natural born fish, though I was a spindly, anemic child. So they forced me to race, and this was a hilarious event. I stood up on the diving block, raced, got out of the pool, I had won, and the people were laughing: I had forgotten to put my trunks on. So that's my first nude experience.

When my father died, my mother just could not handle the fact that my father no longer was around. So she tried to erase her past by moving. At about that time, apparently, I began to start saying "no." I was told to do things, and I would say "no." I was told to behave, I would say "no."

I don't want a family. My family is the X-rated Industry. I don't want to be bothered with anybody else's in-laws, parents, relatives. I have no relatives now. My father died when I was four years old. I'm written up in Who-was-who. He was written up in Who-was-who. He was assistant secretary of the Interior under FDR, before that a federal judge in D.C. He would have been a Supreme Court justice, he was next in line. Felix Frankfurter was his mentor. He taught at Harvard after he graduated from there. But because he was Jewish, when FDR died, Truman apparently was told not to put any more Jews on the Supreme Court. That immediately broke my father's heart. He dropped dead in 1947. I was an adopted child; I was adopted before I was born in 1943. I was one of these grab-bag babies, a war baby. Whatever I came out, I was going to be a Margold.

According to my mother, I came downstairs the day after my father died and said, "How come you didn't go instead?" which I really don't believe I said, but typical stupid-mother psychosis. She put me in boarding schools yet kept saying how much she loved me, which of course was not good for my little-boy head to hear. So I became homesick for a home that was intolerable. I kept on running away from the schools.

I ran away from that school one morning at six, naked. I forgot to put my clothes on. So when I got out of the door and I couldn't get back in, I remembered my pajamas were still there. So I ran across the field, ran across the boulevard. And out came all the teachers, chasing me. And you can picture this poor little boy running naked being chased by these huge men, cars honking, no one ever stopped to ask, "What's wrong, little boy?" I remember this, it's a horrifying experience. A little boy eight [sic] years old, tears pouring down my cheeks, they grab me, beat me real good, throw me in the basement, made me stay down there. That's not a way to bring a kid up. But, you know, I learned with those kinds of experiences and at other boarding schools that the only person I could ever rely on was myself.

What finally taught that to me was when I was twelve years old, my mother finally threw her fat little hands up in horror and said, "I've had it with you; you are a worthless bastard. You're going to Juvenile Hall." So they came and took me away. So I schemed and plotted and literally by hook and crook got to number four, and then number three, and number two. The morning that I left Juvenile Hall to go to Vista Del Mar, I was number one on the ladder. And to get to number one I had done all kinds of interesting things, besides being very bright and very helpful and very good, never an ass-kisser, never a snitch. I never did do any of those kinds of things. I just earned it by brains. You'd answer questions after dinner and you'd move up a couple of notches. I was really good at it.

I woke up that morning and I was number one. And I went to Vista Del Mar. I'm probably the only person ever to cry leaving Juvenile Hall. I was hanging onto the bed, hanging onto the door, hanging onto the chairs, being dragged down the hall: "I don't want to leave, I love it here, I love it here." I got to the home. I was put into a cottage, and I immediately plotted to run away, but they took me to a movie and I decided I had better things to do. So I never did run away from there, but I called up Juvenile Hall. I managed to lie my way into the unit that I had been at, and all the kids were saying they were sorry I was gone. They had missed me.

I'd been there three months and I had really learned a lot about it. So when I went back to work at Juvenile Hall years later, the kids would scream and yell at me, and I'd scream and yell back. They'd say, "What the fuck do you know what it's like here?" I'd say, "I *was* here." I was in a unit that no longer is standing, but I can tell you what the Hall's like. That's how I could identify with the kids. Now as an X-rated personality . . . . In a sense I'm a probation officer in the X-rated Industry: I'm working with overaged juvenile delinquents. So when a kid—an actor or an actress—says, "What the fuck do you know what it's like?" I'd say, "I *am* one of you."

Someone said I'm "the Renaissance man of porn," that's what they call me, because I've done it all. I relate to them. That's why I'm hated by the people who control the Industry—because I don't identify with the adults, I identify with the kids. I've always identified with the kids. In Juvenile Hall, when I worked there, I would go in at six in the morning, I would change whatever I wore into the clothes that the kids wore. I'd put on a shirt, their pants. The only thing that differentiated me was the keys. And I played football with those kids, where I was fair game. (I broke my hand there, I broke three ribs, I got regular busted noses, I got a concussion playing there.) I would be so dirty and so filthy that when I came to dinner— because we never had a chance to clean up—I was stopped by the people at the door saying, "Wait a minute, get back in line where you belong." I had to take out the key and show them the key. It was a great feeling.

I even did things at Juvenile Hall that people to this day don't believe. I used to take kids out. I'd dress them up in my clothes and take them out to dinner at a place where I go a lot, I loved it, and then I would bring them back. The kids never ran away or anything. They loved it. I took a kid home once to his home, which was near Juvenile Hall, for his birthday.

I brought liquor in because it was New Year's Eve. I don't like liquor, I don't drink. I thought that mixed drinks meant that all the booze was poured into one big vat. So I got twelve bottles of pretty-looking liquor. I poured them all into one vat. These kids had all bragged to me about how they were drinkers. I wondered why it didn't smell all that good. I didn't know the difference. The kids drank it and they were throwing up. They couldn't even get up for breakfast the next morning, but they really loved the affection that I showed them. All the counselors chipped in, we got them cigars and a pack of cigarettes, and they had a blast—a big cloud of smoke hanging out over the units.

I used to grind up popcorn and roll it in toilet paper and give it to them and tell them it was marijuana. I hate drugs, but because they said they had to get high, I figured why not hyperventilate them, what the hell were they going to do? You can't smoke popcorn and it smells horrible, but I told them it was Santa Monica Gold, white gold from the beach, and these kids believed it. They believed anything I told them; it was fantastic. I used to come in on Friday afternoon, and if a kid had been bad, I'd come in and stand there and say, "Well, I guess we have to shoot you on Saturday morning." Then I'd walk out. And the kid would go, "What is he talking about having to shoot me?" All the other kids would know by this time, and they'd say, "Yeah, I guess he'll take you out and shoot you, they always shoot one kid on Saturday morning." It was fun. The kids really loved it, and I had a good time there. I really enjoy the X-rated Industry because it's very much like the Hall. The kids are exactly the same, even though some of them are older than me. They want to learn. They tend to look up to me as sort of a Daddy figure.

I was working with this kid, Kim Carson. The way she did it [act in a scene] really was touching. I really, really loved the scene. I hugged her and kissed her and told her she was growing up. Then one of the other girls, Amber Lynn, who had not been in the business very long, began to complain. I said, "You go see Mommy." And she went. And I told Kim, "Now you're Mommy, and you've got to take care of these kids." So I was personally gratified the night of the XRCO [X-Rated Critics Organization] Awards last year that she [Kim] won best supporting actress. We spotted each other across the room, and she ran and jumped in my arms and she just said, "Thank you, thank you, thank you, thank you, I'm so happy." Now that to me is worth as much as anything else in the history of this business.

Those kinds of thank-yous, those kinds of sincere affections are worth a hell of a lot more than anything else I've ever done, because I have helped create a piece of history. So when somebody that I've helped create has made that history—when one of the pages in the book that I've written hugs me—it warms the hell out of me. That's the ultimate form of gratification. When I get a bear in the mail from one of my children, like Serena. . . . All of a sudden Christmas I get this goddamn little ceramic bear, which is now hanging from my little magical bear that hangs off the ceiling: "Brother Bill, I love you," that means a hell of a lot more to me than money or the people that produce and distribute these things.

I want the love and affection of the kids and fuck the adults. It's no different than when I was in Juvenile Hall. Maybe I haven't learned what I'm supposed to learn, but I will always be one of the kids. I refuse to be one of the adults. And I think that what sticks in the adults' craw the most is that I refuse to conform. So many of them have told me that if I only lived by their rules, I could have made so much money and done so well. But I don't believe there should be those rules. So I can't do it; I can't accept the norm; I can't accept their Century City Tower atmosphere, their eight-foot-thick carpet mentality. I won't do it. I'd sooner get down and roll in the dirt with my children and watch over them and have fun with them and listen to them tell me that they do love me.

I'm going to be universally outrageous in the Industry, a universal rebel. The rascal. The bad. But also the Renaissance man. The da Vincis, Michelangelos, the people who were more creative than their peers were thought of as bad boys because they weren't conforming to the norm. I like that. The bottom line of my existence in this Industry is to always be thought of as the bottom line. Not to be accepted but to be thought of: when they mention "the Bear," they say, "Oh, that son of a bitch," or "that asshole," or "he's a hell of a guy," "what a great Bear he is." Instead of "Oh, oh, the Bear, all right," yawn, yawn. The day that I'm yawned over is the day I'm dead. That will be the ruination of my career. So onward and upward in whatever way I can do.

I think that the people in the Industry are in it because they were re-pressed as kids. Sociologically, morally, a lot of them grew up in straight families; they're not from the broken homes, battered children. A lot of them from a very straight upbringing, very middle-class, mundane, normal upbringing. I married one (now divorced). She's a prime example of a woman who grew up in the soft underbelly of America—Littletown, Illinois, a place that fits on this corner of your desk. I have been there. It is truly a town of one school, one gas station, a couple of cafés and fruit stands. She came from that and yes, she started to rebel when she was twelve, she started screwing around when she was twelve years old. Drea is her name.

S: Where does that name come from?

B: I don't know. I think it's a name she used when she said she was hooking in Chicago. She came to me with all kinds of delusions of grandeur about what she had done. Drea is a liar, a patent liar. She is a very normal [ordinary] person who doesn't want to be any more normal than I do. Therefore she has built up this large series of abnormal adventures to glorify herself, but in fact she is a very normal human being. When she came to me, I created the monster from what I saw inside of her. She is a female version of me. She's very powerful, very demanding, very egocentric, very wrapped up in herself and has to be the center of attention. Around me she couldn't be, and finally I think that destroyed her or destroyed our relationship.

We were just at each other's throats constantly. She demanded things from me that I was not about to do anyway. Essentially, she took me off the screen for a while. She is very strange. Then she wanted to get into swinging, which I didn't want to do, because I don't like to swing. I hate crowds, and I don't want to be in an orgy room with people stepping on me. I like one-on-one situations. Somebody stepping on my head doesn't really do much for me in a sexual situation. Drea, because she is a woman, likes being waited on hand and foot. She's a gorgeous woman. My epitome of sexuality is a tomboy, and she's built like a tomboy—tall, thin, essentially titless, three feet worth of legs, small ass, tight, healthy body, and if you roll around with her, she's not going to complain.

I don't like ultrafeminine people who if you muss up their hair they start whining, or you break a fingernail, they have a heart attack. Drea became unfortunately more feminine than I wanted to deal with. She blondined her hair and she began to put on the nails and worry about all this kind of stuff. That really didn't interest me; it did not become ultra-arousing. Then our sex life went down the drain because she took away my alter ego, the screen, where I really enjoyed performing, not the sex, but *performing* the sex. When I couldn't do that any more, I wasn't validating my purpose for being, I wasn't having any fun screwing her. Although most of the time I did, it was great, it truly was the best intercourse I've ever had in my life because I could pound into her as if I was slamming up against a wall. And she loved it, she loved hard, violent sex.

I'm not a great lover. Orally I'm fantastic. I was taught by a lesbian how to go down on a woman, nibble and lick around forever, which they like. Women really do. A lot of men have no idea what they're doing down there, and a lot of men won't do it. There are whole nationalities that won't do it. The blacks are seemingly horrified by oral sex. Mexicans aren't much into it either. They think it's something sacred down there: you shouldn't be nibbling on it. A woman can derive a hell of a lot more pleasure that way than being pounded into because a guy is just bashing away for his own fun.

I think Drea needed this business to really kick up her heels, almost stick her tongue out at her upbringing. The funny thing about it is a lot of people who say they don't like their parents, all of a sudden as they get older, and their parents get older, they suddenly realize how much they loved their parents. Now I think that is hypocrisy. If you hated them when you're young, why bother liking them when they're about to die? You know, I don't think people really hate their parents. It's just that they don't understand the parents any more than the parents understand their kids. So they feel uncomfortable after a while with them: they misconstrue it as hatred. Sad.

My mother and I never really got along, but I have tremendous respect for the woman because she was incredibly intelligent and she did instill in me the desire to write. I saw her interact with all kinds of other people. I didn't *hate* my mother, I just didn't understand her.

Before she died she hated me because I was in the X-rated Industry. My mother died in her mid-eighties. In 1900 (her childhood) making X-rated movies was not the in thing to do. When she was growing up sex was a whole lot holier and a whole lot more sanctified. As far as kids in this business—

S: Let me interrupt you: my fantasy would be—though you're saying it is not the case—that the women in the Industry would be poor, dumb, more like the girl you were talking about who is brain-damaged on Thorazine. That they wouldn't know what the hell they're doing. That's obviously not true.

B: No, oh, no. This girl [the Thorazined one] is an exception. I may not even let her in the Industry. She's such an exception that I'm scared to do further damage to her. Not that the physical stuff would do any more damage, but the mental might. She may snap. She is such a trusting, calf-like human being. I don't really know why she wants to do it. That's the thing I've not yet tapped into. Until I find out why she wants to do it, I'm not going to let her do it. I can't even allow myself to let her work behind the scenes a couple of days just [for her] to see what goes on. She was recommended to me by a man who runs a scam agency where he lures people in: he runs a nickel-and-dime lure-them-into-make-movies-and-become-famous type of situation.

S: Why did she come to him?

B: Because she trusted the situation. To make money. Saw the ad in the newspaper. We have ads in newspapers. This ad was put in by the man who runs this operation. She saw the ad and came to see him. Because she believed she wanted to make money, be a star.

S: How old is she?

B: She's nineteen.

S: Where does she come from both geographically and psychologically?

B: She comes from California geographically; psychologically she comes from a lifestyle of broken homes, a lifestyle of McLaren Halls, Lathrop Halls, Juvenile Halls, all for marginal incorrigibility, which really isn't a crime any more. She just never fit in, and they began to Thorazine her up from a very young age. She is not altogether there. She is totally innocent sexually and very, very uninhibited sexually in the sense that she's exhibitionistic. She asked me if she could go take a bath. She got into the bath and used the powerful water to get off four times in a row. It was a very nice thing to see. I just sat there and watched her. The veins in her head constricted, her stomach twitched, and she went off and she really felt happy and then she curled up on my couch with a stuffed animal and went to sleep. She trusts.

S: You say she's innocent. By that you mean what? You don't mean she's never had sex?

B: Well, she's had sex but she has not had a lot of it. She's had maybe thirty sexual experiences in her life and she doesn't remember many of them. She doesn't really know what sex can do. She's with some guy in his forties who fucks her for about three seconds and gets off and then doesn't bother with her any more. And I am in the position where I don't have any intention of doing anything with her on a sexual basis, because it's not good to screw your own children. I've adopted her as one of my kids. So I have to try and find out where I can put her, where she can derive physical pleasure and mental satisfaction and financial reward, a very difficult triple play.

We [porn people] are a masturbatory aid first and foremost. There is no other reason for us to exist except for somebody to go home and jack off over us. We're not a learning aid. I do not believe we teach anybody anything except how to fast-forward their VCR. So the delusion of grandeur that we have some kind of social redeeming value as a learning aid is a crock of shit. If anybody tries to screw the way people are screwed on camera, they'll rip out every muscle in their back and in their legs. We get into positions that monkeys are envious of, because the camera has to see what we're doing.

They have to see the intercourse. They have to see the angles. The anal sex is even worse. First of all, I don't like to do it—anal sex—because I'm not that good at it. You have to have a certain control of what you're doing, and I sort of stumble into the damn thing. The last time I did anal sex (1977—*Hot Skin in 3-D*), I ripped the girl open, which was not fun. I didn't really like it. I got upset. She loved it. She thought it was fantastic, but I'm too big. It bothered me. I'm awkward because you have to be in a certain angle [for the camera] to do that, and I'm very uncoordinated sexually. You have to get higher up on the top. It's hard enough for me to screw in just normal angles, because I'm very clumsy. In anal, you have to do it in a style where you've risen above the doggie style and go down. I have to then be balanced because the anus is higher. And if she's not accommodating for you, you've got a real problem.

S: Why wouldn't she if she's told to?

B: That's hard for them to do. And the girls are catered to. The men are not catered to in our industry. It's all for the female, because that's who you are going to see when you're going to buy the movie or the magazine. You're not going to buy it because of a man, unless, in the homosexual situation, you want to see Holmes's dick. He's the only man who sells tickets. Fourteen and a half inches worth of meat! That's a whole lot of meat.

S: Is that true?

B: Oh, yeah. I have worked with Johnny on an orgy, not sexually, but I've been at the bottom of a pile of people and he's been at the top. His dick came out over my head. I looked up: it was the opening shot of *Star Wars*. I have never seen anything more frightening in my life. It is truly [gestures size] from my elbow down. All men were not created equal.

S: Women can take a penis that big?

B: They can accommodate him. Think of fist-fucking. Remember, a baby comes out of the damn things. So figure the fist can go into it. To me, fist-fucking is not unnatural. Women really like it if you know how to do it right. It's one of the things that I enjoy practicing [though earlier he said otherwise] when I have the time to do it. If you take the time to get a woman relaxed enough to trust you, it's the ultimate full feeling. Your cock can never be this big [shows fist], and the woman *loves* to feel full. She really enjoys that. Women . . . they have as many . . . well, they have more orgasms. And during their orgasms they can expel a tremendous amount of liquid. So they are basically lubricating your hand for you. But you've got to take the time. You just can't walk up and shove the damn thing in. Because if it doesn't feel good, it scares them, that's the whole thing. But people don't understand that. You know, I used to do that a lot when I was a kid, when I was really learning, when a girl would teach me how to do the stuff. I was taught how to do this stuff by a lesbian. Strange woman.

· · · · · · · ·

PART TWO

· · · · · · · ·

OTHERS

· · · · · · · ·

INTRODUCTION

I have now met ten women in the porn business. Except that they are all females, I see no common features they share that would bring them to that work. As a diagnostician, I see no category they share; as a psychopathologist, I find their symptoms, character structures, strengths, and weaknesses all over the scale; as a therapist guessing how they will fare in life, I estimate their prognoses for dealing with the rest of their lives as *very* different for each. And, for our purposes here—to get a glimpse of how porn works—I found that each came to the Industry with conscious reasons that scarcely overlapped those of the rest.

They are Happy, the next woman to appear here; Nina, a registered nurse who as Nina enthusiastically, lustfully repairs her awkward self, Monica (quite like what we see in multiple personalities, but without the dissociation); Kay, a former performer, then executive in a porn production company, now aspiring talk-show hostess; Chartreuse, a roommate—platonic—of Bill's who, though willing, is rarely asked to perform; Viper, Bill's lover for several years—they live together harmoniously, protectively, lovingly—enraged, magnificently tattooed, wildly rebellious–self-destructive, and unendingly ready, as a performer, for sex with as many men as possible and in any way; Terry, a former fancy call girl, now would-be college student and porn performer; Patsy, a porn journalist who is interested in working—clothed—in porn films, has been invited to play—unclothed—in the films but has not participated in acts of sex in porn films; Bunny, whom all my informants mention as a light-hearted woman they hope the Industry will not chew up and throw away, whom I never interviewed but who sat with my wife and me at an XRCO Awards evening; Porsche, a star; Sharon, a star. Some I list here with their real stagenames, others with complete pseudonyms. No one other than Bill is identified by her or his genuine name (few of which I know, anyway).

The men: Bill, a rebel; Jim, a rebel, his buddy, the "historian of porn," also occasional scriptwriter; Ron, a rebel, scriptwriter, occasional performer in S&M sagas; X, a famous male star, who was brought to me in a medical-psychiatric emergency by Bill and Jim; Clancy, a performer, scriptwriter, director, producer, male erotic dancer; Merlin, a rebel, performer, scriptwriter, director, producer of S&M videotapes; Ed, an S&M illustrator; Terry, a publisher for gay men; Steve, a minor performer, Alex, an ex.

A flaw in this text is the absence of testimony from male performers (Bill excepted) comparable to that from women. I shall take that up via Ron, in chapter 10.

Now, Happy. Bill brings her and her boyfriend, Jeff, in not only so that I can compare her with others in the business but also to show how at least one man reacts to his woman's working in porn. She is small, thin, perky, uneasily optimistic, innocent in the way she wears her emotions on her sleeve, honest, modest in self-appraisal and expectations, high in energy, tenacious, unsophisticated, grateful.

To give you my sense of Jeff, the description should be short and faceless: subdued, nervous.

Here are the first three interviews. Later material did not negate the impressions these created. (She was, at the time I wrote this, well situated as an erotic dancer and sometime porn performer, suddenly and joyously released from poverty, more independent, less subservient to her boyfriend. Feisty. But that was a few years ago. I cannot find her now.)

Chapter 4 HAPPY COMES TO PORN

B: The girl you're going to meet is about to come into the X-rated Industry. What you're getting [to interview] is a virgin with her boyfriend. It's time for both of us to probe and see how it will affect her and how it will affect him, how their real life will now be shattered or cemented by the X-rated Industry. I've given her a name—we collaborated on that—Happy Day. [Bill calls the couple in.]

S: How did you get to Bill?

H: I was looking through the *Hollywood Press*, and I saw the ad for Pretty Girls International. So I called and asked if they needed people with experience. They said no, not if you were born with what God gave you, you don't need experience. So I said okay, fine. So I went there, and there were interesting people there, one of them named Reb, a few people that I wasn't even introduced to, they were just looking at me, which made me feel uncomfortable. When I walked in the room, I was embarrassed because I knew why I was there and they knew why I was there, and that embarrassed me right away. But I turned around and faced the people in the room. There were four: a man sitting behind the desk, salt-and-pepper beard. I focused on his beard because that seemed to be the most distinguishing part about him. He was the size of a bear, a real big, burly man, very outstanding blue eyes, big smile, had a lot of paperwork on his desk.

To his left sat another man, kind of small build, not a bad-looking man, I wouldn't say he was gorgeous, brown eyes, never took his eyes off me, always watching me, which made me very nervous, very uncomfortable. Then to his left was a girl, a model. You could tell by the way she was dressed and the way she carried herself, blond-colored hair, bleached blond. She looked like she was more of a brunette because her roots were dark. She looked at me, smiled, but no words were spoken between the two of us all the time I was there. The smile was one of understanding: "I-know-why-you're-here-and-it's-okay." Other than that there was nothing else from her. And Mark [Bill's writing partner] sat to my right. I was handed an application and asked to fill it out. The information I filled out was very simple, because I have no experience.

S: Excuse me. This is for—

B: Standard model office procedure.

S: But it's for X-rated—

B: It never says that. It's for anything that has to do with the adult film business. It is a simple form—I should bring you one—which says absolutely nothing: height, weight, breast size, assorted measurements, experience, what you will and won't do, which means nothing since they haven't been told what they will and won't do so they don't know what to fill out. I have always been amused by that question. "What do you mean what I will and won't do?" You have to explain it to them. She will tell you that very little was explained. That's how she met me.

S: But it's not under false pretenses?

H: I knew why I was there. I was asked do I know what figure modeling is.

S: I don't. I would think, "Oh, it's for still photographs," but it isn't that?

B: The ad that she answered in the *Hollywood Press* is a definitive ad. The ad is a very large ad. I designed it, and it stands out in the *Hollywood Press*. It says, "Attractive figure models, exploitation, $150–$1500 a day, working in adult features, legitimate (essentially they are) eighteen and up, bonded and licensed," which is Pretty Girl International—

S: What does that mean: bonded?

B: Bonded and licensed means, first of all, "We are licensed as a talent agency," which I've never really understood. We are licensed to break the law, which never made any sense to me. And we are "bonded," which to me means that if you're sent out on a job that the agency gets you and you're not paid, the agency has to pay you. But if you ever go out and get a job on your own, we're not responsible for you. That's what bonded means.

S: But anybody who reads the ad knows that it is likely to be for making videotapes, movies for the X-rated—?

B: By sheer stature of its placement in the newspaper; not on a page full of massage parlor ads. Now if somebody reads the same ad, which is worded differently, in the *Van Nuys Daily News*, then they're told over the phone. Theoretically, she should have been told over the phone that it is nude work.

Now the person who answers the phone, I suspect it was Mark who talked to you over the phone, because Reb rarely answers the phone—

S: Mark is your friend?

B: Mark is my writing partner.

H: The person who answered the phone said, "This is for figure modeling. Do you know what figure modeling is?" And I looked at the phone like he was dumb and I put it back to my ear and I said, "It's nude modeling, I assume." And he said, "Yes." So I knew what I was getting into.

S: I'm still not clear. Nude modeling isn't the same thing as X-rated movies.

B: Right, and everybody who goes to Pretty Girl International doesn't necessarily wind up in X-rated movies.

S: When you answered the ad, did you know that one of the options is X-rated movies?

H: When I answered the ad, I did not know I had options available to me. When I was given options by Reb—when Reb interviewed me personally—then I was given the option as to what I had open to me other than still photography. Then I was asked to go into a room and undress so that pictures could be taken of me. I was prepared for this. I knew this would have to be done. Because somebody [a client of Reb's] comes in and describes something. If Reb feels that I fit what the person is trying to describe, he can show the pictures. So I went into the room, not afraid, I undressed, he was on the phone, he asked me to yell out that I was ready, the people in the room had told him that I said I was ready, he came in, I posed the way he wanted me to pose, he retook my measurements (I was off on one of them, I'm not sure which one, my bust size, I think), and then he explained to me that I have all these options open to me and asked me what I would be interested in, asked me what I would and would not do.

    I put my clothes back on, went back out and then there was another person in the room, and this was the most embarrassing for me. I stood, trying to feel comfortable and yet at the same time being embarrassed by these people watching me and knowing, and really a lot not being explained to me. Reb was about to dial the phone, I was looking at the gentleman who was standing there, a new person. He is good-looking, really good-looking. I would describe him something like—what do you call the guys on the beach—a lifeguard. He looks like a lifeguard, big muscles, wearing a muscle shirt, tattered gray sweat pants, blond sandy hair, blue eyes, and I assume I was staring at the man and I didn't mean to, I didn't mean to make him embarrassed or anything. And Reb said something and I went "Huh" and looked over at Reb. And Reb said, "Go ahead and dream all you want," which embarrassed me even more and I went, "No, that's not why I'm looking at him." I told Reb that I was attracted to blue eyes. And I looked back and the guy had gotten embarrassed and turned away from me, which embarrassed me even more.

By this time, Reb had dialed the phone and told me to ask for someone named Bill. So I asked for Bill. He gave me directions to his home.

S: They now have done a preliminary survey of her, and they're asking you to do the diagnostic interview?

B: It's possible that was how it was conceived. I'm putting together a bondage film to be shot at The Scooter Shop. I need some new, unknown people for that movie, called *The Last Model*. The people I pitched it to thought it was fantastic. They never heard of anything like that before. So I asked him if he had anybody new. And he said, "Yes, I have a girl here named L. (that's her real name); I'm going to send her to you." I made an appointment for her to come see me. I don't care if they know everything in the world about the Industry: when they come over to see me, they're going to find out even more.

S: You didn't know why you were being sent to talk to Bill?

H: I was told that it was for bondage.

S: Not what the job was but that this guy is going to give you some good hard cracks about the reality?

H: Right. I wasn't prepared for that, but my mental image was: a room not brightly lit, blinds closed, curtains closed, very dark, a lot of paperwork all over the place, many boxes stacked, a much older man, maybe smaller, goes by the name of Bill, there's a light hanging over his desk, the only light in the room. And he has a room in the back that I would do this bondage in with all these different things that you would be using to film. It would just be one-on-one. That was my mental image.

S: That it would happen right then?

H: Yeah.

B: I've had a lot worse images than that projected on me. I've had people think I would be sitting there with a little knife ready to hack them to shreds, with salt and pepper shakers and catsup on the table. Nothing ever surprises me. Your image was the typical image that people have of me and the Industry: stagnated sexuality, the cloistered fantasy. They figure they'll walk into one of their own nightmares.

H: But still, I walked into it. I was surprised by the friendliness and the warmth I felt when I got there. When I sat down and I came into this . . . room full of teddy bears? [Laugh.] I mean, there was wall-to-wall teddy bears. And he's very happy-go-lucky, he's very open, very honest, very up-front. He doesn't hide a thing. I liked that. There aren't many people like that, who are open and honest.

He said that he's chased quite a few people out of the Industry, but to me he did not come across like he was really trying to scare me away. I did not feel that he was trying to frighten me. He was honest with me, he told me things that I assumed I would be hearing. I'm not naive. I'm only twenty-three years old, but I've been through a lot, especially the past year. What he told me were just things I had expected to hear. He just told me what I was up against. I learned a lot as we sat together for 2½ hours, and I made a friend. A perfect stranger. And after that 2½ hours, I took my clothes off in front of him, posed for him so he could have a picture for his files. No fear. I was very comfortable.

B: I told her a few things that Reb hadn't. I told her the varieties of modeling she could do: boy-girl, girl-girl, bondage, boxes—fetish, you know—leather wrestling, topless disco. I wasn't so much attempting to scare her out of the business from a sexuality aspect of it. Because she had sexual experiences. But I was trying to advise her, because she does have a child and she does have a boyfriend. As you know, my conscience doesn't need to be beleaguered with other people's consciences. I don't want to destroy other people's relationships. She's happy in her relationship with her boy-friend now, and I want her to understand it was that relationship that she was putting on the line and might do damage to in order to attain the financial rewards and the egotistical rewards of the X-rated Industry.

The sexual rewards are not what she's looking for. I have women who do come to me looking for the sexual rewards. I don't think that's her interest. I think that she's . . . the money would be nice because she earns five dollars an hour driving a truck. She wants to earn a couple hundred a day rolling around; it would be much more fun. You don't get in an accident that way unless you fall off the bed. But she did bring up a couple of soft-underbelly situations: the boyfriend and the kid. Before I had the chance to hit her with my famous line about "What are you going to do ten years from now when you bring home a magazine with you laying there with a candlestick up your ass and your kid says, 'What is this?' Are you going to tell him, 'I was playing the part of a birthday cake'?" It's not going to work that way. She very, very descriptively laid out a scenario of what she would do ten years from now if her kid asked her what she was doing. And I liked that, I admired her.

S: Which is?

H: He's not going to have to wait until he's that age to know. It's going to be up-front. Like I said before, I don't hide things. I try and be as open as Bill. My son is three, from a previous marriage, and I love the child dearly. He's blond haired, has blue eyes, and when he is old enough to talk, when he's old enough to understand is the time to slowly but surely take him one step at a time and let him know this is what Mommy does for a living so that he's not embarrassed when his friends are in the bathroom looking at a magazine and say, "This is your mom!" He's going to go up and say, "Yeah, good picture, isn't it?" instead of running away in the bathroom hiding and maybe crying. He's going to be able to face the reality that that's what I do.

S: [To Happy's boyfriend, Jeff.] So you're the other soft-underbelly, as Bill puts it. How goes it with you?

J: Okay. The thing that surprised me about this the last four or five days is that everything has happened so quickly. I never thought it would do that. I'm much older than L. is. I've always dreamed of doing this myself. I've been very open with sex. I've been married twice. I met L. a year and a half ago. We have a great sex life, still do, I started thinking again of my dream: adult movies and things like that. So what she basically is doing is fulfilling *my* dream. That seems to be the hardest thing to deal with about this whole thing.

S: She's getting a shot at it and you're not?

J: Exactly. I don't know if I've got the guts to do it. I respect her for having the guts to do it.

S: It's one thing having the fantasy and it's another to put it—

J: Exactly. It's another thing going through with it.

S: I presume that you're referring to the question that the boyfriends or husbands may have about whether they want their lady to be screwing publicly.

J: Putting their love on the line, so to speak.

H: Bill says Jeff opened my sexuality. The first time that he had ever done anything about it is asking me if I ever masturbated. Well, I have memories of touching myself as early as five years old but never admitted it to a soul except Jeff. And it snowballed. He started getting me to touch myself in front of him, getting me to enjoy it, getting me to be able to make love to myself and enjoy it, and I don't want to stop. [Laugh.] I love it, I really do. It's a great way of developing who I am. I have discovered so much about myself. I'm a totally different person than I thought I was.

S: That is connected to your thinking you could function effectively in the X-rated Industry?

H: Yes.

S: And before Jeff helped you with this, it would never have occurred to you? Or it would have occurred to you but you never thought you could do it?

H: I would never have had the guts to go through with it. He gives me the courage. For some reason, there is some kind of channel between Jeff and I. I don't know what it is. I can't explain it but I could honestly say that there isn't a thing in the world that I could not do as long as Jeff was at my side.

S: So when she makes love in reality to a blond, blue-eyed, gorgeous man, it will be okay?

J: You used the wrong word. Making love and having sex is two different things. L. and I will make love. If she was on camera with the blond, blue-eyed, good-looking man, she is having sex. That better be all she's doing, but she's got to differentiate between them.

S: And when she doesn't?

J: We've talked the last two or three days about it and I'm convinced that that's the way she will feel about it, that it will be having sex.

H: I also told Jeff that if there's the slightest change in our lovemaking or in our relationship after, say, a few videos or a few picture-takings, or whatever—the slightest—I'll up and quit, no questions asked. [Snaps fingers.] He'll just say, "I want you to quit," and that's all it will take, because I'm not going to jeopardize my relationship for a career. I can't. My career won't last a lifetime; he and I will last a lifetime.

S: Fair enough. The bear that's in hibernation now [Bill being unaccustomedly quiet]—

B: I'm just listening. I know the dangers of the X-rated Industry and what it does in a relationship between two people, one of whom is in it and one of whom is not. Because I lived it myself for eight years with a girl who wasn't in the business. I know that eventually the party not in the Industry can't handle it any more. If Happy comes into the Industry and has limited experiences and then decides it's hurting her relationship and can walk away from it, perhaps then she'll have had the best of both worlds. I don't know if Happy is going to be a superstar. I don't even know if she's going to be a star. I think her sexual freedom—as she puts it, in twenty-three years she's had twenty-three men—will help.

She seems warm and passionate, she likes to hug and she likes to be hugged and she likes to be held. This is stuff that the men that she's working with will appreciate. They will appreciate the attention they get. I suspect Happy will be truly like a cat with a bowl of milk, she will lap, lap, lap until it's all gone. If she can keep these feelings separated and do it as a job . . . . It's not a job, not so much work as a time at bat, in the vernacular of the sports world. Going up to the plate. And if she knocks out a single or a double or a home run—she could even strike out if she's not interested in what she's doing. It's the guy that has to perform. He's really the bat; she's nothing more than the ball. She'll have fun.

It's something rare, this opportunity to catch two people in transition. Right here you have the raw material of what can be a future for them or can destroy their future. Or it can be just an adventure they can share in their own future. It puts me in a godlike position. As my business card says, "God Created Man . . . William Margold Created Himself." I did warn her about all this when she came to the house. That's what I'm primarily interested in. I don't give a shit if she can suck cock and fuck. If she can't, the poor guys working with her are going to find out. I don't think I'll ever have sex with her. I'll probably do the bondage thing with her, because I need brand new people. But as far as having sex with her, it's not good to fuck my own kids. I adopted her immediately because she wants to be adopted. She needs a good daddy. She will tell you about her own daddy. She will tell you about her own family. You need to know that because that [history] is one of the reasons she's into the X-rated Industry: to discover herself and validate herself. She has a past that is not the smoothest of roads. So I'll take a few of those bumps out. I may create other bumps in the process.

S: That's the immediate understanding you would have with her, one you're familiar with in yourself: you can comfort people whose experiences with authorities, parents or otherwise, have been traumatizing.

B: Exactly.

S: You really know about that, and they sense right away whose side you're on. You're on the side of the kids. And the ones who need to sense that will be able to find that in you. The ones who won't, won't see who you are. I presume there are some who talk to you with whom there's nothing in common. But she immediately sensed it, which would predict that there would be a past that would make—

B: Which I immediately went after and which she immediately revealed.

H: I have been through a great deal, and it can start as early as four. I was beaten very badly at the age of four. My father came home. He was turned down for a promotion at work, and my mother got tired of disciplining the child and turned the discipline over to father. Well, father got a little overboard, in fourteen years of discipline he got a little overboard. There were times— there are still times—Jeff will come at me and I'll flinch because I'm afraid of being hit. Jeff has never laid a hand on me, but I still see Daddy. I still have that fear. I still carry that. My father can be right here and now and call, and I'll flinch or I'll jump. I am still afraid of my father.

I love the man, I'm not saying that I don't love him. I don't know if I can go as far as to say I respect him, but I do love him, he is my father, he did bring me into this world, I think it's a wonderful world that we live in, even with all the things that go on around us. I still am able to seek out the beauty in it, and I seek out the beauty in my father and he's a good man. But life with him has not been an easy road and [sigh] there was a year when I was thirteen. On my thirteenth birthday to the following year, there wasn't a day that Daddy didn't hit me or raise his hand to me in anger for something, whether it was forgetting to feed the dog or bringing him a pack of cigarettes instead of beer because I wasn't paying attention to what he was doing or wanted.

I was raised as a tomboy. Jeff noticed that when I first met him, I still carried myself as a tomboy or little boy, masculine features, walked like one, maybe even talked like one, I don't know, worked on cars, I'm proud of the fact that I can tear apart a '56 Chevy engine, tear it apart and put it back together in a weekend and have it running. [Laugh.] My dad taught me how to be good with my hands. He tells me to get him a certain tool, I can do it. But there were times when Dad would drink too much Coors. He'd get belligerent, and I can be cocky and I can have a chip on my shoulder. When our personalities clash, that's trouble. It usually meant trouble for me, because I was the weakest one. He was the strong one, and he had the belt. After my suicide [attempt, see below], I started to resist, started standing up for myself where I would take a swing at him and knock him down. I'll get into that. The early years it would be he'd attack, attack, attack, and I'd be afraid and the flinch and the hands would go up and for every time my hands went up, I got ten more, whether he was punching me or he was hitting me with the belt or whatever.

He's never put me in the hospital. Maybe he held back, I don't know. My mother has tried to get in the way and he's pushed her or hit her to get her out of the way. It wasn't that he didn't love me. It was aggression, anger, all the things that had gone wrong in his life. Whew! When I think of all the trouble that I've caused them. I was a troublemaker; I wasn't the best kid in town. I've been arrested. I've got a few skeletons in the closet, as Bill says. I've had my picture taken for shoplifting when I was a teenager. I don't know if it's on record. I really don't care. I was a teenager, and that's what teenagers do. I never got heavy into drugs; drugs were never really big to me. Sex was never really big for me.

Up until I was fifteen, I was able to handle what was happening to me. I felt like a Cinderella: I was being beaten, I had to do all the dishes, I washed clothes, I scrubbed floors, I made beds, I cooked dinner and went to school, taking out the trash, cutting the lawn on the weekends, helping Dad with his work. That's a heavy load for a child. No play. Everybody that you could ever talk to about my life: "L. never had a childhood, she never sat down and played with dolls." I never played. I don't know what it's like to play in a child-form sense. My son has a roomful of toys. I want him to have a childhood that I didn't have. I want to be able to have the money to take him places and do things . . . . I'm getting off the track.

Everything in my life was work, work, work. And if I didn't do it right, I was beaten for it. I remember one time my Dad took me in a room and beat the living daylights out of me. I really can't tell you how bad it was; it would probably make you sick. I was screaming. That's pretty much what my whole life was like. [Crying.] It hurts. I don't want it to happen to my son. I'd kill myself again before I'd let it happen to that boy.

S: So the suicide?

H: One night I was half asleep. My mom is not one for sex; sex is not a big part of Momma's life, which is okay. And Dad was drunk, and he wanted it and she wouldn't . . . . I was listening to their conversation. Their room and mine are joined by a closet that has no doors on it. Just the clothes hanging in the closet. I can hear, I've got good hearing, very good hearing. I'm half asleep because they're yelling and it woke me up and I'm kind of in a half-state, I'm listening to this. My dad goes into the kitchen, opens the back door. He came back in, came into my room with nothing on. He was totally naked. I was embarrassed by his nudity. I remember looking away, and he said, "Nooky's crying."

I don't know where "Nooky" came from. My dog's name was Montana. So I went to check on Montana. I could hear my dad rustling with a chair in the dining room. I didn't think anything about it, thinking he was drunk, walked through our kitchen, and was stopped cold by my father blocking the doorway, sitting in the chair with his legs spread, holding his cock in his hand, grabbing me by my wrist, grabbed me by my right wrist, bringing me to my knees and telling me to suck on his cock. I was appalled, I wanted to throw up. I picked up the chair and flung him backwards and he fell over, left him, didn't even care, went to my room, and went to sleep. I could hear him as I'm going back to sleep, cussing me out, telling us that women are all alike. Nobody would listen to me that my father had done this to me.

S: Did you talk to your mother?

H: I tried, yes. Relatives: grandparents, aunts, uncles, cousins.

S: What did you tell them and what's their response? It's pretty hard to ignore.

H: This is a fifteen-year-old. Should I say my daddy wanted me to give him a blow job?

S: You hinted and they didn't want to hear what you were intimating?

H: Exactly. I had a conversation with my mom [sigh] in the car. I said, "Mom, if you want to do something"—this is premeditated suicide—"if you believe in your heart that something is right and yet you know it's wrong both morally and legally, do you do it anyways?" I put my mom on the spot. And she said, "Yes, you do, you follow your heart." I said, "Okay." That's all I remember. That was my final decision. I was going to commit suicide on that day. I faked being sick, made my parents angry, I remember that. The minute they left, I got dressed in a white turtleneck, long-sleeved, and blue bell-bottom cords, and white tennis shoes, my favorite outfit when I was fifteen, that's what I liked to wear. I cleaned the house top to bottom. I went through that house in about three hours' time. By 9:30 I was done, everything. It was spotless, I put the chicken on because I wanted dinner ready. I figured, "I'm going to kill myself. They're going to say, 'Oh, she's dead,' no big deal. They're going to walk away and have dinner." I was in a funny state of mind. I really don't understand that state of mind. It would take someone to understand a person's mind at that time. I can't.

I put the chicken on the spit, salt and pepper, got dinner all ready, I think I even put the corn out and everything for them to take over. Laid everything out that I wanted to be dressed in, my rosary, I wanted this one dress that I really like a lot, everything. I remember playing a Shaun Cassidy record on the record player and listening to it. Went and got the pills from underneath my mattress, took all twenty-two in my hand, took a glass of water and I remember trying to remember the quote that Neil Armstrong said when he first stepped on the moon and I couldn't even quote . . . I couldn't remember what it was, but I tried. Took them, took two steps to the door and got dizzy. Everything went numb. I couldn't stand the noise of the record. I was trying to block my ears and just took the record off, climbed up in my bunkbed and fell asleep. Now all I can tell you is the stories that were told me, because I do not remember from the time that I fell asleep to the time that I woke up and started screaming, "Do you know about the pills, do you know about the pills?" Because all that I put in the suicide note that I wrote before I took the pills went to my father, which has been hidden from me. My mother won't let me read it.

S: You don't remember what you wrote?

H: Not at all. Mom said she came in and I was white as a ghost, I was white as my shirt, I was pale. She had just gotten done reading a pamphlet on what to do in case someone suicided. When the paramedics got there, I flat-lined, and they had to defibrillate me to get my heart going again. To make a long story short, I wound up talking to a psychiatrist and psychologists, you name it, and everybody came to the same conclusion: I was not the one who needed the help, it was my parents.

After fifteen, after that episode, I wanted to give my Dad another try. And I did work hard at it, until Daddy and I clashed again. Now I'm sixteen, a little bit bigger, a little bit stronger, starting to run, I've got a good build on me musclewise, I'm not a weakling, and I'm as tall as Daddy. So when Dad comes in with that strap, I grab the strap now. It doesn't touch my skin, and I pull it out of his hands. And then we put up dukes and then we start duking it out, fist-fighting and wrestling. I've wrestled my Dad to the floor, cracked my ribs, but I've wrestled my Dad to the floor in a fight. I'm not afraid to stand up to him any more. And if he ever tries to hurt me or ever tries to hurt my son, which he never will, he's older, I could hurt him. I wouldn't kill him, but I'd hurt him. I'd put him out of commission for a while just so that he knew that I meant business. I've been kicked around growing up. I'm not a fighter. I'd rather make love, not fight. I stand my ground now no matter who he is. I stand my ground and fight my battles on my own. I may do it my own special way, but I'm not afraid any more. I'm tired of running. I'm tired of being afraid.

S: Who else misused you?

H: [Pause.] I'm not going to mention his name: a friend of the family's. It started out as a tickling game—this is what they call molestation, I assume—it started out as a tickling game. His hands started to wander and roam. It started when I was eight or nine and ended . . . I'll tell you how it ended. It was just before my suicide. Because I let him know how I felt. I'd say it happened on about seven different occasions when he started tickling me and started feeling between my legs. The last time he came in and started tickling me. Well, he wasn't tickling me, he was feeling me up and there was no way this man, if he thought he was going to get into my pants, he was wrong, dead wrong, and he leaned over and if I'm laying like this [demonstrates] and he leaned over, it was the right side of his neck and I took a chunk out of his neck. I know I did, I had to, because I had blood all over my bed when I woke up in the morning, all over my mouth. I latched on, and that's loose skin. For an older man, that's pretty loose, and I latched on with my teeth and I bit as hard as I could. I let him know that I was angry, and I wanted him to stop what he was doing. It made me angry. And I remember that fury. [Long pause.]

B: I think the X-rated Industry provides her, in general, escape from the realities of the world because of the over-juvenile version of Disneyland that I provide, of being wanted for what you are rather than having to live up to certain responsibilities. The X-rated Industry has very few requirements except that you show up on time, suck the requisite number of cocks, spread your legs the requisite number of times, perform the requisite number of sexual acts. For you giving your flesh, it provides you a sense of value.

This is the first time I've heard all this. I heard about the suicide but I . . . . Maybe I was saving it for you because this is like bringing you . . . . A dog brings his master a bone; I'm bringing you a series of bones. And you know how to take over a hell of a lot better than I do. Therapeutically—if there can be such a pretentious word for what the X-rated Industry does—she will find herself cared for by an awful lot of people who have gone through the same thing she's gone through. They are all trying to climb out of the same hells that they've lived through. How did I escape these miseries? Though I didn't get along with my mother, everything else was basically fun. I'm shocked at the suffering. I have to say something interesting: she's cried. I have a feeling I'm the only person that sits in this office and doesn't cry. Maybe there's something wrong with me. Patsy [another woman he sent in] tells me she weeps openly here. If I brought other people here . . . . Well, we know what happened with our illustrious superstar that was in here [brought in, as an emergency, in disastrous shape, by Bill and Jim Holliday, whom you will meet in chapter 8]. He was on the verge of bawling his eyes out. It's interesting to see that people can get to this, I think it's the trusting ambience of this office. The hells that people have gone through. I guess an awful lot of people have gone through an awful lot of suffering. I get them and I, in the Papa Bear situation, watch over them and hope that they benefit from the Industry as long as the Industry will allow them to benefit.

They have to give their flesh, and they may indeed sell their soul; what they do is get a nurturing of their reason for existence. The X-rated Industry, like no other place in the world, gives you a reason to exist. It gives you instant reaffirmation of your own self-worth. Maybe you're giving up a few tangential societal mores in the process, but these people need to see a reason for their existence; they need to be validated. And when they see themselves on the screen, see themselves in the magazines, see themselves on the video, see themselves on the cover of the newspaper, they just puff up like peacocks and they strut around and they're delighted.

I'm doing this with another girl right now, much older. I told her I'm going to get her picture on the cover of the newspapers, and she is just so happy. It means an awful lot. People—society—think that the X-rated Industry is corrosive and the acid is destroying these people. They give up something, but they get a great deal more back. It's a hell of a lot more satisfying than the miserable families that people go through. The blessing in my background was apparently that I didn't have that kind of stuff: I had to make my own. I think those who make their own in the long run are better off.

I have very little use, as you know, for the family structure in general. Although many parents have met me and liked me more than they like their own kids, I can't stand the family structure because the family structure demands things. The people get beaten in family structure. People can't talk. So they swing instead of talk. They lash out. I can do much more damage with my tongue than I could ever do with my fists, because I would hurt my hands, and if I hurt my hands, I can't play football any more. I speak in idiotic analogies, but you have to understand what I'm saying: only the ignorant strike out with their hands.

If a person can carry on a conversation, they can do much more damage with their tongue. The tongue becomes the razor blade that can cut out the guts of a human being. I've never met a man in the world who I can't outtalk, quite frankly, can bring down with my tongue. I simply walk away. I haven't had a physical confrontation with anybody other than on the football field since I was thirteen. I realized then that there are people bigger than me and why in the hell should I get hurt. I just call them a few names, which they have to stop and think about. And then they realize maybe they were a couple of those names and I win my fights.

But I did not bring her here to talk about me today. I love talking about myself because I'm the greatest person I ever met, but she is saying an awful lot of stuff. And I wanted to bring this out in your presence. I think it is good for her to say this to somebody she doesn't know, because she trusts you, because I trust you, because she trusts me, because I'm Papa Bear. It's a trauma, but I've always felt the more you talk about the hells inside of you, the less hell it is. Eventually the heat goes away, the nightmares.

H: My father has not stopped drinking; my father has not stopped smoking. And yet his doctor says my father's liver is in the best condition he has ever seen and my dad will drink you under the table. He's not Irish but that man can clean a case in half a day and still be able to beat you arm wrestling.

B: Drinking beer takes no real talent.

H: The only thing is my dad has a few heart palpitations, and he does have a big belly—

B: One day it's going to catch up with him. One day they're going to open him up and find a beer can in there. Listening to these nightmares of fathers abusing daughters and mothers abusing sons, this is stuff I get all the time. I met a guy last Tuesday, he was down from San Francisco, and you know how I am: somebody says they want to get in the X-rated Industry, I'll talk to them. This guy comes down, and he says his grandfather was molesting him from the time he was two years old. And I'm trying to picture this idiotic situation of an older man molesting a little two-year-old kid. What the hell do you see in a two-year-old dick? It ain't going to do much for you. What the hell value is it? I've never understood all the child molesting stuff, but it's more important that it comes out now. It's been going on forever; I suspect it was going on with cavemen.

But I'm not sure everybody in the X-rated Industry was molested, not all of them. I wasn't. I relate to that sixteen-year-old thing where a guy tried to rape me and I said no, I wasn't interested [not told to me before]. Which turned me into a totally straight person. If I ever was going to be gay, that ended it. This guy scared me back into a closet which I padlocked with thousands and thousands of rationalizations. I just wrote an article about it Wednesday, about how I will remain straight to my dying days, because I can't see having my dick sucked by somebody I'm going to slam in the face the next day, on the football field. That's my rationalization for staying straight. To relive the nightmares and expose them over and over is, I think, the most beneficial thing in the world. L. warned us she was going to cry. Then she saw this other poor person lumbering out of here [my office], and I said, "Oh, oh, they come out of here teary-eyed. Be prepared to cry." She obviously cries very easy, a way of venting I don't have.

It takes a lot to make me cry: the Detroit Lions, Yankees, and a couple of interesting movies, that's it. An eviscerated Mr. Stubbs [toy bear alter ego] might make me cry—you know, I go home and find the bear all over the ground—probably because I'd have to vacuum up all the threads. Their [Happy and Jeff's] relationship is very strange. It's strange in the sense that they care for each other, love. The term "love." A relationship ignites but eventually fans down to a warm glow of friendship because we do not continue to love that . . . . I'm bitter because I'm always . . . . My love is for things that can't love back; it is easy that way. It is a very interesting relationship, the kind I worried about. That's why, in my first meeting with her, I tried to convince her that she was putting their relationship on the line, about his being married. [Jeff is presently living with his wife.]

He may be thinking that's none of my business, but unfortunately anybody in my business, their lives, their world, belongs to me because I have to know where they are at all times. I owe it to my industry to be honest with it and with the people [performers] I'm dealing with. And I say what I feel. I don't mince words, and that's why I'm the most hated person in the X-rated Industry. Reb knew when he was sending me L. what I would say to her. He's been upset a couple of times, when he's sent me people he never had a chance to talk to and they've never been seen again. They listen to me for an hour or two, and they're gone. And Reb said, "What did you do this time?" I said, "I told them the truth about the business." And he said, "Goddamn it." But I said, "You want to make a couple hundred dollars in commissions and ruin their lives?" Because Reb doesn't have the time to sit down and talk to people. He's a nice man, but Reb has always been the brawn and I've been the brains in that operation.

H: I should say at this time Reb's a nice man, but I'm sorry he's my agent.

B: Why?

H: Because I wish you were my agent.

B: Well, I am your agent. I'm as much your agent as Reb is.

H: I like Papa Bear, but on a scale of one to one hundred, Reb's one, Papa Bear's one hundred, that's how much difference there is between the two personalities and the affection that I get from Papa Bear that I don't get from Reb. And again, like Papa Bear said, I need it.

B: And that's what the Industry can give to you. The X-rated Industry can provide a type of affection that's unparalleled. It's a bunch of people who need to be hugged and held, and the X-rated Industry provides adulation and warmth and comfort. It is, in a sense, the comfort that a one-on-one relationship cannot provide because everybody needs to have their ego masturbated, to put it in an interesting term. They have to have it fondled on a regular basis, if they have it. Now there are many people in the world who have no ego at all. And there are many people in the world who have no right to have any ego at all, because they don't do anything, don't have any value, any reason to think they're special.

So some people I don't have the time for. But the ones who want to take a chance in my business, they deserve to have their ego fanned, warmed, and cooed over. I'm sure that L. can separate the difference between making love to Jeff and performing her interesting acts on the screen. If she can't, then that's where you two step into your own introspection. I can't sit in as a mediator in that situation. It's very, very difficult. So if L. goes to San Francisco to film, you could go to San Francisco with her but you couldn't be on the set. So you then have real problems—

J: Why is that?

B: It's a fact. Unless he's working in the capacity, we don't invite visitors to the set. This is not a spectator sport. They never want to have the person's mind on anything else except the job they're doing. I used to be very cavalier about that: being told that was the rule, when I first got in the business, I said, "Great; that's a rule to break." Well, I found out that was one rule the Industry for once in its limited intelligence was right. I would magnanimously allow the men to come along with the women. Halfway through the shooting, the woman might have enjoyed the last sex scene a little too much. She would disappear and come back with a black eye, and I would say, "Where did that come from? There are no doors on this set." So she didn't walk into a door. Then I'd have this guy over there massaging his bruised knuckles, and I would say, "What did you do?" And he would say, "She liked that scene too much."

Well, that didn't do much for me. Then, of course, whoever was in charge—this was in '73–'74, when I was still a baby in the business—they would say, "What have you done this time, you idiot?" "Well, I thought it would be nice if this man came." I used to even try to rationalize by getting the guy a job on the crew. That didn't work either, because then the guy felt like he was being used for his $75 or $100 a day. The problem with it is that in many, many cases the man feels inadequate or jealous of the situation. Admittedly the male sex star by and large is a professional lover who is so good in bed, he does a job . . . . They're not making love to the woman, they're making love to themselves. And the King, John Leslie, Jamie Gillis . . . Joey Silvera has so much fun doing it, he talks about hitting home runs and stuff like that. I don't think he cares. But those like Herschel Savage, these people are all putting on a show for themselves. They could[n't] give a shit if they were sticking it into an ashtray, they're having fun, they're putting on a big show for themselves.

I'm to the point now where I believe they could be screwing their hand and getting the same kind of physical interaction. They're all puffed up and prima donnas and putting on the physical show situation. But the woman, because she's the end result of it, is being waited on hand and foot. Like the King makes love on the screen, he prepares the woman as if he's setting a table. I watched him do Drea, my own wife, now divorced. I thought it was fantastic. She was laying there and he was moving her around and stroking this and licking that. It's fantastic, because God knows the guy has made love to what-they-say fourteen thousand women. He should know what he's doing by this time, and he's really good at it. So if the woman, God forbid, enjoys it and has a man who she cares for standing there and all of a sudden he sees a glint in her eye that he hasn't been able to get, then the next thing I know I'm nursing [a woman with] a bloody nose off in the corner. This poor woman's come back and, "Well, he beat me up."

S: Okay. So we're in San Francisco and L. is working and Jeff has been told, "You stay in Los Angeles."

H: That's what he said.

S: You were startled when you learned that?

H: You're right. I know Jeff so well. It wouldn't be so much I'd come back with a bloody eye. I'd probably come back with tears in my eyes, because Jeff would just go like this [imitates a gesture of his] like he always does, he does this when he's had it. That's when he is at the point of no return. He's finished, he's through, it's over, it's done, anything you can think of. If he would be upset at something, say I was sucking this person's cock with the same tenderness that I do with Jeff, I'd go outside and put my arms around him, he'd take my arms off of him and he'd just go like that [gestures], and I'd know I'm in trouble. [Laugh.]

S: Jeff? Let's hear from you. You're going to see this on the screen. You're going to imagine it when you're at the hotel waiting for her to be done with her day's work. How are you going to handle it?

J: It's work. That's all I can say about it. It's her job. It can be handled as her job.

S: When there's a glint in her eye?

J: She won't have it.

B: If she doesn't have it, she's not convincing America that she does, that's the whole thing.

H: The glint in my eye has got to be born of performance, not love.

S: Let's leave out love. Suppose it's exciting, which has its own glint.

B: The excitement is going to be automatic in the beginning because it's brand new.

H: Sure it is.

J: She gets excited at seeing a blond-headed, blue-eyed guy. She gets excited seeing Remington Steele. So that doesn't bother me. Excitement doesn't bother me. I know her difference between excitement and—

B: What will bother you? Definitively, what will bother you?

J: I don't know. I don't think anything as long as she can treat me the same way.

B: She'll come home and she'll tell you about her adventures?

J: Not unless I ask.

H: Not unless he's asked.

B: That's bad. That's very bad. That's where Linda [long-time girlfriend] had me over a barrel and that's why I left Linda after eight years, because I love to talk about what I do, and I figure people like to hear what I do. Linda never wanted to know. After 1974—and I stayed with her until 1980—she never wanted to know what I did. And that really drove me away from Linda because I was so proud of what I did for a living and I had every right to be. When I finally had done *Marilyn Chambers and the Senator* (starring in my first movie), I wanted to tell her. She didn't want any part of it, and yet I stayed with her another six years because Linda's a special case.

We all essentially choose the partner who allows us to perpetuate the images of ourselves that we perceive or who don't require us to alter our own fabric too much. Linda (which I have never said; this is good for our [Stoller and Bill's] own work) had come from a situation where she had very little use for men in general, didn't want to be bothered falling in love. I came into her life, and it was a way to avoid any other relationship. You know, I definitely had everything else going for me, from the ability to perform sexually when she wanted sex, and to get her pregnant when she wanted to get pregnant, and to be intellectually stimulating when she wanted that. All I wanted back was gratification of my ego.

Well, she wasn't interested in ever knowing about the X-rated Industry, and that hurt me. Now Happy is going to come back wanting to talk about what she's done. She will go and work with people that you've heard of. She'll work with household names like Leslie and Silvera and Holmes. (Well, the King may not work again; he goes through these phases where he thinks he wants to retire again. [He is now dead: AIDS.]) But she might work with John Leslie or Jamie Gillis or Eric Edwards. Beyond their ability to fuck and do a very good job of screwing, these people are rather interesting human beings. If you sit down with them, they each have their own little backgrounds and reason to exist. It's just that nobody ever asks them. They're not able to talk because no one ever cares about them more than what they've got between their legs. It's very sad. The Industry doesn't give a damn about what the men have to say, because all they have to do is function. Nor do they care what the women have to say, because all they have to do is function—

S: Now look, that's your situation. They may disagree that it's the same for them.

H: I do [disagree]. Maybe we went too fast when we said, "Only if he asked." He *will* ask, and I *will* tell him, and it will provide a fire, an enticement, that only he and I can share. He's going to ask me, "What did you do? Explain to me in detail what happened in that scene." And I will explain to him—

S: Suppose he asks you, "What did you feel?" Will you still tell him?

H: Sure I'll still tell him. I'll try my best, with the limited vocabulary that I have, to explain to him what is going .through my head, what was going through my body, you know, did it feel good or whatever, whatever his needs are to be. I'm not going to tell him what he wants to hear. I'm going to tell him what happened. I'm not going to lie to him and say, "Yes, I enjoyed it," when I didn't, or "Yes, I had a good time," when I may not have. I'll go in and tell him what happened. I'm going to be honest with him.

S: And your feeling is that if she gets erotically excited you can handle that, if it's at work?

J: Because it's not the same as love.

S: That she's got a body and it's bound to respond, something of that sort. Is that right?

J: Exactly.

S: Bill?

B: Well, we'll see. The future is in the proof of the pudding, as they say. It always bothers me when people get into the Industry who have somebody outside of the Industry who doesn't understand. But if the love is strong enough to hold it together, then more power to it.

S: Have you known of such cases?

B: No. [Laugh.] Honestly, I haven't. What happens—again, like I told you, I'm a pessimist, I have been a [Detroit] Lion fan for lo these thirty years; I have no choice. But the day that they win the Superbowl I'll probably drop dead of a stroke. I would like to be proven wrong, but I know how it goes.

S: Well, at any rate, they stand warned.

B: Yeah. Warned and re-warned. This is the first time that anybody's ever been warned and re-warned in an essentially cathartic situation [with a psychiatrist]. That's why you're both here. Because I wanted you to talk about yourself, I wanted you to get the feelings out, I wanted it on tape so you could understand and keep on looking at it under a microscope because you've yet to have done anything. But the day that you do something is a whole new ballgame because once you have performed your first hard-core sexual act . . . . The bondage [she is to do a non-sex bondage movie before moving on to hard-core] really has nothing to do with that. The bondage movie is not hard-core sex, it's something you'll come home and start laughing about the stupid things that were done. But sex is not stupid. See, you say you had twenty-three men in twenty-three years: a lot of people use sex as an escape from their family situation, what they think will be the affection they've been lacking somewhere else. The X-rated Industry provides a different type of affection than you can get anywhere else, because it provides affection from a whole lot of people who are looking for the same kind of affection. So it's a family affection. The X-rated Industry provides that, but in order to do it, it asks a few things of you: you sell your soul. That's the main thing.

The kid thing [her child] you're handling very well. I remember what you said to me that day we talked. It was amazingly descriptive of what you would do with your kid. You're going to have a lot of people looking stupid around here: "What are you going to tell your kid?" [Mumbles a dumb sound.] There's responsibility in having children. I've been able to avoid having responsibility. I've had them and unloaded the responsibility on other people and see my kids when I want to. I'm a selective daddy. If I want to have the burdens or blessings of being a father, I will say, "Okay, I'll see Goldibear this afternoon." But I am usually quite relieved that I can go home away from this child, as long as I want to—

H: Don't forget that this has all been premeditated, all thought out before.

S: Then I want to ask you what got you to premeditate it?

H: The reason I was able to respond to Papa Bear so quickly and so efficiently with the answers is that it was one of *my* biggest questions: How am I going to be able to handle my son's questions? Because I love my son very much, really, I wouldn't have had him if I didn't, and he's an important part of my life, he's going to be there till one of us drops dead, and I've got to think about him and his feelings. Yet, granted he's only three years old and he's still learning and developing, but I answered myself: "You're going to do what people never did with you"—threw me in the closet, hid from me, talked behind my back so that I couldn't hear, and I had to learn on the street. He's not going to learn on the street; he's going to learn from Momma. He's going to learn everything he needs to know from mother, including what mother does for a living. And I'm not ashamed of it, I am *not* ashamed of being naked on camera or having someone slip his cock into me and have sex with me. I'm not even ashamed that I might enjoy it. I think I will, because I enjoy sex. I'm not ashamed of that; it's a very healthy, natural act.

S: When did you begin thinking you wanted to get into the X-rated Industry?

H: When Jeff brought me out of my shell. It was really funny. Jeff and I have wanted another woman to be a third partner in a threesome. And we searched endlessly for a perfect partner, and I found someone that I thought would be perfect and I brought her to introduce to Jeff, her name was Sally. We worked in the same place. And Sally and I talked on the phone a lot; she worked in another division. The relationship developed so that one night we wanted to go out and have a good time. Where did we go, Jeff?

J: Sailor's Hornpipe.

H: We had a beautiful time. We came back, and they had done their best to bring me out of my shell, where I wound up kissing Sally in a public place, which made me feel good. Nobody looked or turned around or made any noises. I mean, people did see us, but it wasn't as horrible as I had perceived it might be and I enjoyed it. So when we went back home, I was open, I was ready, but they were scared. I had to work to get all this together. Sally didn't want to get pregnant, and so she wouldn't have anything to do with Jeff. Jeff was frustrated, because he wanted so much to be a part of this.

So I wound up making love to Sally, which wasn't that great because she was scared. She was a lesbian; she was not straight. I wanted her to teach me. I wanted to learn, I wanted to know what it was like to be with another woman. I wanted to be kissed, I wanted to be caressed, I wanted to be made love to. She didn't do that. I didn't get enough. I still want to learn, I still want to know, I still have that desire, I still want someone to teach me, to just take me and say, "This is the way I've always done it, let me teach you what I know." And it could have been something meaningful if only Sally wouldn't have been afraid and if Jeff wouldn't have been going through whatever he was going through. I really don't understand what he went through except for the fact that he wanted so much to be a part of it and couldn't.

And at the end, which it lasted all night long, we never went to sleep, we went to work with no sleep. Jeff wound up making love to me and only kissing and fondling Sally, which is not quite the way I wanted it to happen. [Laugh.] I wanted everybody to get equal participation. So I got the *Hollywood Press,* and I found a place in Hollywood that provided for a six-month membership, provided names of people who wanted the same thing: wanted to get together in a threesome situation, couples and women, that you could go out and meet and if you liked them you could, if you don't, you don't.

And we've met a couple of people and only one person that we just recently had a threesome with, and it was the best experience I've ever had. We really enjoyed it very much. She was beautiful and she really helped us be closer and helped increase and intensify our relationship and that's why I said I didn't know, because I'm at that point where I think he's going to stay. [Laugh.] He says he will, that's why I don't know. He does want to stay, I do know that, and I do know that he loves me. What he has to deal with now, he being Jeff, is how to tell his wife that he's not going to move in with her. That scares me because there are two children involved.

Reading through all the ads, all the massages . . . . I was looking for a redhead, because Jeff likes redheads—I saw—I was reading the ads—jobs. Because I figure what's going to happen after something does happen between the two of us and he doesn't stay with me? I've got to find a way to support myself, find a way of earning a living where experience is not required and pays more than five dollars an hour. And also a job I can't get fired from if I've got a cold and the flu. My last job, I was on disability and they fired me. So I wanted something that was safe. If it was modeling or taking pictures for quick money, that was safe. So I looked through all the ads—there was a half-sheet of ads—and I spotted Bill's. It caught my attention because it wasn't in Hollywood, it was on the other side of the hill. I wanted to go check this place out and see if they could offer me what I was looking for, and if possible, I could offer what they were looking for. That's how I found Pretty Girl International.

S: Were you attracted to the idea that you would be photographed nude, be modeling, or photographed having intercourse, or was it that you wouldn't be fired for having a cold?

H: The two combined. I've always wanted to pose in magazines.

S: "Always" means what?

H: "Always" meaning from as far as where I knew what it meant to pose in a magazine. Thirteen, twelve, first time I saw a *Penthouse* or a *Playboy,* saw the beautiful voluptuous women in these pictures. One of my favorite pictures is—I've seen it shot a few times—is a girl in a white dress where she's got the dress all wet and you can see through it and she's either at the beach or by water, somehow by poolside or by . . . . The best one I like is covered moss over the rocks by a running stream or a river by shady trees. That's my favorite. I would love to see myself in a picture like that, in that white dress, sprawled on that rock in the moss and having my picture taken. I might want that for myself. That's why I called, because that is an ultimate goal. But if I can take this further and I can make it a successful career, with Papa Bear's help, I want to do that, too.

S: The first half is white dress, on the moss, by the water, being photographed. And the second half is people look—

H: That doesn't matter to me.

S: I would think that it's a necessary part.

H: Well, sure it's a necessary part. Somebody is going to see the picture.

S: Who are the people—not specifically, I know it's going to be John Jones. When you were a kid, it's a fantasy. Now it's about to become a reality if you want that. All along the fantasy is: I will be posed and they will be looking. Who are "they"?

H: Who do I perceive them to be?

S: Yes.

H: [Laugh.]

S: What was the laugh?

H: [More laughter.] Bill—Bill at work with Jeff, the average man, the average man who buys a *Penthouse* and *Playboy* or *Hustler* or *Swank.*

S: My spaceship just landed a half-hour ago from Mars. I don't know who the average man is.

H: Just your average, ordinary man. Maybe a father of a, you know, three kids, 3.5 cars, the mortgage, maybe doctors, maybe lawyers, but it's kind of like Papa Bear says: if I've created in someone the desire to jack off, I've served my purpose. That excites me. That stimulates my senses.

S: What excites you is the idea that you have stimulated the average man to jack off?

H: Yes, and am able to arouse an individual—I'm at a loss for words—just to be able to arouse another man, other than the man I love. (I've got no problem with him. He's a piece of cake. He's proven.) [Laugh.]

S: That may be important: you haven't proven it with these guys. Therefore, the success of this is if they jack off?

H: Yeah. I've got good sight, and I can see guys watch me. Like today—I told Jeff—I went to the store, and I had six guys following me asking me if they could help me find what I was looking for—I was having trouble finding certain items in the store—so I came home and said, "Is there something that looks different about me today? Why did these guys follow me in the store?" It's not every day that happens to me. It just happened today.

S: Did you dress differently or feel differently?

H: My hair is fixed. I feel differently about myself. I mean, I'm sunburned, I'm a little sore. I had my hair different, I don't usually wear barrettes, I usually wear it down or pull it back, but this time I've got it half and half. I feel good about myself. I felt great waking up this morning, I wonder why. [Laugh.]

S: Why?

H: Ask Jeff.

S: Why?

J: I don't know why.

S: Oh, boy. As soon as she says that, I know why, even if you don't. But that doesn't explain the whole day, at the grocery store.

H: Well, it wasn't a whole day: it was just a few minutes. I had an old guy ask me if he could help me find what I was looking for and followed me around the store as I was trying to find it, and then the manager . . . I mean it was like he just couldn't take his eyes off me, it was like a stare. I'd look back, and he was still looking at me. And I'd look away and look back, and he was still staring at me. And then a couple of the young box boys . . . I looked lost, I guess. I was looking up and down the aisles, and they said, "Can I help you?" I went to go find what I want, and he trailed off following me.

S: I would suspect that you were sending messages—

H: That's possible.

S: But what they were you don't know because you were not aware of it. You must have been feeling more lively.

H: I feel happy. I've felt happy ever since I met Papa Bear. I've never been happier than in the past two months. Since Papa Bear has come into my life, oh, I feel so wonderful. It's just like a breath of fresh air after being in a stale room for so long.

S: Has the average man been looking at you more since then?

H: No. Well, I've seen it ever since I've been growing up as I developed into a woman, since I've been married. These men, they see me and I wonder what are they looking at, what do they want. Do they want to see more and if so, can I provide what they want to see? These men are looking—

J: I think I can interject something. When I met L. she had just been separated from her husband, and she was not happy with her self, her self-image. When I met her she was a tomboy, she walked, talked, acted tomboy. She did not know about her body and how to use it and how to entice or whatever. Since I've been with her, she's really grown up. She's turned into a woman. She dresses like it. Even in blue jeans, she looks like a woman. Before, in blue jeans she looked like a man. She had this belt. I threw it away. It looked like a policeman's belt. And she looked like a tomboy. The same kind of jeans but a different person inside. More guys are looking at her, and she's just been noticing it.

S: Is that correct? You've been noticing—

H: I can see them looking at me.

S: That means that you're looking at them looking at you?

H: I'll turn around, and they'll be looking at me. Not just a glance: they're looking me over. They're watching me.

S: Did you use to look at them and see if they were looking at you?

H: [Laugh.] No.

S: That is, a woman who is aware that she's being looked at sends out different messages. You may not know that. Your receiving is a message to the men.

H: I'm lost.

S: You looked it. I think the gentlemen here know what I'm talking about.

B: It has a lot to do with self-confidence and also self-image. It's essentially analogous to watching animals in a barnyard and how certain animals strut their stuff and some sulk around. The pride that he's instilled in your womanhood has allowed you to emanate that aura.

H: So Jeff has made me feel secure within myself.

B: As far as your womanhood—

H: Go on.

B: The X-rated Industry will go one step further. All you get now is the glances. But once you have in your hands the material evidence that you are a feminine animal: you pick up the *Hollywood Press* and you're on the cover—that's the material evidence. That will make you strut your stuff even more. You send out an aura. I try and find a potential sex performer who can then perhaps become a star, then perhaps a superstar. You gotta be born hot. If the flame isn't there, I can't light it. But I can fan it. I can turn it into a forest fire, because that's what it's all about, and the flames come out and engulf the pages. We talked about what the people will do with the pages that you're on. And if they do that and they do jack off to what you've created, then you've become a porn personality. If they wrap a dead animal in your picture, you're a failure. That's what it's all about.

You will appeal, because of your youthful look and your tiny size, to an awful lot of people very much like your father. The people who look at your picture will be your Daddy—millions of daddies out there who will look at your picture and fantasize fucking you. And that could be the bottom line of the revenge for being beaten all these years. Because they can't have you; you're getting even with all of them. That's what it's all about. Because that's who is going to look at your picture more than anybody else. I laugh when you mention your father is forty-four years old. I'm forty-two. I've seen your father, he looks like he's sixty. That's a man who is in unhealthy shape. That man looks unhealthy.

H: Consciously, I'm not doing this to get back at Daddy. I'm really not. Daddy doesn't want me to do this. He will not watch my movies if movies come out of it. But if this is what I really want, he does support it. So does my mother. She said, "If it's really, really what you want, I'll back you 100 percent, I'll be there for you." I don't care about the uncles, the aunts, or cousins. If they come to me and say, "Look at this, this is you," I'll say, "So, I have to eat. I didn't see you busting your butt to help me find a job." I've gone on thirty-five interviews since I've been fired, and not one has come up profitable. And I've got to eat and I've got to pay rent. Right now money is important to me. I do not want him [Jeff] to support me. I want to make an equal effort in our relationship. I'm really stuck: my ex-husband has stopped paying child support, I had to go to the DA, he hasn't paid in four months. Unemployment only pays $86 a week. That's not a lot of money to live on to try and support a baby.

I want to start working. *This* is the way I'm going to do it. I'm going to jump in, both hands and feet. I want to see what I'm getting into. I don't want anybody to pull any punches with me. Papa Bear won't, I know he won't. I'm willing. I want it. I'm going to do it.

S: Let me go back. What daydream, what fantasy, what situation turns you on?

H: [Laugh.] There are many. I don't know if it will shock you or not but being raped is one, knowing that fear, knowing what it's like. Not to be physically hurt or beaten up, just to have someone, not even know what he looks like, just to have him penetrate me, get off, and leave me, to know that fear, what women go through, a learning experience. He doesn't have to be gorgeous, he doesn't even have to be good-looking. He could be scum. Just to have that fear, it is that fear that I'm after that's exciting. I can't describe the fear, I've never been raped.

B: What about the anal adventure? [She has told him of this when he first interviewed her.]

H: My ex-husband never took time for foreplay. He always penetrated when I was dry. Well, he was having sex with me, and he just flipped me over and put it in my ass. God, it was the most painful thing I could have ever experienced. I was eighteen years old. It hurt. I mean, it turned me off to anal sex altogether. Another man is never going to do this to me again. And I told him, "I'll bite your dick off if you do it again." It was without my consent. I wasn't prepared for it. It was by force. I asked him to stop and he wouldn't stop. When he got off, I rolled over on my back and put my hands and pushed my cheeks together because I was in pain. It really hurt.

S: An actual rape. A traumatic experience. But when you think an erotic fantasy, it doesn't make any difference who the man is; it's that he creates fear in you. That's the essential element, not is he tall or short or blond, blue-eyed, or that he has no face. What counts is he frightens.

H: Right. That he creates the fear during intercourse, during a sexual encounter. Because usually when you're in sex it's love, it's caring, it's caressing, even if it's just sex and not love, there's some feeling between two people or they wouldn't have sex. But not in this fantasy. It's: in, off, and done with. Fear is created because I don't know who this person is, why he is at me. I've asked Jeff to create the fantasy—because he's safe: to be in the house and have me not aware of it and come out of the darkness. When I enter my house, I don't turn my lights on. I like the cool, I like the dark, I like the night. And have him come from behind me and not even let me see him, rape me, and then leave. And then maybe not come back for a few hours and tell me that he was with someone, some of the guys at the bar or something like that.

S: That works?

H: It might.

S: You haven't done this?

H: No, I want to.

S: Oh.

H: You keep referring to the blond and blue-eyed. I'm not attracted to blond and blue-eyes. I'm attracted to blue eyes period.

S: Sorry, the guy in the first encounter that you told about—

H: Well, he had blue eyes and I was looking at his blue eyes. I really wasn't thinking even about him. The embarrassment was caused by Reb saying, "Dream all you want." And I wasn't dreaming. To be honest, he would probably be the last person on earth. He's the type of man that he carries himself like he's God's gift to women. I don't like a man like that. Papa Bear thinks he's great, Jeff thinks he's great. Guys like that may be great. They're great to me because they're here, they're tangible. But they can't beat God, because God is the supreme. God created them in his image.

S: Where does the blue eyes come from?

H: I don't know. Jeff is the first man I ever had a crush on that has brown eyes. I've never liked anyone with brown eyes or been in love with anyone who had brown eyes. That was a change for the good. I know when I look into his eyes I see something that's irresistible. I just can't get enough of it. I can't understand how one man, a simple man, can bring out so much in one human being in a short time. A year and a half but yet taking that—a tomboy—and turning her into a woman. And feeling so wonderful about herself. I'm very grateful to him.

Jeff's not saying anything. Ask him some questions.

S: You take over the interview and ask him. Ask him things that you don't want to ask him.

H: Do you really want me to do this, really, from your heart?

J: [Mumbles elliptically.]

H: Jeff, answer the question.

J: Yeah, I do. Because it's something you want to do. I can see that's something you want to do. [Subdued voice throughout.]

H: That's for me. What about you? Honest, Jeff? Here comes the truth. [Mocking.]

J: From me? No, I don't want you to do it.

H: Why?

J: I don't know.

H: You do know or you wouldn't have any fears about it. And I know there are fears, because I can see the fears in your eyes. Are you afraid I'm going to catch something?

J: I don't trust what's going to happen. I don't know. What I've come up with over the weekend is that I'm jealous.

H: Jealous of the fact that someone else is going to be touching me, or jealous that I'm doing what you wanted to do?

J: Exactly. The latter.

H: What's holding you back or preventing you from taking charge of your dream [to be a pornstar] and making it become a reality?

J: Because I don't have the balls for it.

H: Why?

J: I don't know.

H: Are you scared?

J: Yeah.

H: Don't you think I'm scared? I am, I'm terrified, I am.

J: You've got me behind you.

H: That doesn't matter. Just because you're there and you're supporting me and you're behind me doesn't mean that I can't feel fear. It scares me. I don't know what I'm going to be thinking or how I'm going to respond to another man coming up over me like you do and sticking his cock inside my vagina and banging me. That scares me. What are you scared of?

J: I don't know. I don't think we're here because you think it's my problem.

B: Well, yeah, we are. Because it's your problem. I brought you here specifically. She would have come by herself. What I'm doing for the first time in recorded history is giving a chance for people who have never entered into something [about to enter porn] to voice all of their fears, all of their worries, all of their concerns about one of the partners doing it and the other partner not doing it.

J: Okay. But I'm not here to find out why I don't want to do it. Or why I'm scared to do it.

B: But you did toy with the idea of wanting to do it. As I said, you'll get a chance to look at the transcripts. Anything that you might feel incriminating, you can erase. It wouldn't hurt you to say, in this kind of situation, why you don't want to do it. If there is something that should be brought out, this is the best place in the world to bring it out.

J: I just would rather not.

H: I personally think that Jeff would make a success in the business. I think he would be very successful because he has that way with women. I'm not the only woman to say that. The other women he's been with that I've talked to have told me. He's very complimentary. If he likes something, he tells you. He's very polite, he's very shy, he embarrasses easily, he just has that special touch with women. I think that would make him successful. He's worried about his age and the fact that he may not be able to keep it up or his stamina is not as high. That should be the least of his worries. How do you feel about what I just said?

B: Oh, I don't know what he can and cannot do. How old are you?

J: Thirty-seven.

B: All the main [male] stars in the Industry are in their thirties. I'm forty-two, the King is somewhere in his—he says he is older than I am—John Leslie is my age, Jamie is my age, Eric just turned forty, both Herschel Savage and Paul Thomas are in their early thirties, Joey is in his early thirties. There is only one major [male] sex star, two maybe, that are under thirty years old. So the age has very little to do with it. The men in the Industry seem to be more secure the older they get. It's a very closed society for men, because the ones who are in it don't want anybody else in it. That's their problem. When I was an agent, I would welcome anybody into it—any male who came into my office—without wondering about the ramifications of it.

I should have brought you the article in *Hustler*. I've been getting responses on a regular basis nationwide. I got one from Virginia now, one from Ohio, Florida. I'm calling these gentlemen. They all want to get into the Industry, and I tell them it's very difficult to get up, get in, get off, get out on cue. You're not fucking for yourself, you're fucking for the world. The world doesn't want to see you have fun. They want to see themselves have fun through you. And if it takes four hours to shoot your sex scenes, that's how long it's going to take for you to have their fun. We are nothing more than an extension and machine of their minds. But most of the men in my Industry are within your age range. As far as the sexual stamina, it's all in the mind.

J: I'm not worried about that.

H: Does it have anything to do with your children?

J: Probably, subconsciously.

B: That's the best and most logical answer. People have children they're going to have to answer to. So I don't live my life for anybody except me. I don't live my life for my children, because they're not going to live their lives for me.

H: That's funny. That's what Jeff used to tell me. That he was number one, that he was most important, that he came first. Has that changed?

J: Yes. Since I've been with you.

H: You don't live my life. You're a part of my life but you don't live it.

J: It goes back to where you moved in. At that time you walked around in a shell, just put a dome over you.

H: The dome he's referring to is the dome of protection I . . . . It was like a force field. Nobody could penetrate through it. People stayed away from me. I was very macho, I was very tough. You didn't mess around with me. I was out for blood, if you gave me a reason for it. I was just protecting myself because I had been hurt. My husband had messed on me; he had beaten me in our marriage. It was just a traumatic experience. I just wanted to be protected. I wanted to protect myself, and I wanted to protect my baby. It was just like a big steel or iron shield, something nobody could get into. It was a tough act. I was a tough guy. But I kind of fell in love and he broke through that shield and brought out a swan.

S: Jeff, when you imagine being in the Industry, your reasons are what?

J: Because I like sex, always have, always will.

S: This would be a feast? Because the women would be there? It isn't that the audience is there watching, is that right?

J: Oh, I don't care if they watch.

S: She does.

J: The main reason was because of the sex. It's an easy way of getting sex without having to date a girl for a month or two before you get into her pants. Thinking back, I think that was the main thought on why I would want to do it. And of course it helps if the money is good. And a bit of exhibitionism in me, having the audience watch on the screen. Like L. was saying, ever since I was a teenager I wanted a threesome. I just recently had it. And this is what? Fifteen, eighteen years later.

H: I want to help him. I so desperately want to help him create his fantasies and help them come true. And he's willing to help me make mine a reality as well. There's a lot of love. He's tried with so many other women to get them to be as open and as honest about it as I am, and not a one has lifted a finger to do anything about it. All he needs to do is tell me and I will help create the situations to make them come true.

J: I'm sure you're thinking now that this isn't going to work between us. But my reason for thinking it will is she came out of her shell like she says. She didn't come out one hand, then the arm slowly. She just came out BOOM, all of a sudden, something I wanted, but I didn't expect it like that [snaps fingers].

B: It's hard to control the monster you create.

J: Exactly. And this monster is growing very quickly.

S: When did it come out?

J: A week ago tomorrow, when she found the ad for Pretty Girl International, and the place where we signed up to get names of—

B: What did you join, one of the swingers' clubs?

H: I don't know, it's called—

J: Personal Contact.

H: Personal Contact.

B: They're all the same. How much are you paying them?

H: We paid $150 for a six-month membership. That's for both of us.

B: Yeah, I know. They're good, they're fun.

J: They give you names of people who have contacted them for the same reason.

S: When she was in the shell two and a half weeks ago, what made her change?

J: Two and a half weeks ago we were having problems. For two months . . . first she got sick. Then she got fired. Then Unemployment has been jerking her around, Welfare has been jerking her around. She'd come home and cry and bitch and nag at me. I sat back and said, "I can go home for this, I can go back to my wife and have my two kids running around and hear the same shit." I was real close to just picking up and going. Then I went skiing alone, two weekends ago, and on the way back I stopped and saw my wife and my kids, spent a little time there, realized that that's not where I wanted to be. I'm away from L. and I want to be with her more.

So I left there and went home, and we had a great night of sex. The next day I went to work, came home early because I wasn't feeling too hot after a weekend of skiing. I didn't feel like being at work. So I faked illness, stayed home the next day, and then that was the next day. She woke up, we had a real good feeling toward one another. She said, "I'll be right back." She split for fifteen-twenty minutes, came back with *The Hollywood Press,* I'm still in bed. It's nine o'clock in the morning. She sits there and goes through the magazine and starts circling these advertisements. Later on, she makes phone calls. She comes running in from the phone calls and says, "I found it, I found it": this place that gets us names. That's where it began. Later on, she went to the newspaper and found Pretty Girl International.

S: Now when does her career start? This week?

B: It could start as early as tomorrow or even tonight, depending on what kind of calls I get. The bondage thing is indefinite, it could be this Sunday, it could be the twentieth at the latest. It has to be shot on a Sunday because the Scooter Shop is only available to me on Sundays.

S: What are you asking of her for that?

B: To look scared.

H: I'm excited about it. I'm really looking forward to doing it because it has the fear. I get to create that fear. Bill says I walk out of a bathroom. I look around. All of a sudden I'm gone. I'm taken up [in the air by an infernal contraption]. In the next scene I'm tied up. What's nice is it's the first time that I'm going to be naked on camera.

B: Unless you work before that, we don't know. There are other jobs.

H: Bill is going to be there and that's going to make it nice because it will be a first time, it will help me get broken in.

B: There are all kinds of projects. Reb could find work for her very easily.

S: Why so fast?

B: Why not? She's brand new. A new piece of meat. The world wants to look at new meat. She's a piece of meat; welcome to it. We all start with hamburger and work up to filet mignon. She has the inner resources, I believe, to work into the business and to help the people enjoy themselves in the Industry and benefit from it. Now she's an accepted piece of meat. I kick out all the other ones. I decimate people's emotions when they come to see me. She's motivated. She's looking for something. I need people who are searching. Now it's my job to find paths for her to follow that don't result in having her turn back into her dome. See, she did indeed explode her dome—and yet it is not destroyed. It just sits there, and when she feels that she needs to put a part of her back into it, it's there. A laughing place, a place you can always go. My typewriter is my dome, when I need to climb into my introverted situation. I was introverted till I got into high school and beyond that, into college. I was the ultimate toad. Now I know myself and have learned to explode. But when I want to climb back into myself, I have a ready-made cave full of resident bears.

   You have indeed released her from her dome. Be aware that the dome is there if she wants to go back. A part of her will always go back to it, because there's comfort there, continuity, something she's used to.

I see Happy alone, a few weeks later.

S: Welcome back. Talk.
H: Okay. I've done one picture, the cannibal picture, a video, where I was a piece of meat being washed by two men. It was for someone's personal use. It wasn't for publication. Someone hired this man to do this so that he could see what it looked like on video. If it looked any good then he could hire the original actors, which was myself and two other gentlemen, or find new people and build on it. I know nothing about the man. I don't know who he was, but he paid for everything. I got $150. All the Karo syrup that was used on me and I wasn't hurt. They didn't hurt me. In fact, it was very relaxing. [Laugh.] I got to be washed by these two men. They brought me in, I was supposed to be drugged, they undressed me and washed me—
S: Washed you with syrup?
H: No, no, no. They washed me with soap and warm water, and then sponges. They washed me all over from head to toe, my vagina, my ass, everything. I was just supposed to lay there and be unconscious, with them washing me as they're talking over the different parts of the body and what this meat is like and how it tastes. A lot of improvisation, because the skit that we had was three pages long, and if we did it in these three pages, we were done in

fifteen minutes. He wanted to stretch it out for an hour and a half. So the guys stretched their lines.

After the washing scene, we took stills. I posed, and they posed. They had a switchblade knife, very dull. He showed me that if you stabbed someone with it—he put it into his side—it goes in but it doesn't hurt you. They held it to my neck like they're going to cut me, and I'm looking real scared, then they took pictures. Then they carried me into the bathroom, and they throw me—well, they don't throw me, but it looks like they throw me in—and I'm laying there unconscious and I'm semi-conscious, and they have a saw and they have a knife and they have .. . . it's Karo syrup with dye in it to look like blood—they pour this stuff all over the saw and they pour it all over the knife and get shots of that.

The angles were really tough, because you're working in a room, not on a set where you can work from all angles. He can only shoot from one angle. So everything had to be shot, stopped again, set up, shot. So I'm laying here shivering of cold; it's not the warmest of places. It's in his apartment. About halfway through this scene, they shut the hot water off. (I had had warm water run on my feet to keep me warm.) So I'm freezing, I'm shivering. [Laugh.] The hair was standing up on end plus I'm covered with this sticky stuff. Then I thought, "I've got to dance [nude, on stage, new job] tonight. What if the syrup stains my skin?" I saw it stain one of the guys' hands and I thought, "Oh, no." I rinsed it off real quick in cold water.

They decided they wanted to get real gross. He had bought a cow's heart, cow's brains, cow's liver, all this stuff to get more realistic, like they've opened me up and they're taking all this stuff out. They [laugh]—I don't want to get my hair dirty, it gets dirty anyhow—they throw a towel over my head and they've got the brains sitting on top of the towel and on my shoulder and guts all over my body and blood splattered all over the wall, all over the curtains, all over the floor and all over the mirror and everything. Before that, they took the saw and you can hear my scream, a blood-curdling scream. It wasn't that they were going to chop me up, it was that the water was so cold and I was freezing.

So I'm dead, and they're taking up all these guts. And he actually puts some of the heart on the knife. They poured blood in the heart, and he's sitting there squeezing the heart so the blood comes out. Then he takes the brains and eats the brains raw.

So I'm the star. I get to wash. They help me wash, because this stuff is all over my body. And I'm freezing. I have to wash my hair because it smells like cow guts. I take a shower in cold water. I get dressed. One of the guys goes down and gets my hair dryer out of the van and then we're talking and he has to reshoot the credits because he messed up. He had shot over his credits. Then they fried up what they had. They sat down and ate this meal, this gourmet meal. They were actually eating it—the heart and intestines and everything.

Then my last part—I played a double role—I changed clothes from earlier. There's a knock at the door and they're eating. "Who is that?" And I walk in. All you see is my leg. "That's dessert." It took six hours to shoot, I danced all week after that; I got $250 for dancing plus my tips were about $100 for the week. I'm going to go back to dance. I had a couple of problems dancing, none mentally. After my set I was taking a walk, and one of the clients in the club followed me, started touching my face and telling me how pretty I was and that he really enjoyed my dance. I said, "Look, I'm married, I'm a mother, I do this for fun, that's where it stops." I wasn't aggressive. I didn't know how to react because I've never come across that situation before. He wasn't mean. I tried to be polite. I didn't want to lose the club a customer, but at the same time I didn't want to be in danger.

When I went back, the manager says, "The next time that happens, you tell him 'Don't touch me,' and be firm." He says, "I don't care if I lose a customer, you're the most important thing to me, you're my dancer and you are number one." A man the manager knew came into my dressing room. I had just gotten done dancing. He really came on real strong, made a strong pass: "How about showing me your stuff," he said, "you're not afraid to show your stuff." I said, "When you leave, will you please close the door behind you?" telling him that I ain't messing around, I'm tired, I just got off the set. "I had someone try a couple of days ago to follow me, I don't need this," I said. He's sitting there rubbing his crotch. I said, "Out, get out." So he goes out and tells Michael, "She sure is touchy, isn't she?" Michael said, "I haven't had any problems with her."

I do five shows a night and have five different costumes for five different dances. One time I was supposed to wear my Laker [basketball team cheerleader] costume. It's not sexy, just different. I said, "No, I don't want to wear it." So I wore my silk blouse with my wraparound skirt, which is my best costume, because it takes time to take off and I can do a lot with it because it's a wraparound skirt. I can pull the tie off, and it looks real seductive. It unravels. So I'm having a lot of fun. I unbutton the sleeves, unbutton the collar, pull out my blouse during the first song. The second song starts, and I play. I start unbuttoning and I hide, so they can't see. Then I turn around and take my blouse off one shoulder and move my shoulder around and take it off and show the other side of my shoulder and then take the blouse off and all they see is my back. Then I take the blouse and put it in front and turn around. So I'm still teasing. And I took it off and I showed one breast and then I showed my other breast and I danced for a little bit, threw my blouse right in one guy's face. He caught it [laugh]. He didn't know what to do with it. Then I undid my skirt, because I have to be totally undressed by the end of the second song, undid my dress, and then unraveled it so you can see my right leg, then turned around and opened the skirt up. And I move the skirt to the music.

The light is shining through the skirt and you can see through the skirt, but you can't really see anything. Then I show one cheek of my butt. I show the other cheek. I hold the skirt tight up underneath like I'm sitting on it and move that way. Then I close the skirt and turn around and then I unveil myself totally. And I dance. There's five songs. So I dance. For the next song, I use a prop, a chair. I dance on the chair very slow, very exotic, just moving so they can see my body, basically is all it is. The third song I dance and I get a little bit more exotic. The fifth dance I get very exotic, I get almost down into their faces. I stretch my leg out and my leg may be from here [demonstrates]—a foot away—to their face so they can see. I shave a lot down below so they can see everything as far as my vagina, and I get down into their faces.

Okay, now you can ask questions.

S: How did you know what to do, where did you get the costumes, who gave you instructions, where was the place and how do you know how to dance, who tells you: things like that.

H: Okay. Take one question at a time. Jeff taught me how to dance. He's been to places like the Bucket and places I don't even know where, where he's seen women dance exotically. He was my choreographer. He taught me how to dance to tease. He says as long as you remember to tease, that's the whole idea of exotic dancing.

S: How long ago did he start teaching you?

H: The day before I went to dance.

S: You have never seen it, you didn't really know what to do, and he then instructed . . . . They hired you without your knowing how to dance?

H: Right.

S: Why? How did they know what you were going to do when you got up there?

H: They didn't.

S: Why did they take a chance? You could have bombed.

H: That's true. If I bomb, I don't come back. But after we talked with you, Bill took us to see what she did, and she wasn't doing anything.

S: You mean: just some woman?

H: Some woman, I don't know who she was. She was dancing, and she wasn't doing anything. She was just walking around the stage. At least I dance a bit. The first night I went out there, I got dressed [snaps fingers] and was on stage. I didn't have time to think. No fear. No inhibitions. I just got up there, did what they told me to do: the first song you dance and don't show anything; be undressed by the second song; the third song use the chair or the round, cushionlike stool and stretch and dance with that and walk around it or whatever. I watched her and knew that I had no problems, because I'm not a bad dancer, I know how to excite a man. If I can excite Jeff, I can excite anyone. It just was natural. It was there. It's always been there. I just needed someone to bring it out. I chose my music. Jeff had it taped. He put together my costumes: something easy to take off. Out of my own wardrobe.

S: Before Jeff talked to you, you had contacted somebody about going there?

H: Bill Margold.

S: Bill contacted somebody?

H: Bill contacted the Venice Adult Theater. Whenever Bill gets someone new in the Industry, he sends them to the Venice Adult Theater for experience.

S: And they have how many dancers?

H: One dancer a night for seven nights.

S: The same woman?

H: Right. I do five shows a night.

S: You do five shows a night, and you're the only one?

H: So I do thirty-five shows a week.

S: And you're expected to be there for a week maximum?

H: Right.

S: And then another woman has to be hired?

H: For another week, and then another woman for another week, and I can come back.

S: If they like you.

H: They liked me.

S: If you had bombed, they would pay for you that one night and that would be it? Or would they keep you for a week even if you're terrible?

H: They would have kept me for a week because this girl that was dancing, she wasn't doing anything at all. I mean I could have done what she was doing and been bored.

S: Why do they keep her?

H: Because she keeps coming back, I guess, I don't know.

S: Does the audience care who the woman is or what she's doing?

H: She got a complaint the night we were there, because she didn't undress.

S: At all?

H: She unbuttoned her blouse. It was a man's shirt, which is one of my costumes. I wear a man's shirt with black underwear.

S: And yet they'll keep her for a week even if she doesn't undress!

H: I can't really explain it. I do know that the men liked me a lot because I got a lot of repeat men. As they were leaving, they said, "When's this dancer going to be back?" But don't forget they don't always go there just to see the dancer. They go there to see the two-hour movie, because there's a movie there.

S: Oh, I didn't know that.

H: Yeah, there's a two-hour movie between my sets. And when you walk in, there are all the magazines and all the videos and all the dildos and things like that so you can see and buy things. And they have the little theater— little things you stand in and put a quarter in and you watch a show.

S: So it's a sex shop plus having a dancer?

H: Right. There's four different things that can be done in this one place. They can come see a dancer, they can come see the movie, they can buy things, or they can go in this little arcade—that's the word I'm looking for, arcade. Where I dance there is about fifty seats, maybe seventy. My stage is about as big as this room. I have three floodlights on the ground, one red, one blue in the middle, and then another red. And then I have three red lights above me, one right after another. They're thinking about getting one of those mirrored balls that flashes light. On me. That might make it a bit more attractive. Somebody suggested a strobe light. That light flashing gets me sick, especially if I'm moving. Because I know, I've been in front of one. I wouldn't mind the mirror above me. I think that would be attractive because you'd get it all over the men, you know, and it would be all over me. You could see the little things [flashes of light] on my body. It might be a little incentive; it wouldn't be a bad idea. I wouldn't say it was a scuzzy place, you know, it's not an elaborate theater like the Pantages, but I get treated well. I have my own room. I have a TV, I have a fan in there, a nice fan, a mirror, and a couch.

S: What do they charge the men?

H: They charge the man five dollars, and they can stay for all five movies and all five sets.

S: Five different movies?

H: No, it's the same movie.

S: Your set is how long?

H: Twenty minutes.

S: Twenty minutes? That means that this whole thing is running eleven or twelve hours.

H: Right. But I actually—I dance for like—what did we figure it out to be—an hour and twenty minutes. I start at two o'clock.

S: In the afternoon?

H: In the afternoon.

S: That early?

H: And my first dance ends at 2:30; I can get dressed, come back, be there by 4:10 to do my next set.

S: Are you close enough that you can go home?

H: Yes, I can go home—

S: So your son gets a chance to see you.

H: I do that or I go and eat or go shopping or if Jeff is there, I'm with Jeff. This Sunday I started to dance. So I did the movie and the dance in one day.

S: Did Bill arrange—direct the movie as well? Is he the—

H: Bill's my agent.

S: What comes next?

H: Hopefully, this Sunday we're going to shoot the minibike series, where I get turned into a minibike. He hasn't heard anything from his companions, the people he works with, about it.

S: He, Bill?

H: He, Bill.

S: Will you do me a favor and tell me how the hell you turn into a minibike? I can't see—

H: It starts out I drive this battered minibike to this minibike shop and Bill is the man and I'm reprimanded by Bill for having it in such poor condition. We go for a ride, we fall, I get dirty, he takes me back, I go to the restroom and wash off, come out of the restroom, I'm hoisted up off my feet. They're going to hoist me up so I disappear. Then you're going to see me being tied up with electrical cord and gagged with masking tape—anything you find in a minibike shop—and beat me [laugh], roll around in the dirt, he says, and get oil on him and stuff, and then I'm going to be executed, killed off, and I'm going to be under a rug and then this woman who looks nothing like me but is supposed to be my sister, she's blond and big-busted, the same series of events happens to her and both of us wind up being the new model minibike, one blue, which I'll be blue and she'll be red, this man comes in and is shown the latest model of minibikes, which is her and me. I don't know how they're going to do it but it will be interesting to see. I'm looking forward to it.

S: That's the whole movie?

H: In a condensed version.

S: And where's the sex?

H: No sex in bondage; it's against the law to have sex in bondage, you cannot be tied up and have intercourse. I'll be nude. Being tied up is another fantasy of mine. This whole thing is fulfilling fantasies that I've had since I was a child, this whole Industry. The Industry, to put it in a nutshell very simply, the Industry is beginning to fulfill fantasies that I've had that I have been inhibited by my parents because of the lack of sex, not having sex as a teenager, skipping that whole era, and was thrusted into a marriage and then finally experiencing sex in a marriage and not knowing what other men were like so winding up cheating on the husband to find out what other men were like—the Industry is giving me the outlet to fulfill all the sexual fantasies that you develop as a teenager that you see on TV. It's exciting for me to watch a guy tie a girl up and have her gagged and bound. I used to like Miss Penelope on the railroad tracks when I was a kid. It has to do with someone's mind. I'm not a psychiatrist, I can't explain it. It's just there, it's exciting.

S: What did it feel like when you were a little kid to have these fantasies?

H: Frustrating because I couldn't create any of them to come true. I remember . . . I have recollections of masturbating as early as like three, four years old. I remember being in a crib and my dad coming in catching me. It's very foggy, but I know. I lived it. I know it happened. I was in a crib, a white crib, and I was masturbating or touching myself. I don't know what they call it when a child does it. Frustration. Being in the family situation that I was [in], my dad being an alcoholic, beating me even at that young age, it was a release. It's always been a release. Fifteen was the point where I found it could be erotic. Up until that point, it was a release, an emotional release, a frustration release. When I get frustrated, I play with myself. It would relieve the frustration.

You don't understand me. Okay. You play a good game of racquetball and you sweat and you work up a good sweat and a good game. You end the game, you kick back, you start cooling off, you're relaxed. You've worked out all your aggressions, you've worked out everything that's been bothering you, you take it out on the game, now you can sit back and [sigh], all is great. That's what I'm talking about. Before fifteen, it was a release. When I started getting into my teens and being able to touch myself and become aware of who I was and what I was becoming, which was a woman, the feeling became more of an intercourse where I would use Mom's dildo and things of that nature and fantasize where I had a guy and he might be eating me or I might be giving him a blow job or whatever. That's what I mean where it became erotic. I had fantasies of being tied up and being taken advantage of, fantasies of being raped, fantasies of someone making passionate love to me, two-three people with me at the same time, orgies, whatever my mind could create that it knew how to create. Even with animals. I mean I had some strange fantasies with animals. Before fifteen it was just release.

S: By release do you mean orgasm?

H: I think so, yeah. I really think so. Don't forget, fifteen was the time when I attempted suicide, which we talked about last time. So I really—I lost a lot of my memory.

I was aware of what I was doing, and being Catholic, I grew up thinking, "God, it's a dirty, awful sin." I even believed, going into my marriage, that touching myself was a dirty sin [laugh]. That's why I exploded out of that shell. Jeff brought me out of that shell, taught me that it wasn't dirty, that my body is beautiful, that it's okay to touch it, and to feel good about touching it. Two different people: I'm a different person. My sexual awareness is totally different from what it was before. Now I'll get into the Industry, get some money behind me, get my bills paid off, and then go to school while still in the Industry. I'm not going to work every day in the Industry. There are going to be days where I can, like, go to classes. It may be a long time, but I'll have some backup when the Industry no longer can keep me, when I can no longer survive in the Industry.

S: What does your father think of your doing these public erotic acts if he hasn't any terrible concern about having used you erotically?

H: He doesn't remember, he was drunk that night. I've seen him stand up, walk into the living room, stand there for a minute, walk back, open his drawer and urinate into his drawer.

S: Okay. So you're moving into a world where your fantasies and reality meet, and you're looking forward to it.

H: I'm getting into an interesting profession, needless to say. You know, if I lose Jeff—

S: He's not thrilled with what you're doing?

H: [Laugh.] What's good for the goose is good for the gander. Guys want to go out and play, but they don't want the women to. Jeff is afraid of letting the woman that he loves—because he does love me, loves me very much— letting her go out and have sex with other guys. He's afraid that I won't be able to come home to him and still make the passionate love that I do now to him. Whether my vagina's worn out [laugh] or I'm too tired or I'm just sexed out or whatever, he's afraid. I told him that if there was any change to tell me and I'll stop doing this job and cut it off. I will go back to school or whatever he wanted for me. But he is afraid and doesn't want other guys touching me. He wants to be selfish. But he's dug himself a grave. He's released a monster, and he doesn't know how to control this monster: me, I'm the monster. I don't know if I can control it.

S: You're not really sure that you will quit the Industry and go back to Jeff?

H: There may be . . . yeah, okay, there may come a point where I have to choose between the Industry and Jeff and I will choose the Industry over Jeff if Jeff does not divorce his wife. If Jeff goes through with the divorce, I will choose Jeff over the Industry. The whole thing with Jeff is feeling secure. I need to feel secure in our relationship. I want to give up. I want to be able to tell him to get the fuck out [laugh] but I can't. He ain't got no place to go. He'll go back to his wife, and I don't want him to get back to her. I hate her with a passion. It's a pain in the neck. I just want to let go. If I didn't have a baby and I went off the deep end, I'd probably try suicide again. The only thing that keeps me living is because that baby has no other place to go. I don't want to see him wind up in a foster home.

But I'm at the point where I want to slit my wrists or something. I want to do something drastic, to say, "Somebody help me." I don't know what to do. I really don't know what to do. Sometimes I think going into the Industry is my way of getting back at Jeff for all the pain I'm going through. Sometimes I think: am I just getting into the Industry because he's had sex with so many women during our relationship and sleeping with his wife when he told me he was with someone else, not her? Is this my ultimate revenge, to have any guy that I want and get paid for it? Is it a good reason? I don't know, because I really don't know. The test will be after my first five sex films— actually having intercourse on film or video—if I can still go home and make passionate love to Jeff the same way I do now. I don't think there will ever be a problem, really.

S: Suppose he marries you, and that's just what you want, and then you get out of the business: what will you do about the fantasies that you imagine you're going to satisfy in the Industry?

H: Well, they've been satisfied. They've been taken care of. Just like the fantasy of me dancing in front of an audience. That's on my shelf in my memory bank. I can pull that book down and open the pages and say, "Look what I've done. Here it is, it's recorded. I've done this." You don't need to reread the book, just go back and flip through it. I fulfilled the need. The need to dance nude and expose my body. Instead of getting arrested for streaking through the UCLA campus, I can dance nude and get paid for it and enjoy it. And the men enjoy it. Oh, one thing I skipped over. [When I'm dancing] I have guys jacking off all over the place. I walk out and they're sitting there jacking—masturbating . . . I had one guy climax all over my stage. He got so bad. I just wanted to add that in because I thought it was funny. It doesn't bother me at all. It doesn't do anything for me. It's doing it for them. They're getting off. I don't get off. I don't get wet or anything. I don't get excited. It's fun. It's exercise. I think I lost a few pounds. And I enjoy the money. I caught up on all my bills finally. I caught up on all my bills. I'm real happy. I've got money in my wallet.

She returns again a few weeks later. The dancing progresses.

H: Bill referred me to three places. One was too far to travel. I asked other people about the other places, and they said, "Don't work there; they're no-good places." Then Richard, the caretaker of the Venice Adult Theater, referred me to the Venus Fair in North Hollywood. Well, after I lost my unemployment [benefits], I needed to supplement that loss of income: there is no way that I can survive on a base salary of three hundred dollars [from dancing] and then my tips and support my child by myself and make all the doctors' bills I have from my baby. So I called the Venus Fair and said, "I'm a dancer, I'm looking for a new job. I still maintain the one, but I want to dance some place else when I'm not dancing" (because there is three weeks that I don't dance). So he said, "Come in and fill out an application," and that there would be no problem, they're always looking for new dancers. I said, "Okay."

Well, I had made some phone calls and I picked up the *Hollywood Press* two days before I had made this phone call and called a place called World Modeling, which is another place like Pretty Girl International where they take pictures of models, and I saw it on TV. I saw them interview the man [Jim South]—a documentary about his business. So I went and talked to him that morning and had him take a picture of me and we talked and I said that I'd like to get into video and do video and get into having pictures taken. So he referred me to four places. One place called American Art, another place called Lance Pearse, and two Greek gentlemen that their names I couldn't remember. Well, I called all four when I got home and American Art wouldn't answer the phone, I got through to Lance Pearse and set up an appointment, and called the Greek gentlemen, which only one returned my call and I couldn't get through to either of them. I went to see Lance Kincaid the following morning because I was going to go to the Venus Fair in the afternoon. So I went and they took three pictures of me, three different poses: one with my back to the camera looking over my shoulder, one full face with my bust sticking out as far as I could get it, and just another one with a real pretty smile. And they said that they would contact me.

I left there and I went to the Venus Fair, filled out an application; while I was being interviewed and shown the Venus Fair and what type of dancing is done, Jimmy came in and took over the interview from Mike. (Mike is the assistant manager who has the power of hiring and firing also.) Jimmy took me in his back office and we sat and we talked. I told him exactly what type of dancing I have done, how long I've been doing it, that I have a little boy with no child support that I'm trying to support and I can't survive on this amount of money. And he started to laugh and said I'd have no problem with making an income working there for three weeks and I'll tell you later he was right. [Laugh.]

I'm making more money than I have ever seen, Dr. Stoller. I've got money in my purse, money in the bank, and I've got money in a—

S: Without even trying.

H: Without even trying. I work four days a week; so I work twelve days. I walk away with a hundred or more dollars. Last night I walked away—I worked a double shift, but I walked away with $240 for twelve hours' work. And I don't work that hard [laugh], I really don't. I'll tell you how it's set up. As you walk into the Venus Fair, you have the books and the videos all displayed, all the little dildos and toys and all the little knickknacks—and it's a big room—off to one side as you walk in it's to your right—is the cashier counter, which is a big, oval, horseshoe-shaped counter, and the cashiers stand behind and they take in the money and they help the customers. Behind the wall, behind the cashier, are these little booths and they have them at the Venice where you put tokens in and it shows a movie, a short portion of a video. And they have several of these booths throughout— behind the cashier and beyond the cashier, beyond this area of videos and books. They have several of these booths. (I've never really counted them, so I don't know how many are there.)

In this area of books and videos there is a door off in the corner on the left across the area from the cashier's and you go behind that door and that's where the dancers work. And you walk in the door and there's a narrow hallway that stretches maybe five hundred feet from end to end. At one end is a closet, and there's a small dressing room. Then there's a coat closet, and this is all walk area, and then there's a set of steps. As you walk up the steps there is a beaded curtain that hangs down to separate the walk area and the dance area. And in the dance area there are windows. Now if you can, imagine again a squared-off horseshoe. There are four windows to the right that are small, that if I stood up to it, it would come . . . . If a male was looking he could see from my neck to just below a little portion of my legs so he could see that much in this mirror. It's not quite a full length mirror or window and there's four on the right and four on the left.

In the front, there are five full-length mirrors where he can see from head to foot. Now how these work is the man goes in a door on the opposite side, which is behind another wall where you can't see it. You have to go around to where these booths with the small videos are, the movie video machines, and these men go in the door and they're numbered 1 through 12, and these men put four tokens in. They can get tokens from a machine or from the cashier. A token is worth twenty-five cents so they get four for a dollar or twenty-five for five dollars. And they put the tokens in the machine, four of them, and the light will go out, and they can see in. These are fluorescent lights with two-way mirrors. Now when the light is on—

S: Two-way?

H: Okay, I'm going to explain. When the light is on, I can see the man, but the man cannot see me. When the light goes off, it reverses. I cannot see him, but he can see me. Now at the bottom of each of these windows—because there are two pieces of glass: one on his side, one on my side and the fluorescent lights in the middle of this—there's a dollar bill that sits on the flat portion, on the bottom of all these windows, which is a hint. This is how I earn my money. We're not allowed to ask for tips, but we can ask for their generosity. I'd say 80 percent of the men automatically put a dollar, five, ten, or twenty up there for the girl to dance, in a little hole that's above the window, it's a small talk-hole, these are called talk booths, we can talk to the men. I make anywhere between forty and eighty dollars a day in tips on this floor myself. This is what I average.

Twenty percent of the time I have to say, "Your generosity is greatly appreciated, sweetheart, we're not paid a salary here." Something like that is acceptable; I can ask for that. Now this is the dance area and what we do is we show our body, we're sexy, we're dressed in little sexy outfits and things, something that's easy to get off, or maybe a pair of panties and a bra, something like that, something that's lacy and sexy and I'll get down and I'll show my, you know, snatch to the guy and give him a shot.

S: Can the other guys see you, or are you too much off to the side?

H: If I'm at a full length can a guy from the small window—yes, he can see me.

S: But the guy who you are right in front of sees the most?

H: Yeah. Usually a girl is in front of him. So he's only watching her to begin with.

S: There's more than one of you on at the same moment?

H: During the day there are four girls: two on the floor and two in a booth. And I'll tell you about the booth, I haven't gotten there yet. In the night, there's only two girls. You have a shift nine to four in the morning, which I've worked, which I enjoy, and there's a shift from six to two, which I've worked and enjoyed. I like those night shifts. There's not as much money, but it's much quieter as far as there's not as much traffic. The girls are very pleasant to work with, they're human, they have some faults. I'm sure I have faults, too, which I know I do. But as a whole, I get along with all of them, and there are several and they range in height and beauty and every-thing else, a wonderful bunch of girls, all of them. The talk booths: you walk down three stairs and you have these three talk booths. Now where a talk booth is is just past these mirrors. It says "phone talk booth" in flashing neon lights where the men who are walking out in the area can see this.

And what they see is a piece of glass with red curtains and an open little area where a girl would dance and stand. On my side, where I see it from, is a door and I have a step, I step up into this booth. Now how this operates is a man has a door he can get in, he walks in the door, they're numbered 1, 2, and 3. Say I'm in booth 3. The man comes in number 3 (when he walks in, the cashier is off to this one side). Just to the left and center of the cashier is a chalkboard on top, and they write who is there: Happy in booth number 1, or booth number 3, Jillian (which is a phony name) in booth number 2, and Kristy and Kerry in booth number 1, they're sharing a booth because there are four girls and it's a day. The man says, "I want to see Happy." So the cashier will ring the phone in the back and says, "Happy, you have a booth." I will go to the booth, and the man will walk in, lock his door, and the man says, "How does this work?" and there's a chair for him to sit down and a phone that he can talk to me over, we have phones. If he picks his up, it rings on my side. So if I'm not quite there I know he's in my booth, I tell him that it's a ten-dollar minimum for five minutes. Any time after that, it's two dollars a minute. And we have—it's like an odometer. You press the button, and it counts each minute.

I press it five times for each minute that he pays for. He has to show me his money through a window, a bullet-proof glass, show me his money and then fold it up and put it in a box and on my side it's a glass box, I can see through it and watch the money drop. When the money is dropped, I close my door, I pull the shade, I pull the curtains, which are red curtains (makes me feel like a prostitute), and turn on the light. And I start to slowly undress. I ask the man his name, his name is Bill, perhaps, he asks me mine, I tell him my name is Happy, and we talk. We talk about anything and every-thing. I had a man come and cry, I mean literally tears and sobbing, because he broke up with his girlfriend of five years. I've had a man, last night, talk to me about his being divorced from a woman for five years and came there to relieve himself so when he goes to make love to her last night or this morning, that he could last longer. They're all there for different reasons: some there just to get off, some don't want to talk to me, some want me to be dominant, some want me to be submissive.

The only thing that I've had happen once to me so far, and I've worked nine days, nine shifts so far, is a guy talking about child molestation. I tell him to get the hell out. I said, "Get out of here. You can talk to me as a woman and relate to me as a woman and I'll relate to you as a man, but when you start getting sick on me" (and especially what's going on in my life, in my past, I can't handle it, I kicked him out), "don't even bother coming back and seeing me." He was telling me about how a Mexican woman needed her rent and she gave her daughter for him to give a bath and started getting graphic. And it made me sick. I wanted to throw up. Some guys are nice, some guys just want me to talk to them and tell them how good I think it would feel if we were having sex. So they're actually beating off in this booth and my booth gets very messy, Dr. Stoller [laugh]. I've never had a problem yet with a guy not coming, just like I get maybe on an average let's say, ten, ten to fifteen guys every shift. Every single one of them in five minutes. Some need a little more time and pay for it. But that's the talk booth.

S: How do you work your time? You're also dancing three steps up, you said, with the mirrors?

H: Okay. If it's—we go in shifts—as long as somebody is on the floor to take care of the mirrors, somebody can be in the back with the customer in the booth. And when I'm done with the booth, she'll go in the booth and try and get a customer to come in. We get half of that ten dollars, Dr. Stoller. So if I make a hundred dollars, I made fifty for the day. And I tally it up. Say the Geiger counter reads 059299, I'll write "in 299" and I'll press it five times which would make it "304"; I'd write "out 304." And then that way I can count all the "ins" I have and find out how much money I have and it's half of whatever . . . now if somebody hands me a twenty, I get ten. So I have to count the time depending on whether it's five minutes or ten minutes.

S: Is there tipping in the talk booth?

H: Yes. I had a man—here's a prime example—I had a man yesterday ask me how much I thought I was worth. He would pay me whatever I thought I was worth. I'm not a greedy person. I looked at my bust, and I said, "I think each boob is worth about ten bucks." He pulled out a twenty and put the twenty in my booth, in my thing. I give it to the cashier. She splits it half and half.

They have to take it out to the front cashier in that horseshoe area in the opening and count it out in front of me and split it half and half. And what they do is they add up all the ones and put it on a calculator, and add up all the fives, tens, and twenties and do that, so Ruthie did that for me so I had $100 cash from that, I made $126 in the booth, so I made $226 altogether.

S: Back up one second. Why do some of the men pick the mirror that doesn't show all of you and others do and they both charge the same amount?

H: Okay. It just varies. It just depends on the man's preference. They see our face, because we can lay down on the ground and they can still see us from the small mirror, in the small window. They can just get close and look in and I could (I'm going to describe it): I can just lay down on the floor and do this type of number, you know, lay down on the floor and he's looking right at me. So he can still see me no matter where he is. It's just a matter of a man's preference. They have the long mirrors, and they have the small mirrors.

S: Do you have any theory why, because I haven't. Why wouldn't they all be the same?

H: It's just the way it was designed. Five years ago, Dr. Stoller, there was a brothel upstairs and this area that I'm describing with the mirrors had a bed and all the girls had this bed and they would play with dildos and all kinds of toys, sticking them up and the girls eating each other and having oral sex, you know, with the girls, and they said—at that time there were no laws that were stipulating the rules—the guys couldn't put the money in fast enough, these same mirrors. It's changed in five years. Now we're not allowed to touch ourselves within six inches of any pigmentation [nipples, crotch]. When I'm in a booth, I cannot touch myself. I've had policemen come in already and ask me to touch myself and I sit up and I say, "You push, you're out of here."

S: What's that mean, "you push"?

H: If they push me to try and get me to touch myself so they can make a bust, I'll kick them out and give them their money back. I don't want to deal with it. I'm there to get a man off and for enjoyment and these men, yes, policemen do masturbate [laugh]. Anyone wants to know: policemen do masturbate because they all do. As beautiful—and I'm beginning, every day more and more I believe I'm a beautiful woman—as beautiful a woman as I am, these men whip it out [laugh]. Are there any more questions, because I'm ready to go on.

S: No, that's a pretty good description.

H: I tried my best. It took me two weeks to describe to Jeff what was going on.

S: Let me go back. So you're dancing, either in front of the mirrors or three steps down into the booth and you're—you get some sense of males coming and going—

H: [Interrupts.] You get tired of them.

S: That's what I want to get to. There are males coming and going and jacking off and talking to you, dirty or not, you almost are a therapist for some of them or not, one guy comes in, talks about child molesting; and so forth. What do you make of men? It would seem from your experience that you have information or wisdom about men beyond the average woman who doesn't see this aspect. What do you make of this? What does it do to you? For you? Can you tell me: what's beyond the fact that they're jacking off and the booth is a mess?

H: Number one that—they don't—well, gosh, how can I explain it, Dr. Stoller?

S: Just talk. Don't explain it.

H: When I see the men jacking off in the booth and I get them off, that's fine, I've gotten him off, he feels good, he feels better, he's relieved. That's one less lady he's going to go out and rape or one less disease that he's going to catch. I feel like I'm helping these guys, in a sense being a therapist. They do nothing for me. I mean, some are good-looking men. I've seen men your age come in; I've seen men eighteen, nineteen years old come in. Some good-looking, some total flops, but they're human beings and they have a physical function, a physical need, and I do believe that masturbation is a physical need. It's a release, it's an energy release that people do to release anger, stress, fear, and frustration. The only thing that it does for me is makes me horny as hell when I get home and I want to attack Jeff.

S: You can always see them?

H: I can always see them.

S: What are you watching that makes *you* horny? They are watching you and your body, you're a strange woman, they don't care who you are particularly except that you should look nice and you do the right things, and that turns them on: what's getting you horny? Are you horny at the time or after it's all over you go home and recognize you've become horny?

H: I go home and recognize that I've become horny. It hits me when I'm home and I see Jeff and I know that I can touch him and I can hold him, and he's real, and I can have him without the fear of being arrested for prostitution. I don't have to pay. He doesn't have to pay. It's real. It's love. It's physical. And that's what makes it all worth more. And it has enhanced my sex. I don't think Jeff realizes, but it's enhanced my sex drive a lot, and I had a high sex drive to begin with. I mean, I come home and I attack the poor man at two o'clock in the morning. I mean, "Roll over, Jeff, I want to give you a blow job; I want to make love." "No, I'm asleep, leave me alone." At least I try, that's what makes me feel good. Because one of Jeff's fears that he confessed to me was that I'm going to have all these men, I'm going to be having sex all day on the set or whatever, am I going to be able to come home and want him. So now I come home and want him, and it's like "I've had enough, I've had enough": he feels that I'm going to kill him sexually. He thinks that because I have so much sex with him that he—he calls "it" Richard because everybody calls "it" a dick—that Richard is going to poop out, wear out. I said, "No, dear, I don't think so." I have no problems getting him to a full erection and satisfying him and our needs. That's good.

S: You're not then doing what the men are doing to you: looking at them, turned on by their bodies or by their excitement or by their penises?

H: He'd have to be a Mr. America in order to do that for me. And I've only had maybe one or two guys out of the ten a day that it's like, "Oooh, you're a total fox." They're a turn-on but in a different sense, not a sexual sense, in a sense that he's handsome, he's good-looking, he's got a good build, a good body, a nice-looking cock. That is nice; it's nice to look at. It's like a piece of art that I can admire, and some artists sexually arouse me and it makes me feel like I'm the woman that I am, to look at him. But not to the point where I want to run and go get a dildo and stick it up my cunt and start jamming. No, they don't do that to me. Why I don't know, but I try and be as sexy as I can. My main goal is to try and get them off.

S: I'm trying to find out, among other things, in what ways are women different from men. What about the other women who work there? Do they have a comparable experience? Do you talk about it with them?

Most readers can, at this point (before we go on with Happy's answers), skip the next two transcript excerpts, for they add no new facts to Happy's description. I include them nonetheless so as to converse with colleagues who are also preoccupied with how we, as naturalists, are to share accurately (honestly) our observations. I worry endlessly (most recently Stoller 1985b; Colby and Stoller 1988; Herdt and Stoller 1990) over observers' frictionless reliance on unchecked, uncontrolled (in the experimenter's sense) versions of events. Including these transcript fragments, then, demonstrates a way to seek richer, more reliable reports. Too bad that richer and reliable can mean redundant, dull. But I love redundancy when it serves as a hammer to beat on people's skulls. You should know that I spare you a fourth report, from a man who knows none of the three informants here, who regularly attended Venus Fair during this same period, as he successfully taught himself to move from pedophilic desires to wanting adult women.

It came to pass that I met another woman in the same employ as Happy. (Neither knows that the other has talked with me.) In regard to ethnographic methodology, two points are pertinent here. First, no matter how trustworthy an informant (for example, Happy), it is good to have another who confirms, especially when inadvertently, the earlier one. Second, I find that my study of porn is strengthened, because I have been at it for years, by the gradual development of a community—a web of informants who know one another. Their interplay gives the work a three-dimensional quality not possible when an ethnography uses simply one or a few informants (whose reasons for assisting the ethnographer may invisibly distort the picture without the correction one gets from an informant community).

The first speaker is Norma, talking in the first months of her work. After that, her then-husband Ron, whom you will meet at greater length later.

N: Right now, I'm a stripper. I work at the Venus Fair in North Hollywood, and I love it. I made $184 last night in seven hours, all cash. And I'm behind glass, so I don't have to deal with them on a touchy-feeley basis. They come to a little booth and put tokens into it. Then I become illuminated. Then they put a dollar or other tip through the slot in the top of the window, and I dance for them. If they don't tip, they don't get the show they want. It's a blast! A real ego stroke, guys all day telling me how beautiful I am, what pretty tits I have, what a nice smile I have. The girls are really pleasant to work with, much less catty than the girls in the B&D clubs, from what Ron tells me.

My girlfriend Dolly had worked there. She said they were looking for a new girl. She thought that I'd love it and that I'd be a big hit and that it would be quite lucrative. So I went over there. I didn't even audition. They just hired me sight seen, dressed. (Some girls are hired and never even show up. It weeds it out. They're prepared for that.) I did end up dancing that day. They had just let six girls go: they need new girls, new faces and asses. But there are girls who have been there for two years. If they are good earners and have good attitudes, they stay. If they aren't nice to the customers, they get booted. I started out at one day a week, and now I'm working there three or four days a week.

S: How does it go?

N: Okay. There's two sections. There's the live-dance area that I just described where the men are in a little enclosed booth. There's also an area called the "fantasy booths" or "talk booths," in which the man has to pay a minimum of ten dollars and he gets five minutes with the girl, still separated by glass; a telephone in each side. You talk on the phone, and you give him a private showing, and usually they jack off. You have to have a strong stomach for that. Some girls don't. I can be turned on by it. A surprising amount of attractive men with nice bodies. I'm aroused a lot of the day, that's another plus. Tease and frustration, because we're not allowed to touch our genitals or breasts. That's against the law.

I talk dirty to them. They see my rings [nipple and genital piercings], my tattoo. They peg me right away: Many of these guys are interested in S&M but have never talked to anybody about it. Ten dollars for five minutes and two dollars a minute after that. Then there's the live-dance area, twelve different booths that the guys go in. Usually there's four girls on the shifts I work. Usually I work a 12:00 noon to 7:00 P.M. or 3:00 P.M. to 9:00 P.M. Last night, I worked 7:00 at night till 2:00 in the morning and had a very good night. The other girl was sick; so I got it all. Occasionally, the guys freak out and can't handle it: my body, my piercings. They won't give me a tip and they leave.

May I draw you a diagram of the room? Here's the live-dance area, several girls here. A bench here that we can get up on. And windows all around, each window surrounded by a booth. What happens is: you see a light go out, which means the guy has dropped tokens in. So you go up to dance for him; you take your clothes off. If he doesn't put a dollar through, you inform him that his generosity is appreciated. For some reason, we are not allowed to outright ask for a tip. If he doesn't put it through, you try and entice him a little more, but not spreading the legs. If he still doesn't, you tell him you depend on their generosity because we're not paid a salary, which is true, and tell him it will inspire you to give him a good show.

You do what you can. Most of the time you can get a dollar out of them or more. Frequently they keep putting tokens in. Four tokens is a dollar, which turns the light out for a minute. So it costs two dollars a minute here also. Some stay five minutes and put five dollars through. It's fun taking each dollar out at a time. Strange conditioning. With my rings, I'm a novelty. A lot of the guys have never seen or heard of it but love it right away. So it's fun most of the time. It's pretty exhausting. It's more than dancing; it's wriggling and writhing and squirming and humping. Very physical. I come home pretty sore, muscular sore.

Now Ron.

R: Even a hard-core committed exhibitionist like Norma can get sick of that job. She got sick of the company, for one thing, the girls. She doesn't work for an audience; the guys are on the other side of the window. She doesn't have much real contact with them. Even in the fantasy booth situation, she does most of the talking. They pretty much just masturbate. Unfortunately, the contact with her coworkers is a little more social, and it drives her crazy. Some bright women are attracted to these jobs, but overall they're not. It is a job for a woman who hasn't much faith in anything, in any abilities or appeal than the sexual and who needs lots of cash to support a drug habit.

Not stimulating company for someone as lively, curious, and restless as Norma. She gets bored stuck in that glass booth with those girls all day. It drives her crazy. Large parts of Norma's personality go unused. Very frustrating. She's bitter that society pays well to do this and poorly uses skills we value. She really loves doing her [legitimate] work, but the best offer she's had so far was at a remote location that would take her away from home for five weeks at $250 a week. She makes on a really good day at Venus about $250 *cash*. What society values and what society pays for is not so good, but I guess it has always been that way.

She's also seduced by the money. Norma likes money, and this is one place where she can get it. Doing this job hasn't gotten the desire to be an exhibitionist out of her system. Since it doesn't really satisfy those urges, she ventilates them elsewhere. They are not based on the kind of relationship that exists between herself and a client. I think that exhibitionism is a hostile act from a woman as well as from a man. She thinks it's sweet and innocent. She thinks she's a bubbly, ebullient, lively person who just likes to show herself off. She doesn't understand that what she's really doing is shoving this up somebody's ass.

I think it comes from her family. Classic. It's her mom and dad she's pissed off at. Particularly her dad in some strange way, although it's the mother who caused the trouble. She sees her father as a passive figure who has to be engaged. This is a way to do it. Her work at Venus Fair doesn't satisfy her need to exhibit herself, because there the victims are too willing. Norma likes to do her exhibiting where it will shock people, or where it is at best inappropriate but she can still win people over with her charm. The borderline that people into consensual perverse behavior walk: they do it in part because it's socially unacceptable. They're not antisocial personality, don't want to be ostracized, don't want to be criminals, don't want to do bad to anyone or have anything bad done to them.

This is why people into S&M eventually let their straight friends know about it. I find myself telling people about my intimate life before I know what their reaction will be, afterwards thinking, "This person will only know about me that I'm a crazy sadist. They'll never know what other kind of human I might be. Why did I sacrifice my chance to be taken seriously with this person?" I'm more troubled by this than Norma is. She just shoves and then has a laugh over it. She doesn't much care what people think; if people don't like it, that's their problem.

In any case, working in a strip joint no more satisfies an exhibitionist's needs than working in a B&D place satisfies an S&M person's needs. After I've done a heavy session in S&M video, I don't have the terrific high that I have from having done a really great S&M session. I just feel tired and frustrated and bored and glad I got my money and glad it's over and worried that we're going to get arrested. When I do it in my own life, afterwards I feel euphoric.

H: Every woman is different. I've been told that there is one who got so wet— moist—with her vaginal juices from being excited that she would leave a big wet spot in her booth. I mean, she would have to lie in a wet spot all the time, because she just flowed that much with excitement. Now guys have told me . . . I can only see in the reflection of the window, because I can't see my reflection when I'm in the booth, I'm lying there with my legs up, and they'll tell me "Oooh, you're nice and wet." Now I might be. There have been times when I'm not only on the dance floor where this has happened, where I've had to run and go get a napkin and wipe discharge, because there's so much wetness there.

S: But you're not aware of genital excitement at that time?

H: No. It only hits me when I see Jeff. I've come to the conclusion it's because I think about him all day long. When I look at a man, I'm not looking at the man, I'm looking at Jeff, I see Jeff, because that's who I really want to be with. When a person's in love, I believe that they can't stop thinking about the person that they're in love with no matter where. I don't care if he's a thousand miles away, his face will always be there, and I'll always see him. He's just a very sexy man. There's just something about him. It's a turn-on all the time. And he tells me the same thing: there's something about me that always turns him on.

S: But that's not necessarily true of all dancers, you're saying?

H: No. I know it's not true, because not all the dancers are married or have a relationship. In fact, several of them are single. There is one that's married, into bondage: she has earrings pierced through her nipples, earrings pierced through the outer lips of her vagina, her pussy—

S: She's dancing with them?

H: She's dancing with them.

S: And that's okay with the men? They like it? Or they don't?

H: Oh, sure, they love it. Oh, they love it, they think it's great. They tell her in the booth. I'm sure they want to pull on them and bite on them and everything. I don't do it to my nipples because I want to nurse. I want to have another baby, and so I want to nurse. I'm afraid that that would interfere with my nursing, I just wouldn't do that. Oh, I would do it, I would get at least my nipples, I wouldn't do "that" because I would be afraid of getting hurt having sex. But, you know, to have something small like that wouldn't be too bad.

S: For decoration?

H: Decoration.

S: Not for erotic excitement?

H: It could be for erotic—you could wear a heavier gauge earring and the guy could pull on it just like pulling on this [pulls ear], it doesn't hurt. If you'd yank on it it would, but to lightly tug doesn't hurt, just like if I were to grab it and pull on it, or he would grab it and pull on it. Because when I told Jeff about her (which I did; I tell him about all the girls; I try to describe them in detail to him, so he has a good image, like you, of where I'm working because he won't go to see), his eyes lit up like "Would you do that?" I said, "After I have a baby, I'll think about it, but not right now. Two have boyfriends like myself and the others are all single, all single, and don't date. They've gotten to a point where they don't have a need for men.

Maybe it's that they're there all day long with them they don't want to have to deal with men any more after their day is done, which I think is possible, very possible and very true. Let's put it this way: I can walk through the UCLA campus now and not look at a guy in a way that I would before I started dancing. You know, "Oooh, he's cute," and check him out. Now it's just kind of like I'm more interested in getting to where I'm going, and I'm not interested in looking. I don't really look. I've asked Jeff, I said, "Do I really look?" Once in a while if a guy is going to . . . . There's a guy on Jeff's softball organization, the teams that they play against, there's this one pitcher and he wears these white baseball pants, and his ass is shaped really nice, like Jeff's, and I just [gasping noise] "What are you trying to do?" I look at him, admire him a bit, and I go on with my business. So it's nothing major or drastic, where I'm hanging out the door of the car [panting sounds] panting real loud and just drooling all over the guy. I don't do that anymore, where I used to: "Oh, baby, you're cute."

S: You've seen a lot of men.

H: I've seen a lot of men.

Chapter 5 **KAY, AN EX-EXEC-EX-X**

Kay Parker was, for almost a decade, a popular sex star, highly respected, then and now, by my other informants as a lady. Biologic time and servitude as a performer alerted her good sense, so she moved on to different areas of the Industry. She is slim, graceful, intense, wary-covered-by-willingness-to-inform, dressed tastefully in casual Southern California style: high-heeled black shoes, net socks, slacks, blouse, and sweater—none of the flamboyant, sex-starved, sparkly dumb starlet number; discreet, experienced make-up; re-laxed/practical coif. Nothing hypererotic, but not demure or prim. English actress accent. Holding herself poised, with all movements self-contained. Controlling the conversation with the skill of an old hand at interviewing. She knows the value of being private, and—sensibly enough—she is not into the pride in rebellion that dominates Bill and my other informants in the production end of the Industry (and that lets them be so open from the moment we meet). Kay, in contrast, offers a relaxed yet formal, thought-through rendering of her expertise.

The first time we talked, Kay was director of public relations for a major X-rated producer and distributor and enthusiastic about her opportunities there. When we next talked, she had left this company—unmet promises—and was trying to create herself as a talk-show personality, hopeful that her experience as an erotic performer could be translated into a broader sagacity for a radio or television audience. What follows is taken from our first interview.

K: Okay, I'll jump right in. I really believe that the adult film industry has created a lot of myths; we're so subjected to advertising in the world that it becomes a subtle form of brainwashing—even in the adult film industry.

I'm sure there are, within that, very common fantasies. Off the top of my head one would be a common male fantasy of watching two girls—two women—make love. It seems to be one of those formula things that has stuck and stuck and stuck and stuck, and yet the funny thing is after about eight or nine years of this work, I realize that I'm also very turned on by very sensual woman-woman themes in the films, something I was afraid to admit for years. As if it makes me a lesbian, which I am not. It turns me on in some cases.

What I find happening now, though, is there is a sociological change going on. Many people in the adult film industry are talking about romance, they're talking about the couples' market, of course, because promiscuous sex seems to be on its way out. Maybe because the disease factor, ultimately AIDS, has everybody scared stiff. But I also think it is just significant of the times we live in. From the sixties to the seventies it was a whole different era: "make love not war," "free love, free love, free love." I'm confused. All of us who were back there in the sixties—long hair and no bras—now are responsible, hopefully "adult," making a living and doing whatever and finding out that those sixties attitudes are passé. What is really important to us is a very fundamental, instinctual thing: Have we really changed that much? Are women still not basically territorial individuals? Is the male still not instinctively wanting to take care of the female and all that other kind of stuff? They're questions that I've been asking quite a lot. I was involved in human potential workshops several years ago, and I facilitated one of my own. I discovered some interesting things about people in general, you know, and about blacks, and communication between male and female. What that was all telling me was that yes, in fact, people do latch onto an ideal and it becomes a scapegoat for the truth. What they're really saying is one thing, but they are putting out double signals. What they're really feeling and experiencing emotionally within themselves is a totally different thing.

And I was guilty of the same thing. When it came right down to the nitty-gritty of "what do you, Kay, want?" I want a husband and I want children and I want a house, and I want unconditional love. But that's just me. I call myself a child of the universe. I watch a lot of what is labeled as love out there, and to me it's not loving at all. It's something quite different. Even the people in the Industry, even the actors and actresses in adult films—there is this common belief that we're nymphomaniacs and sex perverts—not so. Many are very rational and very normal people in their individual lifestyles. When we get in front of the camera we're able to either become the exhibitionists that a lot of us are or to live out fantasies in front of the camera. It's a fascinating syndrome.

When I got into the Industry about nine years ago, it was a baby industry. The only X-rated films anybody had ever heard of were *Behind the Green Door, Deep Throat,* and *The Devil and Miss Jones.* The three classics. Then suddenly up popped all these film makers, and it was a good industry to be in: a growing industry. At that time there were many, many, many X-rated movie theaters across the country. Since then, three-quarters of those theaters have closed down. Something like fifteen hundred theaters six years ago, and it's been reduced to less than five hundred. So it is not lucrative to shoot on 35-millimeter film (which is a far more expensive medium than video). VCRs are going into dozens of millions of homes all over the world. People can now watch these films in the privacy of their own home, they can let it all hang out in terms of what they want to see and do. It really changed the Industry. In the beginning of the video boom there were high profits both from shooting video product and from transferring the existing 35-millimeter product to video. A lot of the producers made a killing. One such film that I did was a very controversial film called *Taboo.* The original *Taboo* was a story of an incestuous woman; she seduces her son. It put one company on the map, it sold a fortune in copies.

S: Did you get paid for each day and that's it [that is, no royalties]?

K: Yes. Flat fees. No royalties. But I don't talk about that any more. I'm not a person who holds grudges. What's past is past. And, yes, I wish I had royalties [laugh]. I'd be retired by now. But then everybody started learning video skills. And now, 95 percent of the product is shot on video, much to the public's dismay, because it can't compare to those old 35-millimeter films. In my position as an actress and as a PR [public relations] director, I heard about lawsuits. We hear from the people who are opposed to it, but we don't hear from the millions of people who are watching it in the privacy of their homes. They've done market research studies of just how many people are into adult films. They've come up with figures like one out of four video tapes rented will be an adult tape. And it's reported that in some parts of the country up to 50 percent of those people renting adult tapes are women. People are finally coming out of the closet.

S: About this shift to more romantic stories, is there a change in taste or just that films are being made for an audience that always had that taste?

K: I don't think the people changed. I think it's more a case that the audience can stand it. In came the women, and the women said, "We don't want to watch this garbage that they're cranking out." And they're right; it's garbage. The standard formula has been: seven sex scenes per film or more. One of those sex scenes had to occur within the first about seven minutes; at least one of the sex scenes must show a cum shot, preferably in the woman's face or on the chest; one lesbian scene, woman-woman; and an orgy scene. That was the formula. Well, when the women started watching these things, they said, "What is this crap? I don't want to see all that junk." I've been screaming my head off about this for years. Exterior cum shots are abnormal! We don't do these in our real life. We women don't run out and make love to the first sexy woman we find! We don't enjoy orgy scenes for the most part. And one sex scene after the next seems just simply bullshit. But this is a male-oriented business, and the men had the power.

S: Why did it develop in this way? Whose idea was it? Was it a correct idea? Was there a huge audience for this or was it just that nothing else was being produced?

K: Well, remember: back in the days when these producers were forming this formula, the biggest audience was the raincoat crowd [isolated men masturbating under their coats]. They were catering to the gentlemen who went to adult theaters. Who were these guys? I don't know. The three or four times that I've been inside an adult theater, they seem to be older. I didn't see that many young guys; I did see minorities in there; I saw a lot of adolescents in there. I think it's highly unlikely that you'd see lots of businessmen. And if they did [go], they would disguise themselves. They would wear raincoats [laugh]. Bear in mind also that adult theaters are more expensive than regular theaters. So it wasn't just the bums off the street. It would have to be people who had money in their pockets. Then, right after I moved to Los Angeles, about eight years ago, one started to see more couples going to the theater. I actually went with friends, couples. It wasn't comfortable for me, though.

S: Because?

K: Vibes. I was into energy, and the energy wasn't . . . . It was strange to me. Maybe because I was an actress, and I was maybe fearful that I would get recognized.

S: It wasn't because you were with friends, and it wasn't because you were seeing yourself? It was because you were seeing yourself through the eyes of the audience that was there?

K: Probably, probably. But even at that, one would go into an adult theater and it would not be even a fourth full, very scattered clientele. I couldn't understand how these theaters could stay open, but they did get a trickle of viewers all day long. Then women began to open up in terms of their acceptance of sexuality or whatever. And it's the "whatever" that still has me boggled, because it seems . . . . The difference between men and women, the basic difference, was that men could have indiscriminate sex and enjoy it each time; women couldn't do that. They needed the emotional involvement (or maybe I'm speaking from my own experience).

S: The question you're raising is: Was that male-oriented, fetishizing-women pornography really on the button? Is it possible that you could make movies that would also turn on men where there was some relationship between men and women?

K: Well, the women I speak to these days don't seem to want that. But we also know that there are thousands and thousands of women across the country saying, "No, I'm not going to let you (husband) watch that garbage." But if we bring in a product that appeals to her sense of sensuality and eroticism, then she will let him watch. She will even go out and bring the tapes in herself.

S: Did you women who were making the earlier films feel that you were being used? Or did you say you were being professional, like an actress in a straight movie, who tells herself she doesn't feel she's being used?

K: Well, as an actress . . . I'm unusual in that I was a trained actress before I got into the business. So I only took acting jobs, things that I considered to have some meat to them in terms of the acting in the role, in the character. And I was very fortunate because I appeared in some good budget films. I was steered in the right direction, and I followed my intuition, and I had some great roles in the beginning. Then things started to change. That's why I dropped out of the business, because I'm not able to perform sex the way it's done now. When the Industry was on its way up—a baby industry starting to form itself—I was happy to be on the bandwagon. I was also happy to inject whatever I could into it in the way of real emotion, which I have done. They need that again. It's called putting the heart back into it. I felt right from the beginning that even though we were making pornographic movies—there were classics that have some very poignant moments in them, films with real stories; and even though the formula existed and we had to pump out so much sex because that's what sold the damn thing—there were nice moments where I didn't feel exploited. I never felt that I was exploited, though it was a semi-exploitative industry.

S: That's what Bill told me (with whom almost everybody disagrees about many things, apparently). His feeling was that the working people, as different from the producers, shared a lot and were not exploiting each other. And that made it a group of friends or acquaintances, whatever hatreds also might exist, that you were all understanding of the problems of getting a product out as compared to the people in the big-money part of it, who may have been exploiting everybody. Is that your—

K: Basically, yes. This word "exploitation" has been so overused. I think it's ignorance. Just ignorance. Somebody found something that worked: whatever was the product they were putting out, it worked. Did they really intend to hurt anybody by it, or did they intend to steer anybody wrong? I don't really believe that. Businessmen wanting to make money, we meet them every day. I can't hold that against them. But, by the same token, I say, "Okay, guys, that was then. Now it's time to change." Women are so involved these days.

Now there is such competition between the top three or four companies: everybody has cranked out all this merchandise. How do we sustain a position in the marketplace; how do we get people to buy our product over this other person's product?

S: Who is "we"?

K: Company president and vice-president and all the other people that constitute a company.

S: Do different companies, like the Hollywood studios used to, have actors or actresses stay with the same studio? Or does everyone move around: you get whoever you can for this particular script, including the writers, the directors?

K: There are a couple of exceptions in that two of the young superstars signed contracts with a small company. They do that because the company has come to them and said, "Ginger, sign this contract. You'll own half the company essentially, but you can only work for us." One such actress, Ginger Lynn, is one of the top actresses and a nice, nice, sweet girl, seems to be very well balanced. She owns part of the company. She can only shoot video for them. She is at liberty to shoot film with somebody else. Ginger is very beautiful, a very outgoing personality. In my eight years of performing, I could not have been that extroverted. I could not let it all show the way that she does. I was still always holding some back. But she's incredible, a wild little creature when she gets up there on the screen.

S: Is this genuine, or is it just putting it out for the camera?

K: Sometimes it's genuine, and sometimes it's . . . . I've seen one of these young ladies look up to make sure the camera is on her, and I say, "You little devil, you."

S: And yet up to that point she has looked as if she was totally into it?

K: Right. But I knew her. She's very, very conscious of the camera, whereas Ginger . . . Ginger tends more to be totally present and not to get outside of herself and wonder about what's going on around her . . . . Some consider going into legitimate movies.

S: Is that available?

K: Yeah, if you don't get too big [in X-rated films]. But if you're too big, I don't see how you could break off and just go into Hollywood.

S: The world out there wouldn't allow it? Wouldn't they try to chop her up for her past?

K: Yes and no. There has always been this idea that you can't make the crossover, but I've done it. If you've got the right attitude, you've got the will to do it, you can do it. You just have to meet the right people. And I've always said for myself that it just took an agent courageous enough.

S: I can't believe that. It would take more than will. I would think there are a lot of women or men who just wouldn't be competent.

K: I'm a good actress. I've won a bunch of acting awards. It had been my goal—though I'm inclined not to hold the goal anymore—to win an Academy Award. I didn't feel it far-fetched at all. To be in the right place at the right time, the right person standing right there. You come at them with all of your power: "I can do it." There are many women in the business now. Several actresses (or I should say ex-actresses) have raised money and made their films. I haven't particularly cared for their films, because they still conformed to a certain form. It kind of worked, and it didn't. But that's all right. I'm thrilled that they did it and they deserve a lot of credit just for doing it. I'm in a very fortunate position because the company is behind me. It's a strong company, and I've got distribution. It's right there. There's no way we can go wrong. The interesting thing is that—I heard this from a friend who edits hard X-rated products—soft X, which the product on the cable networks—

S: What's the difference between the two: whether or not it shows an erection?

K: Yeah. No erections. No penetrations. You could see a man going down on a woman but not actually see his tongue touching, that kind of thing. A pretty fine delineation.

S: On cable they don't have hardcore?

K: No. Well, there are a couple of satellite networks now that do show hardcore, but your basic cables don't.

S: What about the motels? Do they still exist, the motels that advertise whatever they advertise: hardcore? Is that soft?

K: I believe it's hard.

S: If you want the hardcore—the whole thing—you've got to get a vcr?

K: Right. But the reason I brought that up was that my friend who was working at one of the other companies says they are gearing up to have the largest soft-X line in the country because there are so many areas now which prohibit X-rated but will allow soft-X, and they feel that they can pick up that marketplace. Most companies have always cut soft.

S: What do you mean "cut soft"?

K: Edited. It's becoming more lucrative to cut back to the soft. So it really does tell us something about what's happening.

S: Bill's version is, "Oh, yeah, the stuff that we're making, some of it is terrible as far as production is concerned, but we're right on the ball with cum shots in the woman's face, and anal, and horror." You're telling me something different.

K: Even with the companies that are getting into the female fantasy product what we've also seen is a radical climb in the S&M market, the real hard stuff. It's touch and go right now. The sexual climate in this country is not that positive right now. So it's going to be interesting to see what effect, if any, [the Meese Commission report] will have. But even with that, some companies are still making this very raunchy product.

S: By "raunchy" you mean S&M?

K: Not full-out S&M. I don't think they'd dare do that. But it's definitely more raunchy. It's real, you know, kind of—no, no, not physical violence—but just really what I call real lustful sex, you know, just real hard-driving. They've got some titles on the market—I don't want to mention any names because I don't like to do that. They just have a whole different approach. Their belief is that many people still want to see real hard-driving, lustful sex. I'm sure that's accurate. They want to see people get down on their knees and pound away. They like a lot of the anal stuff. But they still play by the rules basically. In other words, you're not going to see anybody whipping anybody. You might see them doing it teasingly: you may see them acting it out; you may see—and you do—all the black leather and the studs and the dominatrix and S&M types playing with a whip, but they are not using it.

S: Why will they not do the actual S&M? What are the penalties; what's the price they have to pay?

K: The LAPD [Los Angeles Police Department], first of all.

S: Are there regulations?

K: Well, I'm not even sure what their regulations are, but they obviously have them, because every once in a while they swoop down. The last time they did that, they were looking for something which had to do with urination. That's an absolute no-no. Of course, they're always looking for child pornography.

S: Are there laws that protect distribution, or can people pirate?

K: Well, the laws which exist apply to all marketplaces.

S: Even for X-rated films?

K: Sure. There's one famous case about a company up in Canada that, unbeknown to the distributors in California, pirated their product for years. The gentleman made himself a bundle of money till finally one of the producers went up there and caught him doing it, raided his stores, took all titles off the shelves, walked out with the stuff, and set off a huge lawsuit. It dragged on for years, and finally the Canadian made a settlement with the distributors. But another guy just did it [pirated]. Who's to stop you? You've got two VCRs and a good duplicating machine: that's what he did. He put his own labels on them. You could still find him floating around up in Canada. He's still doing that at some level, according to some sources. Now I went up there and I worked a show for the first company. I met one of his partners, who treated me like a queen. I felt nothing but good vibes from this gentleman. But the other guy—his name is still mud as far as the distributors go. I don't know whether they would do business with him or not.

S: What about other women who have been in the business? How has it gone for them? I imagine that you're an exception.

K: I'm a total exception. First of all I got into the Industry at a much later age than most of the women do; they're usually in their early twenties, eighteen, nineteen. They have to be of legal age, they have to produce a legal document. Early twenties seems to be the average age and very wet behind the ears.

S: What usually happens? They don't end up like you did.

K: No. Oh, they'll meet a guy and get married, or they'll just go off and do something else, or they'll stay in the business. I'm different. I've always had a mission. I'm really not the norm at all. The lifespan of an actress in adult films is on the average three or four years. The public will get tired of her. (There was a time when that wouldn't happen, because there wasn't that much to choose from.) I was very cautious never to overexpose myself. A lot of my success yet today, my popularity, I attribute to my not overexposing myself: "Don't work so much that people are going to get tired of looking at you." The problem, though, is that in order to make a living doing it, you've got to work constantly, especially today.

In my day, you might work five or six days on a film and that's got to keep you going for a month, two months. I would take off for maybe three months if I got enough money. But they can't do that any more. The pay rates have dropped. Video projects, on the average, are shot for between twenty to thirty thousand dollars, one- or two-day shooting schedules. Now within that kind of a budget, what do you suppose your budget for talent is?

Not very much. So your stars may make five, six hundred dollars a day. Anything less than a star is going to make a lot less than that. Kids early in their career only work one or two days at the most on a shoot. So they walk off with five or six hundred dollars in their pocket. But that doesn't get them far these days. So they've got to be working constantly. They've got to work twice, three times a month to keep a roof over their head, if they're going to work exclusively in the business.

Some of them will moonlight as dancers. There's several young ladies who have their proverbial act together. They supplement their income by dancing in nightclubs. It's a very lucrative business, but that means going on the road. And working in nightclubs is hard work, but they can make a lot of money. Sheri St. Clair is one such actress. She's a very sweet girl, very good head on her shoulders, she's in her mid-twenties. She does these kinds of things. She goes on the road, but she also works on films an awful lot. She works constantly. And that's a shame, because—

S: That means that she's risking her career because she's in so much?

K: I think so. I think so definitely. Producers can get tired of using you. The producers are always concerned about bringing in new talent, new faces. It's harder today mainly because of AIDS. It's a very small family of people in the business. That way you can monitor people: you know who they're sleeping with. If they begin to be promiscuous outside the family, they're blacklisted.

S: But what about herpes, gonorrhea, syphilis [and since this interview, AIDS has entered everyone's awareness]—one person gets it and you've got an epidemic.

K: Well, of course, herpes is controllable.

S: It's controllable but—

K: It's controllable to the point where you will find people working in the business if it's in an arrested state.

S: And nobody worries about that?

K: They don't seem to. They work with them. I don't see that there's any secrets in this business. If you have it, everybody is going to know that you have it. There were a couple of actors in the business who were known to have herpes. If they had outbreaks, they would, of course, go off and take a break. Come back and they'd be cleaned up. In my years in the business, I only had two scares. Once right at the beginning of my career I got a call from an actor I had worked with, and he said, "I'm not sure, but you'd better get down to the clinic and get therapy or get some tests made." So I did, and my test turned out negative. So it was just a scare. But it was immediate [snaps fingers]: the moment anybody suspected anything, you called every-

one concerned. And the other time it was just my own feeling about somebody, and I said, "No, I don't want to work with him." I didn't feel
confident that he was clean.

S: What do you do if you don't like somebody?

K: Well, I've never really come across anybody that obnoxious in the business.
There are people that I don't feel as compatible with as you would on a
personal level. Because I'm committed to the part, usually I would just use
acting techniques to get along. There is always something I can use, you
know, like they may have pretty blue eyes. I use whatever technique I know
for getting past that.

S: Are the men—again generalizations—are the men sensitive enough to
know if a woman is doing that? I can't believe they're not.

K: Well, that's one of the problems for the men. This is why I say to a lot of
people, "Give the ladies in adult films a bit more credit than you do,"
because many times we play psychologists. We sit on a set with somebody
and you have to apply all your skills as a very feeling, understanding,
diplomatic individual. Otherwise the scene is not going to happen; you're
going to be there all night.

S: It's how you do it.

K: I tell a very funny story about working with an actor who had not long been
in the business; this was like his third or fourth project. He was fresh out of
est training. And this man ran every number on himself in the book. Very
heavily Jewish—tremendous Jewish guilt, heavy ego, did not want to get
kicked out of the business. (We didn't kick anybody out.) My point of view
to him was: he had already fulfilled his contract as far as I was concerned.
He did an excellent job of acting, he and I were portraying husband and
wife, and everything had gone very smoothly so far. He might have even
done one sexy scene. And I said, "Look, what does it matter if this [erec-
tion] doesn't happen? It really doesn't."

S: I thought it would. Don't they need him?

K: Yes, but in this case they had shot enough sex scenes anyway, they could
have easily have done without it. But he said, "No, I really want to go on
with it . . . blah, blah, blah." Finally the director called me and said, "What
are we going to do? Can he make it?" I said, "Give me a few more minutes
with him." And, you know, as a supporting actress in a position like that,
you obviously do whatever you can do to assist. But it got to a point where I
was exhausted. I had no more tricks up my sleeve, as it were. I'm talking on
a physical level. I simply realized that all I could do was just be there with
him, just be soft and tender and understanding and just shoot the breeze.
Usually what happens in a situation like that is that the crew will be sent off

set, clear the set, let the man prepare. That's embarrassing but typical. That will happen. But this particular gentleman was very sensitive.

What the director would usually do in a situation like that is say, "Do you want the set cleared?" The person will say, "Yes, clear the set." They'll say, "Okay, we'll be right here; just give us a signal." So the director will ask the cameraman to keep a watchful eye in my direction, and I do my little hand signals. [With this man] the crew started to come in, I'd go [gestures] "Don't come in," or I would say [to the man], "Let me just have a word with them; you just lay here and rest." I'd go out and talk to them. Finally the director came and said, "Look, we have somebody standing by that will stand in for him," I said coldly, "Thanks for telling *me* that." First of all, they hadn't told me that. I said, "That's all very well to do that, but you should get my approval first of all." So then I was mad. But it was okay, it [the substitute] was somebody I knew, a typical stand-in—

S: I don't know what that means.

K: Well, it means that—

S: He [the stand-in] could guarantee an erection?

K: Right. So he could stand-in. Then they just shoot a very close shot of the genital anatomy. It's called an insert. You've heard about inserts.

S: Not that one.

K: So they can cheat a lot: they'll shoot the other person doing simulated stuff [that is, they simulate success for the original man by substituting a close-up of the stand-in's genuine success]. I said, "I can't break this to him right now; this would be just devastating." And he said, "Well, what do you think?" I said, "Let me try once more. I know what it means to this guy." First of all, I had some simpatico going for him. I could see that he needed this. He was going to do a number on himself if he did not fulfill his total commitment. He was just going to load himself with such guilt. I could see that, and I said, "It would be really nice if you could give him that extra time." He did make it! I went home, and I awarded myself the highest medal. I was exhausted. What it took to just hold to that person, not to lose my patience, not to lose my temper, not say, "Oh, the hell with it," just to hang in with him. But that is what happens to all these guys, and of course the young girls, they don't know what to do. The poor guys have this extra added burden of having this young ding-a-ling there who doesn't understand what's going on. That's why producers would much rather work with professionals. On days like that, they definitely respect me. But he made it, got it on film to prove it. But it took an awful lot of doing.

I went home and said I never want to see another penis as long as I live. But those are the realities now. The sad thing is that back in those days, some of those scenes were poignant, they had story, they had emotion, they had people interacting who communicated. You just don't see that any more. It's like get in there, cut, take off the clothes, back into the bed, cut, we'll do a little of this, a little of this, and then we'll just go for the hard stuff, and that's it. Out the door. It has become very dehumanized. That's what I resent.

S: Does it ever happen—I presume it does—that two performers get together who really—not necessarily love each other—but [smacks hands together]?

K: You mean want to go at it?

S: Yeah.

K: Oh, sure.

S: Not just for the moment, though they both happened to get excited, but where they really are lovers, at least temporarily?

K: Oh, yeah. I had several experiences where . . . I fell in love with my leading man in one shoot. He was just an absolute cutie-pie. He was much younger than myself. In those days, I had a thing for young men, and he just filled the slot. It was the first time he and I had met, and I fell instantaneously in love with this young man, so much so that the sex scenes . . . . People say to me, "What is that one scene?" This is the famous *Taboo*, the original. There are a lot of *Taboos* on the market now; there's a whole new series which just came out, called *Taboo American Style*. We're not talking about that. It was made about seven years ago. I was the star of it and played this boy's mother. There's a scene in this film where I seduce my son that is so hot. The energy is so profound. It's not so much in what we're doing, it's just what is coming over the screen. It was real. And I maintain that if it's real, you [audience] feel it.

S: Do you then take it out after hours or is it enough—

K: We did enough just to do it on the screen. Because, for the most part, women never get to climax [while performing]. A lot of them claim they do. I didn't. For me to climax and orgasm is a very sacred moment that takes time. We never had that kind of time in the movies.

S: Why do the other women claim that they do? Is there an advantage in the business to claim it? Or is it some kind of athletic prowess?

K: No, I think they're a little bit more extroverted than I am.

S: Wait a minute: they're claiming it or they're doing it?

K: They claim that they do it.

S: It's the claim. You don't have to be an extrovert to claim it; you can claim anything.

K: Right. But it's only the ones who claim it who seem to be extroverted. It might be some ego trip. I have heard women say, "I won't let them stop the camera till I come." Okay [laugh]. But I was never about to ask a producer or a director to do that for the sake of my satisfaction. I came close. But my commitment was to be present. It's an attitude you're taught. You must be present. I did that to the best of my ability. The purpose is to be in the sex scene, whatever that takes. Bear in mind that in terms of photographing the sex scenes, it takes a lot of different moves, different angles, close-ups, long shots, explicit, nonexplicit. Even the worst actors in the business can usually at that point act real. Without the words coming out of their mouth.

S: [Time runs out.] Thank you. You are very generous.

K: I'm always more than willing to share with people such as yourself because ultimately I think it's for the highest good of all the family, that's how I look at it.

Chapter 6 NINA, WHO IS MONICA

Bill said he had talked to Nina Hartley, an up-and-coming pornstar (now one of the few great stars), who was to attend the X-Rated Critics Organization Annual Awards ceremony. A few days later, she called and we arranged our meeting. During the awards ceremony, Bill brought Nina and her husband over to meet my wife and me. Nina struck me as wholesome-pretty, bubbly, not glamorous, neither the Marilyn Monroe parody of sexiness nor the sullen burning-with-sex vamperoo, with a big smile and a game-trouper look about her.

The day after, in my office, she is unrecognizable: big, thick, pink-tinted glasses held on by wires, different hairdo, minimal makeup, effective, practical, pleasing, no performer-exhibitionism. She is dressed in black stirrup pants and blue sweater; colorful, stylish, not garish; no ass wiggling or breast blimping (not at all like some of the women last night). An RN off-duty. Her husband, Dave—no studlike demeanor—is out getting coffee for the first part of the interview. Also present is Bobbie, a woman in her forties, mildly plump, dressed for a rainy day, a very present member of an avowed ménage à trois.

S: How did you enjoy last night?

N: I had a real good time. It was only the second awards affair I had ever been to, the first one after having done a substantial number of movies. So it was real exciting to be part of the gang [laugh], the film gang.

S: You won an award?

N: Yeah. It was certainly fun and important. This particular award is given by the critics. With AFAA awards, it seems like you can nominate anybody if you pay a certain amount of money. But here no one owes anybody any favors. That makes it more important. The critics who watch these movies for everybody else have more experience than anybody else, have a better body of knowledge to weigh each individual scene or movie as good or bad.

S: [Explains his work.]

N: That's real interesting to us. I'm a registered nurse. I graduated last June [1985] with a B.S., magna cum laude. At that point I'd been making movies for about a year and a half, only on weekends. And I'd also been working as a stripper after school one day a week until I got out of school. (My first movie was March 1984.)

S: Did the people at school know where you worked?

N: Not at the time. During my senior year, two friends found out. One day, on my rotation in Maternity, a friend came up: "You're a really good actress." All I said was, "How did you like it? Which one did you see?" And a friend who watched movies with her husband rented a movie that I happened to be in where I play a sex therapist. I wore the same glasses I wore at school. When a woman wears glasses in a movie, she has to be a teacher, a secretary, a doctor, an executive; someone obviously very smart and educated. I looked pretty much like myself, which is very rare for me [in a film], and she recognized me. It was the voice, too. That was okay: she and her husband watch these movies; they don't have judgments about someone being in them. She knew me as a good student, as a nice person who also happened to make movies that she enjoyed watching. That was really nice.

This other woman was of the feminist philosophy that pornography is harmful to women, and though she also believes that what consenting adults do is okay, she had conflicting feelings about viewing pornography: she didn't want to see it suppressed but was not very comfortable with it. They both were very supportive and wanted to know more about it. I stay in contact with the married woman and keep her abreast of my movies. She enjoys that. But she kept my secret. Months later we went to lunch. She said, "Several other people at school know what you do now." I went, "No, oh, my God! What do they think?" Because I'm so different in school than I am as Nina: the way I dress, talk, and everything. She said, "Well, they think it's pretty neat. They know you. You're a nice person; so it can't be too bad if you're doing it." So I went: "Far out." I thought they'd all be shocked to death.

S: You don't practice nursing?

N: No, I'm afraid not. As a new graduate, to really learn nursing in the actual clinical setting, you have to work full-time for a year or two. You work hard. I'd work three or four times as many hours for half the money. I find doing what I do is much less stressful than being a professional nurse. It's not time for me to undertake that level of responsibility as a professional health care provider. Being in the movies is helping me to develop parts of my personality that were stunted during adolescence: how to socialize, how to be at a party, how to interact with members of the opposite sex, how to be a social being, how to be empathetic and caring. I was a recluse throughout high school. The hassle of learning to socialize seemed too much trouble for what you got. So I said, "Forget it." Now I'm going through now what most people do before they're twenty.

S: How old are you now?

N: I'm twenty-five. A lot are twenty-three and under. Then twenty-eight to thirty-five, not many, and they've been in the business a long time and established themselves; they have a reputation and a following. And then there are a few in their forties who make occasional movies still, who started ten to fifteen years ago, mostly now have moved into production, writing in magazines, publishing magazines. It is very hard for a woman to start in this business at thirty and expect to get anywhere. She'd have to be one hell of a dynamite thirty-year-old, because the fixation of society is still toward young girls and young girls' sexuality. Very few people, as consumers, appreciate the mature woman's sexuality: the "I know what I want, I know how I like it, I'd like to please you, I'd like to have fun with you, let's just do it" kind of attitude rather than the pedestal sex or the virgin sex. People still want to see a face on screen who looks like it never even said "damn," sucking a cock. Hopefully it will change.

S: Are you then chosen for parts specifically because you are older?

N: Oh, yes. I get more of the young married, the secretary, the professional—I'm a doctor, etc. I rarely get anybody's daughter roles. I don't look like people's idea of "daughter." Because acting in the business is generally so bad, they rely heavily on visual stereotypes. You look at a young actress, she's a girl, so when she says "Daddy" to somebody, you believe it. When I say "Daddy" to an actor, you're not going to believe it. I don't look like people's concept of eighteen. "Eighteen" means diminutive nose and a little round mouth and little pouty lips.

S: Like Bunny Bleu?

N: She's twenty-two! You'd never think it. She weighs ninety pounds dripping wet. She plays coeds, cheerleaders, high school girls, Daddy's little girl. She gets those roles because she looks it. So when she goes, "Oh, that feels so good" or "Oh, I've never done it before," you believe her, because she looks like she's never done it before. I have played roles where I said, "Oh,

I've never done that before," but I don't play an eighteen-year-old who has never done it before. I play a twenty-three-year-old who has never done something before.

S: No great actresses.

N: Few great scripts. No time to make a mediocre actress into a good actress. Which can be done with editing and direction, but you can't do it in two days. You have to have someone who fits the bill right. So older women play the mothers and the secretaries and adult women roles and then there are the girl-women roles, and people pretty much don't cross over.

S: I must say I would *not* have recognized you today [as the woman on the stage last night].

N: [Hearty laugh.] Yeah, I like it that way. I like to be able to walk down the street and not have anyone go, "Hey, didn't I see you sucking cock the other day on a ten-foot screen?" I don't want that. I want to attract that attention when *I* want it. So I'm very pleased that I can look so different. What shall I call my real self? Monica, if you want. Monica, the one that's behind Nina, wouldn't shave her arms; wouldn't shave her legs; wouldn't wear nail polish; wouldn't curl, tease, and spray her hair; wear makeup or tight skirts. Monica's sexuality is more toward the blue jeans, cut-offs, bathing suits, real natural. That's comfort, how I want to go out in the streets. In high school I wore men's overalls with plaid work shirts, Birkenstocks, and a braid and wire-rim glasses, real plain. But underneath it all, I wore bikini panties. I wanted to be comfortable with outward sexuality, but that was only after I met Dave and Bobbie.

I grew up in Berkeley, the home of radical feminism, antisexism, and anti-objectification. I fit into that real well. But I was different inside. I was turned on by reading pornography since I first got my hands on it. I loved looking at *Playboy*. I loved reading the *[Penthouse] Forum*. I gravitated away from the S&M stories or the spanking stories and toward horny-young-girl/horny-young-boy, let's-have-fun, let's-experiment stories, because I was that kind of girl. If I had had certain friends, I would have done a lot more experimenting than I did.

Now, Nina does the whole glamour trip and wears clothes that are overtly sexual and not useful for any other purpose. I like short shorts because they're sporty and sexy at the same time. Nina has bought the clothes that are strictly sex, can't be used for anything else because that's what Nina is. Nina adorns a fundamentally strong and able body with sexual clothes that enhance natural beauty, not cover up a weak "unthreatening" body with fussy clothes.

S: When you are Nina, are you Nina or are you Monica playing Nina?

N: I'm Monica playing Nina, but Nina is very carefully thought out. She's what the three of us [Bobbie, Dave, and Nina] believe is the ideal fantasy woman. For some people the ideal fantasy woman is six feet tall, big tits, legs up to the armpits, blond hair, and no brains. Not Nina. Nina embodies physical fitness: she leads a healthy lifestyle. I don't smoke, I don't drink, I don't take drugs—

S: Wait a minute: "me," "Nina." Is "me" you or Nina?

N: Sorry. Nina is the embodiment of Monica's concept of ideal sexuality: what Monica is, plus the qualities we think a perfect woman would have. Monica has a lot of the characteristics of the perfect woman, but she may need adding to or refining. For us the "perfect woman" is physically fit, has a healthy lifestyle, wholesome, no smoking, taking drugs. I rarely stay up late at night and party. This perfect woman also is educated in lots of fields: social sciences, liberal arts, the hard sciences. She's well rounded. She didn't specialize in crass economics, for example. And she has a healthy attitude toward sexuality. She's not guilty about sex. She is sweet and understanding, but she won't let herself be walked on. She understands men and their culture and women and their culture and how those two interact. She has an intellectual, analytical understanding of people and fits into it in a very conscious manner. At the same time, she's a compassionate and giving person. She doesn't just flail around and go through life bouncing off of, reacting to people.

S: Is that what Monica would have done as a teenager?

N: That's what Monica would have done, yeah. In fact, I felt really inept. Nina, the perfect woman, is mature. She has youthful energy because she enjoys life and sex and being physical. She enjoys athletics and enjoys feeling good. But she is mature: she can delay gratification. She can give to others. She is mature in that she has found peace within herself and knows herself very well, has come to an understanding of herself. The "perfect woman" has steady relationships. Now our concept of the perfect woman is not monogamous, but she has stable, on-going, committed relationships. I happen to have one with two people whom I'm most committed to: Bobbie and Dave. We're a stable trio. We've lived together for three and a half years now. [Still going strong in 1991.]

S: That's what you meant last night when you said [on receiving her award], "My husband and my wife"?

N: Yes. I talk about my wife and people don't really understand.

B: Until they meet me and watch the three of us interact. Because our relationship is still, even in this world, a very unusual thing.

N: Yeah. And through having to act out the character of Nina, Monica *has* become more mature. I am more responsible now about time, more responsible about taking on adult responsibilities that most people know by the time they are twenty or twenty-one. Berkeley is very intellectually sheltered. You don't have to know a lot about the games that average Americans play with each other, vis-à-vis power, pecking order, etc., to live in Berkeley. You come out into the real world and get thrown for a loop. So Nina is having to learn how to be an adult in the world, and Monica is taking notes in the back room. As I am Nina more and more, Nina and Monica are starting to meld. Nina's not hard for me to portray, not an alien identity that I have to mangle myself to fit into, but rather a facet of Monica's total personality. It fits, and we're constantly fine-tuning. It's a conscious decision to use Nina to work on undeveloped areas of Monica's existence. A safe arena to grow and experiment in. The role-playing give me focus. I think it's a healthy way to work on personal issues.

S: You don't mix them up?

N: No, no. I never slip, and no one else makes the slip either around me.

S: [To Bobbie] When she's Nina, do you feel differently toward her?

B: No, because I see the same person. Nina is an image that she puts in front of her, for the public: the hairdo, the makeup, the nails. It's an attitude. It is her profession. She needs to be "on." It's not like a split personality. I don't ever feel that. I feel it's like she's gotten dressed up and gone to work: as Nina. But the names, the shift, helps us think: "Okay, it's job time now, it's time for her to be on; we need to be supportive." She tends to play a very feminine role at home, and she's very supportive of us, both Dave and myself. I have a very masculine, very independent side. I'm not that domestic, I'm much more aggressive, much more assertive than the norm for a female. I need a wife. But when she's Nina, she can't be my wife in the same way. I then have to step into the background and be supportive of her in order to help her be on.

N: Yeah, when Bobbie comes home from work, I cook dinner, I do most of the shopping.

B: I can sit back and read my paper.

N: I bring her coffee and something to nibble on. "How was your day, dear?" and she tells me about the day. While I cook dinner, she talks to me in the kitchen, goes in and greets the other guests. That's fine, I like being somewhat domestic. I'm a terrible housekeeper, though; I won't clean house, but I do love to cook and I don't mind doing the shopping. I have a strong family tradition of love being expressed through cooking and feeding. Not bad it you don't fetishize it.

B: But when she is being Nina, it has to be the opposite, because then she is the center of attention. She's the focus, and she needs to be supported. It's the difference between private and public, actually.

N: Um-hmmm. Our private life. And our public life. We're all three aware enough and analytical enough to see what's coming minutes before it's happening. We constantly shift gears. So it's not a mental strain if I'm home in my sweats, chopping vegetables for dinner, and then dressed up and going out in a miniskirt and boots.

S: What about sexually? Are you Monica or are you ever (I don't know whether I'm going to get the right word) Nina or Nina-oid? Do you [Nina] ever portray yourself differently to you [Bobbie] in these regards, or are you [Bobbie] making love to the same person?

B: Oh, yes, it is the same person.

S: Does she sometimes put more Nina into it or just—

N: No, no. It's Monica being sweet, and Monica-being-sweet is Nina. Nina is the idealized Monica. Obviously in real life, in my personal life, I can't be sweet all the time. Nobody expects it; nobody desires it. But when Monica is sweet, that's Nina.

S: Supposed you're dressed up as Nina, you went out, you come back, you're in your Nina outfit, and you decide to make love, still there's no difference?

B: That's still Monica.

N: That's Monica. Home alone behind the doors, it's Monica. I don't know if I should give my secret away, but Nina is quite calculated. She is the essence of the three of us: unique, semi-utopian. We've worked out nonmonogamy, and we're totally comfortable with it. It's a growing relationship, not stagnant. Very supportive. And it works. My name changes from Monica to Nina, but Monica's essence is what's coming out. Nina is the mouthpiece. I'm not inculcating from a base of anger or hatred, but love and a desire to share the beautiful things we learned.

B: We have created very calculatedly the image of Nina in order to get across important ideas about sexuality, about human nature. She liked the idea. She has always been fascinated by porn; we all loved it—

N: Porn, performing art, theater—

B: She's a theater person. And when we started talking, it was more like a joke—

N: I didn't get to see that much [porn] as a teen. I didn't get to see many of the early classics that are still good sexual movies. Instead, I saw some poor ones: "This is it?" So mechanical, so [makes distasteful sound]. Occasionally a fun scene or a funny scene or a really erotic scene, but they seemed to happen by accident rather than by design when two people really were turned on to each other. That's what I'm trying to portray on screen. In the early days, I think, more women made porn because they loved sex. They were hippies. It was beautiful for them to do it. Now these are all young girls—we'll call them girls—young girls in the business. They do it not because they *love* sex or they enjoy sex but because the money is good. Their hearts are not into the essence of the work. But the look of the people has gotten better in the Industry. Attractiveness. Physical well-being. Physical health. Because it's more acceptable now for pretty women to make these movies.

The point I was trying to make eluded me. Oh: So I'd look at these movies and say, "I could do that at least." And Dave and I, during lovemaking, as a fun fantasy, talked about me being in the movies. Then I put a mirror next to my bed and got comfortable with the idea and the reality of seeing myself make love: "You're sweating, you're in a weird position, you're panting, making funny noises." You say, "Who's going to want to watch this?" But I'm very visual, 50–50 voyeur/exhibitionist. So I love to show other people, and I love to watch other people who enjoy showing. It's very easy for me to go in and out of voyeurism/exhibitionism.

So I would get into watching us make love: "God, when we do it this way, it *does* look good, it *does* look sexy, not silly. If I close my eyes, I can feel so sexy right now, whatever position I'm in," and I open my eyes: "And I look sexy, too. Far out!" [Nina adds, on reviewing the transcript: "That was important from a feminist point of view: I can be sexual even though I don't look like society's standard. But it is *real*, and therefore powerful."] So I got used to seeing myself in sexual positions, legs spread, legs up, legs apart, all messed up, giving head, whatever. Got used to it and got into it. I learned how to make a better picture. I'm a dancer at heart. So it was easy for me to use my body to make a pretty picture. I'm blessed with a nice figure, that helps. Then I started working as a stripper. I worked it for a short time in a club in San Francisco, the Sutter Street Theater, now defunct, and did a live sex show with a woman in a circular room with one-way mirrors all the way around, which in turn opened onto private booths with a curtain and a tip slot. So I took what I learned in front of a mirror and used it in this room. Because here were one-way mirrors, I saw myself. But I knew behind curtained rooms—[at this moment, Dave, who has been in the cafeteria, enters; she greets him]—I knew that there were men. So I shifted from dancing to the mirror to dancing to the man behind the mirror and learning how to be visually sexual that way. That was a good step. That only lasted three or four months. The club closed. I loved the job and learned a lot about myself.

So I moved to this strip place in San Francisco called the Mitchell

Brothers Theater. It had a big stage with continuous nude dancing, stripping. So you'd go on and dance two or three songs and end up naked. That was basically the format. The performers could choose their own costume, their own music, their own dance, they could do whatever they wanted to out there. It was a totally free artistic environment. The only requirement was that you had to end up naked. So I moved from the private booths to a live audience, did that for two years and loved it, loved dancing, and got into really very sexual shows, had a dildo act. This was San Francisco; it was legal to use a dildo to show penetration as long as it wasn't a man doing it. And I got girls up on stage with me and we did girl-girl shows, eating pussy right there at the edge of the stage, no audience touching. I loved doing that, and in between your shows, you'd put on underwear or bathing suit or leotard and go into the audience and sit with the men, and that's how you made your tips. They would pay you to sit with them.

A lot of the girls had regulars. That was nice. The girls who worked there for a long time developed many regulars, sometimes two on the same night, just people they saw a lot who came back. I really liked that aspect of the work, because I was in nursing school then. So I was into trying out my nursing theories [laugh] and also because I do care about people's sexuality. I see a lot of pain and distress out there about sex. I did my best to set people straight. I'd give them medical advice, about VD or the female orgasm response cycle, just little bits of knowledge plus a lot of friendly support— "There, there, that's terrible"—TLC. Sitting there and rubbing on their lap in time to music, or cuddling or whatever. I would never actually make out with them, because the idea of kissing strangers grossed me out [laugh].

They weren't allowed to touch your breasts or your genitals, and you weren't allowed to use your hands on their crotch either. But lots of the girls used to sit on the laps and rock in time to the music and wiggle around. We called it "lap dancing." I earned a lot of tips that way, because I'm very good at it. I liked to do it. I liked to turn the men on. I liked to make them feel good, and I got paid for it, too. That was nice. I liked it because they went out feeling so well. And I liked bringing some of the men to orgasm that way, if they could get off dry humping. You know, I never did break the rules, I never did touch anybody where I wasn't supposed to, but if he could get off doing this, great, that's great! Far out! It was nicer than being with a prostitute, because I was much more giving, I think, than the average street hooker can afford to be. Obviously a lot safer, because there's no actual genital-genital contact. The disease factor was nil, but it was very intimate: I'd whisper in their ears, I would say nice things to them, I would hug them, I would kiss their earlobe or something. It was a very intimate experience.

Almost as intimate as fucking. I did that for two years, and when I graduated [nursing school] and went to doing movies full-time, I really haven't been able to go back to dancing because of scheduling. I didn't want to either. Now, I dance in clubs as a featured entertainer and come in for six-day gigs.

I got into movies because I met—I don't want to tell the whole story—but I got in contact with this woman who was an English teacher who got into the business while writing her master's thesis. Someone said to her, on a dare, "Why don't you do a movie?" And she did; she loved it. She had a great time doing this movie. Her stage name was Juliet Anderson. She developed a character for the Swedish Erotica series called "Aunt Peg," a very independent executive woman, you know, based here in Los Angeles. She made her first movie at age forty and became a star. [Some time later, Kay described Swedish Erotica:

K: Loops—we're talking 16 millimeter, but then they upped it to 35 millimeter—maybe a half hour, not much story—then sixty-minute, wall-to-wall sex tapes.

S: When you say sixty minutes, you mean a real story as different from loop?

K: "Loop" means wall-to-wall sex. No story, no story. Just throw a couple of people in the studio and tell them to go at it. Shoot it, and that becomes a movie. Swedish Erotica came up with a formula that became very successful: shoot three different segments with different people, put them on one sixty-minute tape, and put it on the market. And it's good quality pretty people, everything is clean, nice, and natural-looking sex, pretty set decorations, nice makeup, beautiful lingerie. It's the tops, it's classy. Even though it's just wall-to-wall sex, it's the best that you can buy. It's not like it was years ago, when there were only two people in this little basement somewhere, and it was dirty and the soles of their feet were dirty. That was a joke. So Swedish Erotica, I think it was called, developed this formula.

S: This was Sweden, the country, or just a name?

K: No, just a name.]

D: Ever since Nina has been talking about being interested in it and found her exhibitionistic side in dancing, I began immediately to entertain the possibility of her being in movies, but we didn't know anyone in the business, didn't know where to go.

N: You just don't know.

D: And you hear bad things. I'm not at all sexually possessive but you might say fanatically protective. I don't even like her riding taxis. [Laugh.] I don't trust a lot of people today. I think that sexual repression and sexual dysfunction are major reasons I don't trust people. So I told her about this woman I had seen dancing two years prior, featured as a porn star doing a striptease and then answering questions from the audience, while the regular show was going on at the same time in another part of the building where she (Nina) worked later on. And I heard her conversing with the audience and talking about how she got in the business. And I went: "Ah-hah, that's a real woman." She even sounded feminist. And I went "Interesting." So I thought if I ever ran into this woman, or if I ever knew how to contact her I would. . . .

But down at the corner of our street was a little supermarket. There was this woman, and I was sure it was her: her look was unforgettable if you've seen it a dozen times in two hours of her films. I didn't say anything to her. I went back home and told Nina that I had seen this woman I'd been telling her about, and she started pinching me in the arm. A week later I saw her again, and I approached her. I figured she would think I was just another fan pestering her. When I told her about Nina, she [Juliette A.] figured it was a line to try to get to know her better. She gave me her card and said to send some pictures of the lady in question in the letter. She thought she'd never hear from me. She was really shocked when she got the pictures and a typed letter, not typical for this business. [Laugh.]

N: Right.

D: I like telling that part of the story to show my overseeing her for her safety but also that I want to give her all the sexual freedom she can possibly want.

N: I was concerned about my safety as well. I'm Berkeley, I'm feminist, I'm middle-class, I don't do weird, risky things. I knew you didn't just go up to a strange man and say, "I want to make fuck movies." So this woman who was feminist and educated was a physically safe entry to the business. That was the only thing I was waiting for: how can I do it and not end up in a car trunk? That was it. The horror stories are pretty much unfounded. I haven't heard any horror stories about women getting into the business by force.

D: The worst we've heard is when a boyfriend or a husband is abusive.

N: At home.

D: It really is unrelated to the films. It's usually that he wants her out, jealousy. He's getting more and more jealous and more and more insecure about his own masculinity, his own virility, watching these well-endowed men fucking the shit out of her on screen and then thinking, how can she want me? So they start to get more abusive and they may be into alcohol or some drug or something, and those are the only horror stories that we've heard.

S: I didn't get the impression last night that this was a group of people who are doing murderous things to each other.

N: Nah, nah. No, not at all.

S: It looked like the annual Boy Scout reunion. Not in its content but—

D: Almost. It was celebrative.

B: It's the Industry convention, a one-night convention.

N: Right.

D: There's this Jewish girl, and raised incredibly protected, I guess, who is a production manager now in the business. She moved down here and did some TV commercials, and somebody asked her if she would do an "X." She needed the work, so, okay, she did the production work on it. While the first sex scene was going on—she had never seen one before, but she really believed this stuff about shame—and she whispered to some technical person working on the film, "What do they do with the bodies when they're done?"

N: She said, "How could anyone want to do that and be alive afterwards?" It was so embarrassing to her.

D: Ashamed, total shame. And he looked at her, and said, "Boy, you really believe that?" And she said, "Yeah, I was raised in a good family, and I just can't imagine anybody facing anybody after doing that." The idea of performing something so intimate and private was such a debasement to her—

N: A fate worse than death.

D: A strict Catholic or a strict Fundamentalist Protestant, you might as well be dead if you had sex in public. So that terror was in her. It reminded me of all my early fears when Nina would sit there watching a porn movie with me, saying, "I'd like to do that; I bet I can do that." And I'd say, "I would love to see you up there doing that, but I'm worried about you." Plus we're feminists, and so many of our movement friends are so antiporn. They just believe that graphic display somehow leads automatically to a degrading form of objectification.

B: They see objectification as degrading.

D: Tell about the bookstores in Berkeley.

N: A used bookstore. Directly across the street from the one adult theater in Berkeley. They had Western, science fiction, home care, etc., etc., erotica. I would go in there at thirteen, fourteen years old in my overalls and drag up a chair and sit down and read the erotica. *Lust in the Afternoon, School for Wives,* all those pulp novels. Dreadful trash. The whole time I was reading them I was scared: "Oh, my God, someone is going to say, 'How old are you?'" That's all they would have done: "How old are you?" I would have told them. I obviously wasn't eighteen, and they would have said, "Well, maybe you shouldn't be reading these books." That's all anyone would have done in Berkeley. They wouldn't have called the cops, they wouldn't have called my parents, they wouldn't have made a fuss about it. But I would have felt embarrassed. But no one ever came up to me and said, "Excuse me, young lady, should you be reading those books?" I would sit there reading the books; I had to keep my legs together to read them. It was great, I had a great time: "Oh, this is a turn-on." I would read passages mostly that dealt with inquisitive teenagers getting together. Those are my favorites: a woman who was horny and ready to do something about it. She would admit to it: "Oh, I'm actually horny right now." Rather than suppress it and go eat or clean the house, she'd want to do something about it.

So I'd look for a passage like that and get tingles between my legs. I also babysat for friends who had an adult collection next to the bed, *The Joy of Sex*, the factual books, and storybooks. I went back to the same one or two over and over. *The Pearl* was my favorite, a Victorian underground periodical, hard-core. I hated the spanking, though, always have.

I used to daydream about sex all the time. I loved thinking about sex. I didn't do much about it till I was eighteen. A few fumbles. I didn't like it. I didn't want to be with another virgin; I didn't want to be with another teenager. I didn't want to be with a teenage boy who didn't know any more than I did: I needed someone a little more knowledgeable. As it turned out I should have gone with the teenage boy, because the guy I ended up with, who was older, was the most incompatible lover I ever encountered. However, since I started at the bottom, I could only go up. I was still daydreaming a lot sexually.

I daydreamed about women. I was attracted to a lot of women in high school, but I didn't do anything about it till after graduation. I didn't know who might also have the fantasies. I didn't want to expose myself in case they might totally freak out and tell everyone, "She made a pass at me." The best place to grow up gay in the world would be some place like Berkeley or San Francisco. But still, kids are kids. You don't go up and say to someone, "I really think your tits are nice." You just don't do that, but there are lots of girls who have nice tits. I would want to go up and play with them, and I wanted that not to be a big deal. I wanted that not to be offensive or a total freakout for them or weird or shocking. I wanted them to be able to receive it in the spirit in which it was given, which was, "Gee, you have nice tits. I would just love to squeeze them for a second and make them feel good. They look nice; what do they feel like?" Now why couldn't I go up to someone and say that and ask her permission to fondle her tits and have her go, "Oh, sure." That's all I wanted. No big deal. Obviously, I knew enough about social graces to know that it *is* a big deal.

D: Another problem she encountered: Boys ask girls out, but she wants to do the approaching, she wants to pick her girls and to approach them. So, from puberty on she's been afraid of rejection. Now I know what all boys have to go through. They risk rejection with each invitation. Women need to be more sensitive to that fact.

N: Dressed up as Nina, not many heterosexual men are going to refuse me if I turn on the burners enough, unless they are totally religious or something like that. That's fine, but with women, you don't know. Some of them might be closet "lipstick lezzies." "Lezzy" is a colloquialism for lesbian. "Lipstick lezzy" is one who is very feminine in appearance as opposed to the more radical lesbian who wears the blue jeans and the flannel shirt and is more masculinely dressed, not male-defined. A "lipstick lesbian" likes to look like the women in the magazines. She pays attention to fashion and looks like a girl. But she likes women and likes her women to also be feminine. "Lipstick lezzy": girls who look like girls who like girls who look like girls. They often get turned off by dyke-like women.

In all the men's magazines, the girl-girl photo layouts feature very feminine, male-defined women having fun with each other, not bull dykes. Those images have helped women conceive of the idea of making love with another woman. Obviously, though, we need to expand the concept of what is "pretty." That's very valuable, because women have a lot to gain from going together sexually. They can get from each other a lot of what they're demanding from men, the petting, the romancing, the kissing, the fondling. Women can do that for longer while guys quickly find themselves with the painful irritating presence of an erection trapped and confined. If you make out with a guy for ten, fifteen minutes who is attracted to you, then they get an erection. That's what happens when men get turned on (speaking from a man's perspective): "I get turned on to you, honey, so I have an erection, and it hurts in my pants, can I take it out? If you are turned on to me, you should want me to be turned on to you. That means I get a hard-on, and it just has to be taken out of the confines of the pants because it hurts." But girls love to be turned on in tight pants; they get to squeeze their legs together. They want to make it last, not just come. It's that difference.

A lot of feminists don't believe that the three of us can be true feminists because we have sympathy and empathy for the male turn-on and what happens to him when he gets aroused. It shouldn't be such a big deal to get him off, because it's no big deal for him. Why should it be a big deal for you [any woman]? Not that you should do it if you don't want to, but don't resent him for his biology. Working at the O'Farrell Theater and seeing guys turned on and feeling compassion for them made me realize that it's not a big deal to get them off. And they're so grateful afterwards, they're so relaxed, *then* they can give to you. There's an old Yiddish saying, "A man with an erection is in no need of advice." And that's right. If he's turned on and needs to get off, he can be nice to you later, he'll talk to you later, he'll take you out to dinner later, he will listen to you, learn your name later. He *wants* to do that. *If* you can do it without hidden and unspoken resentment or contempt, and without being a doormat.

Most men do not just want to get off and forget about you. If they like getting off with you, they'll want to keep seeing you. Men are not evil that way, they're not genetically deficient that way, but when they're turned on, they get that insistency, they get that pushiness, and they seem grabby and inconsiderate, and women start feeling "all he wants is my body." First, try tuning into your pussy, learn how to be connected with your pussy, and, if what he's doing feels good, start with that and enjoy it, move with it, direct it, follow it, whatever feels right, and then afterwards, "By the way, my name is so-and-so." He will love you for your understanding. Women have, I think, very unreal expectations of men and how men are supposed to act, but if a guy is attracted to you and he's not ugly or awful looking, you should be flattered that someone nice looking is attracted to you, which means you look nice. It's crazy that women take all the time and effort to look good and then reject men who respond honestly to that effort.

S: How many women in the porn business agree with you?

N: They don't even think in these terms. Very few.

S: They're not political creatures?

N: No. No. No. And if they are, it's not politics like this: they just don't think anyone should mess with [get rid of] pornography. Attacking the Industry is extremely unwarranted and misdirected. (Obviously, when I defend pornography, I'm not defending child pornography.)

S: Is it a turn-on—I know this is a standard question—during the actual work, or are you working?

N: With some people, it's more work than others. The work is a turn-on because I like performing for the camera. I like my sexuality, and I have a very good idea what my sexuality is, and I want to communicate it to you.

S: It's exciting *because* of the camera?

N: Yes. I want to communicate it to you, because I think you should hear what I have to say. How I say it is through my body, through the noises I make, how do I do this guy, this woman, that's my message. If I was with someone I especially liked, the chemistry is there. And if the woman takes control and gets crazy, gets aggressive, they love it, they want sexually aggressive women who can just go and have a good time.

Not acting but doing. Sometimes, say I've got a bit of menstrual cramps and I still have to do a scene. Then there's a bit of acting. I'd rather "Oh, rub my back, baby." But it's not bad; I'm not doubling over. A lot of people have to work with headaches, lots of people have to work with sore hands pushing a wheelbarrow. Sometimes I have to work with a sore uterus or a bit of a sore pussy. A certain level of discomfort I'm willing to put up with in my line of duty: leg cramps, slight backache, whatever. But beyond a certain point I'll say, "I can't do this any more." And if I've been working a lot and my pussy really is pretty sore, I'll go to the director ahead of time and say, "I'd like to keep this as heavily oral as possible, because I've been working a lot and I'm a little sore." Most directors are nice guys and try to accommodate me. Or if I have a bum leg and there are certain positions I can't do, I let them know, and they won't do those positions. They are very understanding.

B: But even though you get really excited, because of the awkward positions and the constraints of the directing and the time available, you can't really be orgasmic all the time.

N: Yes, yes. Some positions are not what I would do at home. While they may feel good, they might not in real life bring me to orgasm, because I like to be in certain positions for that. But I know some women can come that way; so I will enact an orgasm. I get turned on working. I get turned on fooling around with the guy ahead of time [before filming starts]: he eats my pussy, I play with his cock. I do like it, and I do get aroused, and so the noises come out. I try to make them real. I pay attention. I turn on the volume. I kick up the intensity a bit because it is a movie.

B: And you're an actress.

N: And I am an actress, I'm an erotic actress, and I'm very proud of that. And I'm proud of being able to portray realistic erotic activity even when I might not be [uses sexy voice] super turned on and having a super time. But I'm never having a *bad* time, unless it's two in the morning and I'm really tired. But then everyone else is tired, and everyone else wants it done as quick as possible. Professionalism takes over. So it gets done. That is about the worst. Actually, the *worst* is having to fuck at eight o'clock in the morning, which doesn't happen very often, or really, really late at night after you've been on the set all day. Most of the time for the woman it's very easy: you don't have to get an erection; you don't have to worry about all that. You just have to go out there and be pretty, at the very minimum be pretty, and let yourself get fucked. I take it to the next level and really practice being there for my partner without being weak or losing my identity. It's a great dance: look nice, help him, let the camera see, have fun. I use the situation as a Zen meditation.

Now you're not going to get very far in the business if you do just that, unless you're very beautiful. People in the audience and people in the production end of it *want* to see a woman having a good time. If she can *really* have a good time, great! You are in the right business. They love the fact that I can take control of a situation without appearing to, just by turning up my enthusiasm, going, "Wait, how about this? I'll try this." "Okay." And I'll just start doing it and everyone starts filming it, and it moves things. That's easy. My work is very easy to me, it's natural to me, I always wanted to be a courtesan or the madam of a classy whorehouse. A courtesan is not just a whore; she's educated, she's educated on how to satisfy a total need. Or a madam. I'd love to be a madam. I have been making my fantasy whorehouse in my head for years, having complete control over the erotic environment. I think I have something really special, and if I could present it in a way I think is best, I think people would respond to it. However, I'll never know until I have more artistic control.

If I say I won't work with X, Y, and Z, you can't change my mind. They'll get somebody else. Either they'll replace me or they'll replace him. So you know if you don't like someone, you don't have to work with them. I don't hate anybody in the business, but with certain people the chemistry is better. You just get along, you fit better. With some guys, they may be nice, but I have to try hard to be comfortable around them.

D: Excuse me. There are people that you interact with who are old pros [who know their jobs]. That helps a lot in every way even if there isn't great chemistry between her and, say, Jamie Gillis.

N: Yes, two professionals can have a lot of fun together.

D: Solidarity among outlaws. Not like the bimbos that they fuck: the eighteen-to twenty-four-year-olds. Most of them are airheads. But a lot of the guys recognize her intellectual background. They respect her. If you're welcomed into the porn scene, it's unbelievable. It's an extended family.

N: Yeah, it's a big family.

D: In fact, she almost feels like she's going to an X-rated country club. So many Jewish people involved with it. She's just having a ball. [Laugh.] You run into each other on the sets, and you haven't seen each other in a couple of months, and it's like old, long-lost relatives and family reunion.

N: Right. Like Tom Byron. He's a young man in the business, and I hadn't seen him for a while. I love working with him, but we hadn't worked together in a long time. So it was heavy flirtation, grab-assing, grab his cock, like "I'd love to work with you, I have a great time working with you. We're just going to have a grand old time out there." There are very few people that I want to associate with outside the business on a close personal level.

D: Everybody treats each other with amazing respect and gives a lot of space,

more than you'd get in any other business in the United States. They defer to
mistakes, they allow them, they tolerate them. It's just amazing, the toler-
ance. There's a little catty back-biting, but that exists in any business in
which you try to climb the ladder, especially in the entertainment business.
But of all the entertainment businesses, it's the most tolerant, the most
forgiving, in all ways. But we really don't like the Hollywood influence:
very shallow, nonanalytical. I come out of the tradition of the New Left, a
Marcusian. As a social scientist I see Hollywood as a focus of cultural
decay. It defines our culture, and it spreads out throughout the whole
country. I see Hollywood as a cancer; it has destroyed our fucking society.
Next to the suppression of sex, it's the most efficient reinforcer of modern
human alienation. I'm a socialist. A Marxist can take great offense at
unrestrained profits and unrestrained colonial violence and I feel that Hollywood blatantly glorifies these negative values. Hollywood could play an
amazing role in making the American experiment work. But what happens
is just the opposite.

Chapter 7 WHERE ARE THE MEN?

Though, as you find herein, I have talked for years with men in porn, none is primarily a performer. Bill and Jim (chapter 8), who know almost all the actors and actresses in the Industry, at times have tried to get men to tell me what it is like to do this work. None has. Ron, a writer (who speaks to us at greater length in chapter 10), gives his explanation.

R: There is an absence of male voices [in everything that is reported on X-rated performers]. These guys have to do some talking. I think their experience is very like that of the women. It will be difficult for an angry feminist to argue against pornography only in terms of exploiting females when they've heard the voices of male performers.

S: In addition, there is the risk of my book in itself being seen as exploitation "because the only people he talked to were the women: a man who is a professor using his power on the women". It's very hard to say, "Look, they never called. (Margold gave six male performers my name. Only one called, none came in. Then two others. One came in one time, and it was very good stuff; he never came back. The second came in because he was in trouble with everyone in the Industry. He never came back.)

R: My theory assumes that both men and women in this business have sexually exploited backgrounds and that you can't understand this business without understanding that. And it's time to rip away the false assumption that sexual exploitation of minors is a thing inflicted entirely upon girls by older men, as if there is no sexual exploitation of male children that results in certain behaviors in those children when they become adults. A political bullshit that serves the interests of feminists to believe that only female

155

children are sexually victimized and exploited. It serves the interests of men who are preserving a macho facade that they could never ever have been victims of similar exploitation.

Let me withdraw the words "exploitation" and "victim". And "molestation." Call it "early sexual experience." Not because my own views of this are value-neutral—they're not—but because I am avoiding inflammatory language. But basically I believe that early sexual experience is the distinguishing characteristic of the person most likely to become a part of the sex industry or a sex performer: it is as true in the men as in the women.

S: We have to get data. At this point you do not have data like you have on women. This is a suspicion that could be checked out if you'd ever get them to come in and talk. Is that what you're saying?

R: Right. I've had tantalizing bits from guys who have talked to me, but overall, I find male porn performers to be among the most close-lipped, guarded, remote individuals I've ever known. They really keep to themselves and each other; much more than the women, they are extremely clannish, a subculture within a subculture. They maintain, I think by choice, a separation from the women they work with, from the crew people they work with. They keep to themselves on the set. The girls mix much more than the guys do. The girls mix with the crew, they mix with the producers and directors, they get out there, they schmooze, they press the flesh, they fool around, at lunch they sit around with the other folks and chat and flirt.

The male performers are always off in a corner with just each other. The dressing room is the girls' territory, the girls' locker room. And if there's a cast lounge or a crew lounge, it is understood that that is the guys' area. They hang out there. Sharon [a star] has said, "It's the guys versus the girls in this thing." And not much social contact between them outside of work either. Friendships are pretty rare between male and female performers. And relationships all but unknown. It's rare to see a couple in which both parties are performers unless they perform as a couple. Full-time male performers are a small group of men who are difficult to get access to. A little tribe that doesn't let anybody in.

S: [If they were to talk with me] would they come clean?

R: Well, that's the question. I think they're afraid of fucking up their own process by examining it.

S: They're right.

R: They're superstitious about their dicks, and it's understandable because their dicks are their fortune.

S: It must be a pretty complicated Rube Goldberg psychological structure that allows them to do it. Maybe that's unfair.

R: Uh-uh [no]. I see external evidence. It seems like a meditated process: they go off by themselves for awhile before they do their scene; they rest; I suspect they fantasy [fantasize]; they masturbate; they come onto the set masturbating, they're getting themselves worked up. . . .

S: The girls "fluff" them [that is, cater to getting the men excited before H-hour]?

R: No, not at all.

S: I thought that's . . .

R: That's history, though "not at all" is not fair to say. The older [female] performers in general are nicer about that. The younger ones seem not at all interested. The older ones make an effort. Often performers who are about to do a scene will closet themselves for a few minutes before they come on. The male performers are the ones who invariably are concerned about the schedule. For instance Jay, a wonderful performer everyone likes, uncomplaining, and a very good player, came up to me on the shoot before last and said, "I see that you have me in the schedule with the regular scene first and then I have anal. I would prefer the other way around in the future, anal first. I said, "Why?" "Because they're [anals] difficult for me to do" (indicating to me that he doesn't like them much). "I will play stronger in my first scene than in my second; I want to be at greatest strength when I have to do my most difficult scene."

That's simply practical and mechanical, which as a man I can understand. If I'm going to have two orgasms in eight hours, the erection in my second session is probably not going to be as strong as in the first. But at another level it is something psychological he's saying: "I want the maximum physiological advantage for dealing with the thing with which I will have greatest psychological difficulty." Complex mental processes surrounding what they do that they're afraid to examine. They're afraid it [potency] will go away if they have to talk about [examine] what they're doing. An example of this is Miles Gloriosus, whose real name is Bud Black. Bud doesn't acknowledge to anyone in his private life that this [porn] is what he does. This is a man who has been in this business ten years and has probably made a thousand X-rated pictures.

S: Wouldn't some people in his private life have looked at pornography?

R: He claims that he has girlfriends he meets in straight life who he does not tell what he does, that he has relationships with them until they find out, and when they find out, it's the end of the relationship. He has a whole other life that we don't know about, and presumably the people in that other life don't know anything about this. That seems to be the pattern of the male performers. The male performers do not seem to identify with the culture of pornography. You don't see them doing the promotional stuff, for instance, that the female performers do. I think that the most common false pretension of the male performers is that they're just horny regular guys. A lot of false jocularity. They try to act like a bunch of fraternity brothers.

S: Can you get one of them to talk with you?

R: If he talks honestly, he will be identifiable. There are fewer of them [than the women], and therefore the details that they drop make them more identifiable. There's a thousand [exaggeration for effect] new female faces that pass through this industry in a year, but year after year it's the same guys over and over. We'll take in one or two new guys a year. Others will try and wash out by the dozens. Mostly the same guys. The guys who can do this can work a great deal, can stay in a long time, and they do. So if they mention that they worked on a certain picture or did a certain scene with a certain female player, anyone from the business who reads this book will say, "I know who *that* is because I remember that scene." So they expose more when they expose. Anyway, let's try it. Let me work on this. It's very hard for men to talk about sex except in a socially acceptable, locker-room fashion.

S: Also, the people in your world have put themselves in a position of being the handful of humans on the face of the earth who represent male heterosexuality, and they, literally, are the only ones it is possible to see, even in Mozambique.

R: They are *it*, and they carry that heavy burden with them. Though the female performers elicit sympathy for their situation, the male performers' circumstances are probably more trying. They probably need the sympathy more and get it less. Someone always wants to help, save, support, and otherwise come to the aid of damsels in distress in this business. But the distress of the men is private and does not inspire much sympathy. In fact, I think it inspires resentment from other men. Other men look at these pictures and say, "Those lucky sons of bitches. They get to fuck all these great looking girls. I wish I could be one of them." But when I watch them work, the impression is not of men having a good time. It is the impression of men doing a grim piece of work.

S: Pounding rocks on the chain gang.

R: Absolutely. And under tremendous pressure, with the knowledge that one or two failures and they're out. There's no mercy. The way the male performers are treated on the set if they fail to perform is chilling. It's as if they've suddenly come down with some terrible communicable disease [when they are impotent].

S: Which might be true! Society is a communicable disease.

R: If a guy fails to perform, they throw him out. "Get out of here, don't come back. Whatever your problem is, get it out of here." So having to be under that kind of pressure and knowing that if it happened on three consecutive pictures, you'll probably never work again. Anyone can have a one-day washout. Of course, that will immediately get around. And they might be allowed a second at bat. But if they strike out three times, they're out. They're gone. So that's tremendous pressure to be under.

Chapter 8 **JIM, THE BIBLIOGRAPHER**

Jim Holliday is a lot like Bill, which helps account for their being friends. Both are intelligent, articulate, filled with humor and chuckles, self-contained, and free of long-term intimate commitments; contemptuous of establishments, institutions, orthodoxies, and pomposities; salted through with a twentieth-century version of frontier America.

Jim is accepted as the historian of porn—the bibliographer, the scholar who knows every publication, references it with exact accuracy, knows its contents, and can quote what was said by whom where and who did what to whom when.

Like Bill, he is in porn not for money or free sex but for immortality, and like Bill, he impresses his version of our erotic myths onto the world.

He is a youngish Santa Claus—bearded, burly, jolly, proud of being straight-forward, energetic, a raconteur, with an optimism about his unending smoking that would make even a tobacco-state senator blanch. He comes to my office dressed like a logger.

He describes himself in his latest book, *Only the Best* (Van Nuys, Calif.: Cal Vista Direct, 1986), as follows:

Jim Holliday found his way into an infant video industry almost by accident. Due to the lack of accurate adult information available to consumers, he was one of the pioneers of the second wave, reviewing for mail-order companies in the '70s and compiling the first ever *Adam Film World* Special Directory in 1980. He wrote HOW TO BUILD YOUR X-RATED VIDEO LIBRARY in 1980 and the surprise best seller, THE TOP 100 X-RATED FILMS OF ALL TIME in 1982.

His degrees are in Radio-Television and Communications from Ohio University, and he still entertains the notion of someday adding a Ph.D. in adult film history. Before discovering the existence of adult entertainment, Holliday was a history teacher, football and basketball coach, disc jockey, carnival promoter, writer, chef, and professional travelling telephone salesman. He once spent an entire year hitchhiking around the country. His ability as a phoneman brought him to the attention of people in the video business.

Jim is currently a consultant for various adult and video companies and a reviewer and columnist for *Hustler's Erotic Video Guide*. He also writes a column for *Adult Video News*. Holliday can be seen with Marilyn Chambers as the film and video reviewer for MCTV cable network. The 37 year old bachelor lives in a secluded garret one block off the Sunset strip in Hollywood, California. [p. 249]

S: I have no agenda that I'm aware of.

J: Okay. Well, I'm here because Bill Margold thought I could help you find out about our Industry. Jim Holliday is the name I write under.

S: All right. Who is Jim Holliday?

J: Jim Holliday is a commentator on human conditions. If you listen to two knowledgeable people in the Industry—we're talking about major video companies, adult film executives—one of them would say, "In every sense of the word, Jim Holliday is a genius; he is also stone-cold crazy." That means he's aware that I have a strange code known only to me. As he puts it: "He listens to the beat of a different drummer, in this case his own drummer." I respect people's privacy, people's property, and people themselves. But other than that, I won't do anything I don't want to do. I'm willing to risk everything—financial security, personal relationships, anything. If I don't want to do something, I just won't do it.

That's selfish, but Jim Holliday started as just a farm boy in the Midwest who was told by his high school guidance counselor, after getting over fifteen hundred on the college boards, "Well, you'll probably be accepted at *one* of the colleges you apply to." I applied at five colleges: Cornell, Penn State, Illinois, Ohio, and Emerson College in Boston—radio and television. Within three to five days I got acceptances from all of them.

My academic career was similar: seventh grade, straight A's; ninth grade, A's and a couple of B's; beginning high school, A's a couple of B's; senior year, a couple of C's; freshman year in college, 3.6, come home and hear "Couldn't you do better?" Fifty-five hundred freshmen and I was one of 125 invited to the dean's home? Everything I ever did until I was twenty was something you were supposed to do. You go to college and four years later you graduate. Then an unusual summer job: I got hooked up with carnival people and acquired the street smarts to go with the book learning.

Then eight years ago I decided to have some career ambition and got into the adult film industry, strictly by accident. I've always made my living on my wits. It's easier for me to sit in an office and work as a telephone salesman. That's how I made my living. The video industry was just starting, and people were looking for phone men. They paid decent money. Then I decided I wanted to be the best in the world at something. I studied film in school, but no one had documented porn films. Now having played all the games academically and in the normal business and carny [carnival] type world, the high and low—my code is still not sucking up to anybody, not kissing ass. I look around today. A lot of the guys I went to school with, in the radio-television school at Ohio University, are heads of radio departments; a couple are even producers in Hollywood. These are the same idiots that I went to school with, they're just twenty years older, and now they've achieved acceptance without really doing anything to justify it, in my mind. I harbor no grudges for anything. The choice I made is my own. In the seventies, I clowned around, made a lot of money and retired at twenty-three, took four years off, did things like manage bands, write songs, just to eat and sleep.

But the porno world offered me an opportunity. People would say, "Tell me the truth: the porno world is a bunch of gangsters who make money in spite of themselves." The gangster thing is open to interpretation, but those who think the mob run porn are a bunch of dummies. Anybody with anything on the ball can make money in porn. So I just kept my mouth shut, never let on to anybody that I had "impressive academic credentials," and just proceeded to be thought of as "hey, that nice, smart farm boy from the Midwest who wants to write books." And I'd written books. I guess that's why I've gotten where I am. In 1980 I was with a large video company in Hollywood, consulting for them and running the mail-order business. They also made porn films and owned theaters. People came to know Jim Holliday through mail order and magazines and one-shots [articles] I have done.

Because I was in mail order, I talked to people who were calling in orders. A guy would call in and I would learn just one or two things about him: the fact that he was a stamp dealer and lived in South Carolina. So, because of my memory, when he called he got the personal touch. It's nothing more than that—"Hey, Jones, how are you? How's the stamp business?" That makes this man feel like, "Here's a stranger in this world who knows something about me and seems to care." So I developed about two thousand friends that would call, and I would tell them my impressions of the value of any video-porn, strictly porn. Jim Holliday may be the most normal person in porn. The person that I am sits back and everything I do is calculated. But I approach it not from an intellectual and not from a jerk-off, raincoat mentality. I approach it on what I think of this stuff, figuring that I'm normal. And, hey, it works. These people buy the films I recommend, and they come to trust me.

I was making good money. A couple of years ago I turned my back on all that money. I'd gone to a different company, the same type of position, vice-president, so to speak, that's what the trade papers ran, I didn't even want a title. I really am fairly unassuming in that respect. I simply turned my back to concentrate on writing the story book [summaries of the stories told in noted porn videos]. Right now, Jim Holliday is probably perceived by people in the Industry as the most knowledgeable person about film facts and the people that make films. He's also regarded as somebody that was a video executive. So I do know the people, the executives as well as the performers, a jack-of-all-trades who is being counted on now to come out with a book called *Only the Best* and after that the ultimate encyclopedia [of porn]. Within the core of the Industry—the maybe two thousand people that make their living in what the media labels pornography—they consider me the expert. . . .

The difference between what *I* write and what the magazines write is that I concentrate on factual accuracies. Magazines that disseminate the information on the latest films to the American public: *Hustler's Video Guide, Adam, Film World, Velvet's Erotic Film Guide, Cinema Blue*—I refer to them as stroke books. You know, not the *Hustler,* the *Penthouse,* or the *Playboy,* but the lower-echelon stroke books.

S: What does that mean, "stroke books"?

J: A book you can pick up to masturbate by. I'm not proud or ashamed, I'm curious, a commentator on the human condition. I have never personally masturbated to dirty pictures or what the world perceives as pornography. I'm fascinated by people who do, and I find out that a hell of a lot of people do. "Stroke book" is my term for anything designed to arouse or stimulate, which is essentially the purpose of erotic material. Maybe the difference between them and me is I found personal sexual expression in different forms.

My college fraternity, which was, quite honestly, an animal house, used to formulate the opinion, "Let's go out today and ask strange women on the campus, 'Hey, do you want to fuck?'" I found out that if you asked twenty people, one girl is going to say, "Sure." You go up and ask a girl to dance and she says, "No," I've always been prepared with a line: "Well, that's all right, I've got to take a shit anyway." I slough off fear of rejection. I don't know how I arrived at it, but I do believe I'm right. . . .

I mistrust most video companies. Invariably they try and pour shit down my throat—shit meaning bad porn for me to review. I'm independent of all companies now. Ten years was enough. I go through life: "It's all one big game and see how much wool you can pull over people's eyes." I'm afforded the luxury of saying, "I only have to work two and a half hours a month." Jim Holliday Enterprises. I sell my knowledge: "You can trust him."

S: [Looks at flyer for porn distributing firm.] Are you Cal Vista?

J: No. Cal Vista is a video company, the vice-president in charge of things out there has engaged my services. He knows Jim Holliday is a magic name. I do it for him out of loyalty and trust and friendship. I could do it for, I suppose, just about any video company. The frightening thing is that most of the people connected with the adult industry are three-piece-suit graduates of Wharton—you know, University of Pennsylvania business school. They're just nice people. You've heard the classic line: "In porn, you don't fuck to get the job, you fuck after you get the job." I know enough about the entertainment world and Hollywood producers and actors that are themselves porn groupies: "Hey, send me over—can you get me a chance to meet such-and-such [pornqueen]?" "Yes." Five hundred bucks changes hands. . . .

S: You're not in the business part of porn? You don't act in it, you don't direct it, you don't write scripts, you don't distribute it?

J: No, that's not true either. One of the reasons Bill suggested I come here is I might be the complete, one and only, total jack-of-all-trades about porn.

S: He didn't say it quite that way. He said you'd probably know more about it: you're the historian.

J: Yes, I can tell you all about the films [who plays in each, the director, the storyline], but in the area of writing scripts, that comes from my days in the video business as a video executive. Executive. That's a term I've run from. But, yeah, they said I had to have a title, and I said, "Okay, how about 'Creative Projects Director'; that sounds real schmaltzy." I've done many successful scripts. I have even directed an entire feature by myself, but under pseudonym. I've been involved in all the behind-the-scenes wheeling and dealing, and I'll tell you an honest thing: the first time I ever went on the set, I was the writer of the script, and they told me writers have to be around. There aren't many intelligent people, that's the problem. I'm known as the garbage mind, the guy that knows trivia. There is no way I can discuss art, literature, music with most people in the adult film world, because you're talking over their head and I don't want to be condescending. One of the true joys I have in life as a commentator on the human condition is playing humble farm boy from the Midwest.

Like in Trivial Pursuit [an information quiz game]. Invariably it's a New Yorker who thinks he knows more than he does. I come in as just a humble "aw shucks" guy. I play it nice until it's time to go for the throat. I want him to walk out of there truly humiliated in front of his friends. Therefore, you talk to all of the people in the Industry: "Yeah, Holliday's a garbage mind; he can tell you everything you want to know about a TV show or music or films, or even porno." But that's not enough for me. I could say to you, "Bring in the best guy UCLA has about the Civil War, and we'll sit down," and this guy is going to go away saying, "How did a porno guy know all seventeen lieutenant generals for the Confederacy?"

I've kept a lot of this secret from people, but Bill knows, because I've talked to Bill. Bill is one of the few people in this business with monumental intelligence. All of this is part of the "commentator on the human condition." I just go through life watching, enjoying. As a published author. As Jim Holliday, separate from the magazines.

S: What do you mean "separate from"?

J: The magazines are self-serving, self-promoting. Whoever pays for the advertising, they want their films treated kindly. I won't do that. I have made concessions: I did things for *Hustler* simply because in the porno world *Hustler* is the Bible and I don't mind my name being associated with the best. I will not have it appearing in little crummy magazines. They quote me. Someone from the magazine will come up and say, "What are the ten best films that women would enjoy?" And I will give them my honest opinion. I do it, free of charge, simply because I want that to be in there to counterbalance the idiocy that they're going to wind up publishing from other people who make a very cavalier determination. I can't lie to the people. I want people to know that *Every Woman Has a Fantasy* is the single best film I've seen in five years. For everybody, men and women.

It boils down to: what is erotic? Though we can go out and find a dozen people in West Los Angeles who can only get total fulfillment by masturbating on their wife's shoe, I really believe, based on the response of most people, that what I perceive as erotic most people perceive as erotic. So I can't be branded as a guy who enjoys films where there is fist fucking or urination or some odd eclectic taste. I stayed away from the Meese Commission people who were out here. I knew (a) that it was a witch hunt and (b) if I went in and said, "What I have to tell you is that, hey, 10 percent of the people that look at pornography in my humble opinion should be behind doors and should be shot, and 90 percent are perfectly normal and healthy," all they [the commission] take is what they want to hear, without recognizing that, hey, 40 percent of society at large should probably be taken out and shot because they're stone-cold nuts.

I take great pleasure in baiting. I've got to be honest with you. I will bait people all the time, to get whatever kind of response I want to get from them. And I don't do it for personal pleasure or satisfaction. I do it just to bust somebody's balls. The honest statement would be: I hate people. With fraternity brothers . . . I used to start in with, "I hate people who . . . ," and they would say, "Cut it off right there. You hate everybody." To make a statement like, "I hate 97 percent of all the women on earth," they're immediately going to label you as some sort of weirdo or misogynist. I do that just to provoke them without saying, "By the way, I hate 98 percent of all men."

S: That makes you a philosopher.

J: Okay. Yeah. Why not become a cross between a philosopher and a social commentator? Because Lord knows I've met some of the greats in America and have come away shocked. I met one of the five great sexologists at his institute. They're accredited; they have degrees. Off the record, my opinion is they're a bunch of mid-forties-to-mid-sixties middle-aged crazy people who want to climb into a hot tub because they can't get much [sex] on their own. They've got credentials. I'm impressed. . . . These are people that get quoted in everything. I went before an audience of intense feminists. I played clips [segments of videos]. Then I realized I was in over my head. These were intelligent people. So I wound up with a draw. I said, "Hey, you'll have to forgive me. I'm sorry I showed you that Marilyn Chambers clip. You have to take the whole movie in context," got off the hook as being some sort of porno guy, you know, at least fit their stereotype, came out somewhat drained, sat down in the foyer, ran into the great expert, introduced himself to me and I did the old "aw shucks, gee, I'm really impressed," recounted from memory all his credentials, and said, "I'm pleased to meet you."

The first thing out of his mind—or out of his mouth—was, "Jim, how big do you think John Holmes is?" I was kind of shocked. I figured I'd get a little more from an eminent doctor. So I told him: "John Holmes is advertised as thirteen and a half, some people say fourteen. If you ask me, no more than eleven," which is the whole hang-up on male organ size. . . . Do you want to know about the lunchbuckets?

S: What's a lunchbucket?

J: Lunchbucket, meaning people that I personally feel are in real trouble, emotionally, monetarily, as human beings. For instance, I finally met one of the people who had been talking to me on the phone from the very beginning. He was a physical disaster and truly was an example of people that need erotic material as a surrogate for sex. The physical appearance, the fact that he couldn't see well enough, had to take a bus to work, it struck me that he probably already—late twenties—had resigned himself to the fact that he could probably never—

S: That would be a lunchbucket?

J: Not really. He was an intelligent lunchbucket. No, he's in the area of deprived sexually but certainly no threat to do the things that anti-porn forces feel porn watchers do. He's never going to rape anybody. My perception of most people who have watched porn—theatergoers as well as the cassette crowd—there are distinctions, but they basically fear and mistrust women, by sheer lack of personality become subjugated to the women in their lives, and in some cases outright hate women. The guys who go into a porn theater go in there. . . . If I was going to write a book, a cute title would be: *What Is Porn All About: Blow-Jobs and Losers.* Quite frankly, they don't get oral sex at home.

The fantasy of the blow-job is unbelievable. First I discounted it as "Aw, come on." But no, the blow-job is the one thing the average American guy wants from his woman, but his significant other will not perform oral sex on the man. Therefore he seeks release in a porn theater. At the extreme are people that actually fear and hate women, who will never be able to relate to women in real life. But they are not the threat to go out and do the damage. The Pussycat theaters have a fantastic slogan that I'm surprised the anti-porn forces haven't capitalized on. It's something like, "For those who never knew and for those who will never forget." Does that not smack of losers and old guys? People want to keep stirring the pot just to fuck it up and make it more complex. . . .

Coming into this business I did not believe, for example, that [white] women fantasized about black men, that women fantasized about being taken by force or raped. But once I talked to a nurse who ordered tapes for the doctor. She might order him ten at a time, and she'd occasionally stick a couple on that she wanted to see. One day I asked, "What's your fantasy?" "I fantasize about a big, black cock in my mouth. What woman doesn't?" The standard old thing is from North Carolina [mimics North Carolina twang]: "Jim, we have a tape club here. A bunch of the fellows get together." That means you're either all bachelors and never could relate to women or you're all frustrated married guys and instead of going to the Elks or the Moose sitting around shooting the shit about North Carolina basketball, you get together every Thursday night and watch porn. You're all looking for jerk-off material.

Getting back to "garbage minds," it's a sales tool. Let's say you're calling from Athens, Georgia. The first thing out of my mouth would be,

"How about them dawgs" [Southern accent]. That signals to him, "Let's discuss University of Georgia football," from present coach Ray Goff to Charlie Trippi in the old days: garbage mind stuff. I talked to a guy from Lexington, Kentucky. He ordered ten tapes. So I gave him ten minutes of time talking about U.K. basketball and listening to his frustrations that "we all went south with Tom Payne," which is my cue to become his racist buddy and say, "Yeah, the minute Kentucky got them niggers, boy, we all went down hill, didn't we?"

Yes, I may be a cardboard man, but it's all very carefully crafted. To give you an example of racism. The guy in Georgia said, "I'm looking for a film [accent again]. Is there a film where a white guy screws a nigger chick doggie-style?" I said, "Let me think. There are all kinds of films like that." "How about in the snow?" I said, "Yeah, I'm thinking." To condense it, there was a foreign film called *White Heat* with a black female and white male; believe it or not he screws her doggie-style in the snow. "Does he come in her mouth?" "Oh, man, you're doing this to me, hang on a second." I open the drawer and whip out *White Heat* (I track films, have the—)

S: What does that mean, "track"?

J: Document what goes on during a movie—

S: You've got it written down?

J: Yeah. I look at the chart I made. I've got my symbol for the ejaculation, and it's on her back, as most doggie ejaculations are, come on the back or the ass cheeks. I said, "No, I'm sorry he doesn't." "Well, shit, I don't want that movie." "Goodbye, fucker." The guy has asked me a question that only I can answer and when I tell him he doesn't pop in her mouth, I have to reflect on what is going through this yo-yo's mind. As an amateur psychologist, I have to wonder what kind of pent-up frustrations are in this guy's mind. Let's say their fetish is lactating. "A film does exist with a woman lactating, and yes, if you want to know medically, a woman doesn't have to be pregnant to lactate. The woman's name is Chris Cassidy. She does it briefly in this film, but you're going to shell out sixty dollars for a tape to get three minutes of this? Man, you're better off taking your dough down to the corner hooker and keep asking until you find a woman capable of lactating."

This is the 20 percent that are so frustrated that porno is never going to satisfy them. They want the Linda Lovelace dog movie because . . . . Or they want a movie with a pig and a woman. As someone who has become jaded and has watched over seven thousand porn films, I now say, "Why do you want this?" If I'm going to spend my money, I sure wouldn't spend twenty to fifty bucks to watch two minutes where neither the woman nor the pig is having a good time. But, regarding a matter that the national agenda has deemed important, incest: I firmly believe it's a whole lot better for a guy to watch a film where the models are made up to look like they're eleven even though he knows—he won't admit it—he knows they are eighteen. It's better to watch that than act it in real life, not that they would. In that sense pornography is a short circuit to maybe two years down the road when a few more wires get crossed.

S: You don't get turned on?

J: Oh, no, I do. I have what might be the ultimate *Hustler's* scale: a film is rated from totally limp to totally erect. Totally limp, one-quarter erect, half, three-quarters, fully erect. Because of corruption and advertising and special interests, they rate many films as fully erect. But I am the ultimate *Hustler*. Jaded as I'm supposed to be, if I have an erection, that is definitely a world-wide turn-on. When you become a new adult film reviewer, you face several risks. First, you're going to compare the films to Hollywood. Therefore you pan every one, because they're made for peanuts. Secondly, you're dazzled like the mainstream critics were about "Deep Throat." "Oh, boy, oh, boy, we saw a stag film on the gas station wall years ago, but here is fucking and sucking right in front of our eyes, and hey, this turns us on." And they went ga-ga over an average routine film. These mainstream guys have made porno chic a household word. So in that sense you become aroused often and eagerly as a novice critic.

Once that wears off I estimate I fought off being jaded five times—I'd be a liar to say I don't become aroused. I just don't become aroused as often. Films aren't as erotic as they used to be. They're catering to all kinds of esoteric tastes: the couples market or "what women want in porn," which to me is bullshit. Women object to a cum shot in the face, but women want tasteful raunch just as much as men. There is no difference. Psychologists, mankind, men have been studying women for centuries and still come to the conclusion you can't figure them out. So why bother? Why exert the energy to try and determine what women like when women are no different than men? One woman is going to like what I like down to a "T". Another is going to like filth. Another is going to want to lick guys' shoes, which I would personally find useless. Bondage I find useless and ridiculous. Most of the time it's executed so poorly. My personal life behind closed doors, if any woman ever suggested I put on a little rubber suit, my code would just say—there's a line that I have: "I don't play soap opera games." Which means when I walk out the door, you're not going to call me tomorrow to have the little bullshit conversation and I come back and everything is wonderful. I don't play "fight and fuck". When I walk out the door, I'm gone. "The silly little rubber suit drives me to see that you're a yo-yo. I want nothing more to do with you. It's nice knowing you, no hard feelings."

But I get turned on by these things, a very few, but I do. Out of 7,000-plus films, closer to 8,000, my book will detail 250 that really turn me on. I'm not afraid to deal with rape because "I'm going to offend someone." Some of the most stylish erotica ever filmed deals with rape. In porno, far more than in mainstream Hollywood, the rapist gets his comeuppance even if it's just a throwaway line at the end. But that's the big area that feminists and antiporn forces are attacking us on right now. Like Bill Margold, I have one-liners to throw out: "Your contention is that there seems to be a rape every time you turn around in porno. There is only one difference between you and me, and that's that I've seen 5,000 more films, and any time you want to sit down and go over the list, you're going to find out you're a goddamn idiot." There are fewer than 10 percent that deal with rape, and the majority of them use the rape as a justified plot point.

To define what I've always looked for—the normal—in fuck films is pretty people preferably (it doesn't matter, but that's a bonus), plot, production values, in a healthy setting, pretty people enjoying themselves. But the Ice Goddesses, the "10s" I knew all through my first twenty-five years of life, the flawless perfect women you see in porn—what I call the Annette Haven School of "Hi, I'm a '10,' I know I'm a '10,' now I'm going to lie here and allow myself to be penetrated." Whereas give me a "6" that enjoys sex and really gets into it, has an enthusiastic smile on her face, enjoys what she's doing, I'll take that any time. Bill is the same. When I talk about the "10's," I'm talking about fewer than a dozen women in the history of adult films. But they are usually the least erotic. . . .

S: Okay. Tell me about the Industry.

J: The standard line is that they're gangsters that make money in spite of themselves. Distributors and manufacturers make the money. The manufacturers make the cassette. Technically, a distributor is merely someone who handles various and sundry lines for different manufacturers. There are very few, they do exist, three-piece-suit businessmen who would be perfectly at home as executive vice-president of Sears Roebuck. Less than a handful, but they're not gangsters. They got into this strictly for the money. It's as if porn managers are managers of McDonald's suddenly turned loose in a new field that has no pioneers. You don't have to play games. You can make it on your own in porno, because it's got the reputation of being so sleazy, and who'd want to be in porn? So your guy that started out as McDonald's manager is now an owner and a company head in the adult field. He's just as brilliant a businessman—more brilliant—than Hollywood studio heads, as brilliant as any of your bankers, any of your steel company executives. They're not gangsters, but above that level may well be.

Bill has called this "a playpen of the damned." I call it "refuge for the restless." That's how I got into it. I had no intention of doing anything. I wanted to be a Jack Kerouac and just wander around and enjoy and not be pinned down doing "anything." "What do you want to do today?" "Well, I think I'll sit here and watch the Interstate Bridge all day and if I want to curl up and sleep, then I will." That's how I got into the Industry and I will never leave it. People don't believe it, but then they don't understand my code. I have found a home. If someone offered me a quarter of a million dollars a year to go elsewhere, I would not turn my back. Part of the code is the personal defiance, arrogance, giving the finger to the straight world. "Gee, why haven't you lived up to your potential?" Well, it's because I got straight A's in seventh grade, took a look around, and had no use for that any further.

All right. One of the first times I ever went on a porno set was as the writer but also as the guy that had put the cast together based on my knowledge of what the people of America really wanted. If necessary, I will suspend disbelief and assume the producer tried to cast everybody else in the Industry and couldn't. Therefore he had to settle for a fifty-year-old woman playing a teenage virgin. I'll buy it. That's the Industry. You have to give them leeway. You don't expect Eric Edwards to be Laurence Olivier, but you're not going to see Laurence Olivier do a pop shot in his movies. I walked on the set knowing I was going to have to sell this film and guide it through its creative process. I was terrified that I was going to embarrass myself by getting an erection as soon as I saw the action. Lo and behold, everything everybody had ever said is true. I found myself two feet away from the lead, a precious little girl from Michigan who trusted me when we met fully clothed in the office and wanted me to "write great lines" for her. I found myself standing two feet away from a totally nude woman that America would give their eye teeth for and found myself caught up in, "This is a job; hey, it's no big deal." It's been that way ever since. Everybody goes through it.

Some time later, Jim finished his book and brought me a copy.

J: The procrastinator finally got off his ass and finished the book. The subtle farm boy, just off the turnip truck. A couple of people have read it, and they're impressed, very impressed. I can't really, "Aw, shucks; I just genuine thank you," because my goal was to become the Pauline Kael of porn. The publishers expect to sell between thirty-five and fifty thousand copies over the next two years at a cover price of twenty dollars. To their mail-order list. The average guy. They'll sell probably six or seven thousand to those people. The rest will go to various video distributors at a marked-down rate. Then through the video companies they will move about thirty-five thousand. That's pretty much what my other books have done. The book will stand on its merits. Even though it's a cute little book, it is the definite statement. Bill Margold was looking at bits and pieces of it throughout [the writing]. We were talking is it worth the money, because, unlike a lot of people in porn, I don't want somebody [customer] thinking they got a raw deal. If they're going to shell out twenty bucks, which they probably worked three hours to get, I want them to be happy. They will be.

S: Your deviousness is to be straight.

J: Yeah. And there's fun in that. Before I even got into this business I was a con man. I worked in the carnival. We sold circus tickets for handicapped kids; that was one of the scams I worked on. I would get hold of, say, the UCLA faculty list and call them at their office. "Hey, Dr. Stoller, Jim Holliday from the Shriners." I'm lying, I'm not a member of the Shrine; I'm [only] authorized to do their solicitation. "I know you're busy; I know you haven't got time to bullshit; all I'm asking is ten bucks to send seven lousy handicapped kids to the show. I know you can swing it." I developed my own spiel so that about 70 percent of the professional people I talked to . . . . Those little ten bucks add up. We did send the handicapped kids. And we oversold the tickets thirty-eight times over. They weren't all hand-icapped. To me, that's conning. That's the carny.

   The straight world drove me into it. A lot of people that are porn fans— your average guy in Louisville, Kentucky, that buys three tapes a week, he probably thinks I have the greatest job in the world: "He knows all the performers; he goes to all the screenings." Every time they see me in a magazine, I've got a tuxedo on: "He's got life licked." I'll take some satisfaction and refuge in their opinion. They're crazier than all hell. They have no way of knowing how tough it can be, but I chose it. So when Henry Kissinger says he's the foremost authority on international diplomacy mat-ters, I'm the foremost authority on porn.

S: But is that a complete con? It isn't.

J: No, that's the truth of it. The real world forced me into . . . . They didn't force me. I had a million choices: I just could never see myself being one of these nine-to-five lunchbucket commuters that lets some guy tell them what to do all day. You know, there's rebellion there. But with respect to other people and their property, there's nothing antisocial. I want to grab people by the throat and say, "Will you understand I'm telling you the truth?"

S: Your rebellion is extremely complicated as I see it: it has to be ultimately based on telling people the truth. That is tricky as hell. You may not always tell the truth [laugh]. I know you don't. But you have set yourself a very difficult task, and you've succeeded at it. There's a certain amount of risk. You've always taken the risk because it was worth the game. And I suppose there's almost no better place than the porn business.

J: The very nature of the porn business made me fearful, because it's so easy. So I still have to play the game within the game.

S: Tell me more. But I don't know what I'm asking for yet.

J: Well, how about some of the people that you've talked to now . . . since I have been here? I tried to hook you up with Kay Parker.

S: I talked with her. . . .

J: I know. My argument to Bill is: instead of sending dimwits who think they know something, take this raw hunk of clay and find out what motivates her. Well, you have seen one person; Kay is slick, stylish, sophisticated, and hiding.

S: I know that.

J: Okay. Kay is our jewel, but she's not going to tell you what you want to know. But, oh, was she slick in the process of not saying anything, and sweet and—

S: She was. But she made it very clear she wasn't going to tell me anything [beyond what she should], and I appreciated that she would come in and talk to me when she wasn't going to tell me anything.

J: Okay. Bill thinks she's not controversial: perfect for the talk shows.

S: She's not controversial? You mean, in a public way she's not controversial. But she's complicated.

J: Yeah, she's that. Kay is special.

S: And if you talk with Kay it's all right to quote me.

J: Oh, I, no, no, I don't discuss—

S: No, it is. You are free to say anything.

J: But I will not say . . . . In that sense I'm the Pollyanna of porn. I can provide you with the closest professional insight you're going to get from anybody in porn. I make no bones about it. I've just studied the field more than other people, and I'm not as easily fooled as . . . . Kay is perfect in front of the television camera. Any hostile minister or some nutso, antiporn guy is going to melt. How could Jerry Falwell scream venom at Kay Parker when she's sitting there saying, "My sex life was enriched by porn"? And it was.

S: It was very valuable for me to talk with her. . . . She wasn't looking for anything. She was doing you or Bill a favor.

J: I know.

S: And I need that because I need to see the defense. Who else?

J: Well, you talked to one of the primos, Nina Hartley. There is what modern porn is all about, in a nutshell. I assume Nina talked to you the way she would talk to me when we're somewhere just shooting the shit.

S: I talked to Chartreuse.

J: This Little Miss Trinket wants to be a porn star supreme without ever having to do the act. I put her in the "Yes, Bill, take care of her, but I don't want to hear it" category. Now she wants to be the Trophy Girl at our next ceremony [X-Rated Critics Organization Awards]. Amber Lynn was the Trophy Girl, and Nina Hartley was the Trophy Girl: it's an honorable position. So I said one night in front of Chartreuse and Bill, "I'll tell you what. You make three videos or films where you have a substantial role and you are the Trophy Girl." Margold had no idea of what I was doing: I was whacking her over the head so that once and for all I threw out enough ground rules that she would never be able to comply. So I didn't have to hear this shit for four or five months. . . .

S: I read in the newspapers that Traci Lords, etc., etc. Is there anything in that [arrests of producers because an underage girl was used in films], and what does that indicate for your part of the business: sales?

J: Oh, yes, that's my job to know it historically. Let's start with what the police are doing: waste of time, and absolute horseshit. The latest rumor is that the FBI is investigating producers who used her. "These porn companies knowingly used an underage performer; therefore porn is bad; therefore we've got to end it," the epitome of our government wasting their time and taxpayers' money.

   Nora Kuzma from Steubenville, Ohio, moved to California with her mother. She was attending Redondo Beach Junior High or somesuch. She started by doing nude modeling. The bottom line is: if you look at the woman physically, this is not an underage girl, this is a mature woman. You hear stories fourteen, thirteen. She probably began nude figure modeling when she was fifteen, almost sixteen. In 1984, on May 7, she would have been sixteen. She went to a modeling agency and registered as Christy Nussman, age twenty-one—

S: Where'd she get a name like that?

J: There's a real person that exists. When Channel 4 went to break it, their computer guy, their nutso that sits there putting all the facts together so that the bubbleheads can read it on the air, gave me a call. This guy calls me, and I'm not going on camera. That's my low profile: these other guys want to go on camera and spout horseshit. I'll just tell him what I know, who to call, and help them any way I can, because I trust this guy. He put an end to a child porn story from Iowa a few years ago, and so now my number is in his book. I got the call the day that the Los Angeles people raided the office which is semi-headquarters for Traci Lords's corporation. You saw her at the show accepting her award: an "it's about time" award.

S: Is she blond?

J: She was the one that was up there with Gazzari, the gangster-looking guy that owned the club. They gave her the special award, because she couldn't win any of our regular awards. They gave her a special award because they're idiots.

The kids at her junior high school knew she was modeling and knew she was in porn. They knew that Nora Kuzma was Traci Lords. They're not going to tell their folks. I understand that. I went to two of the first three guys that ever used her on film. The first time she ever worked she had no intention of doing hard-core. She just did a split-beaver, you know, beautiful-girl-gets-naked-and-spreads-her-legs. The guy went back later and said, "Hey, I've got to get some explicit footage of you. Otherwise I'm going to be the only guy on the market that doesn't have anything". She made hard-core when she was sixteen. These two guys, no way they're bullshitting: they swear they had no way of knowing. This girl came in with identification, through the agency. They're not policemen. They believed she was twenty-one. The first guy who performed with her thought she was twenty-one. This is a mature woman. And that guy told me all about how secretive she was and how she didn't really say anything to anybody. Yet we find out these kids at her high school knew all about it. How can they come at the Industry when she supplied false identification and documentation she got from the duly constituted authorities of the real world we live in? She went to Japan with their passport.

They give us no credit for self-censoring. Margold has a cute line: "When they find all these sex offenders, they also find a Bible and *TV Guide,* but they are more interested in linking *Hustler.*" Cute. The specious chain of evidence that the Meese Commission put together, without consulting social scientists, without consulting anybody who might know; the American public would believe me. I could prove [by selecting the cases] that the government, the U.S. Congress and Senate is overrun with homosexuals. They're allowed to get away with their chain of evidence [that is, pseudoscience], and nobody can throw it back at them. They bring in child pornography gratituously [to show that all pornography is evil]. My answer is: "You idiots! Is a pedophile going to watch *Little Girls Blue,* which has eighteen- to twenty-year-old women depicting thirteen-year-old junior high students with pigtails and braids?" I ask you, is a real pedophile going to get off on watching grown women pretending to be children?

As for the Industry, it would be good to get these "Chicken Little" companies out of business [by threats of legal actions]. Half of them have no business being in business, because they're screwing up a good thing for everybody. Right now, porn sells. I could make the best film ever made, you could make the worst video ever made, and depending on the packaging, it's going to sell the same number of copies. I'd almost like to see a little policing just to get the crap off the shelves. I've been beating my head against a cage for years trying to get people to take home three or four really good movies, but all they want is something extremely salacious. P. T. Barnum and H. L. Mencken are my best friends. Nobody went broke underestimating the ignorance of a bunch of low-rent idiots who couldn't name their governor, their congressman, the secretary of state. They are dumb, incredibly dumb; I wanted to write a book called *Americans Are Not Just Stupid; They're Incredibly Stupid*. But I've learned through the carny, through the ability to con these people: you've got to forgive them because they're really good people. They're idiots, but they're good people.

S: Let me back up. Tell me about your carny life. I'm looking for resonances with the present "carnival" in which you work, the X-rated Industry.

J: It started when I was just fifteen; summer job time. I am one of the most normal people that America produces: if your basic, upper-middle-class WASP with appropriate sensibilities is normal, then I'm your American normal guy. My father was an influential executive with A Corporation. The other kids, whose fathers were mill foremen or advertising salesmen or lesser people in the company, got nice jobs pushing brooms at the steel mill over the summer, the old nepotism. My father looked at me and said, "There's one word that's not part of my vocabulary: nepotism. Go look it up." So I did and realized I wasn't getting a job at A Corporation, a cush job where you don't do shit and you make big money over the summer. The only physical labor I would ever tolerate was caddying on the golf course.

So, not wanting to be a guy that worked at a hotdog stand, I answered a phone ad to sell magazines and found myself earning thirty-six dollars a week; this is back about '63 or '64. We'd sell magazines one day and the next get on the phone and pretend to be direct-dialing from Cleveland, even though we're in Pittsburgh: "We're calling from Cleveland. Did you get the survey yesterday? The boy [actually himself] took the survey. I hope the boy was courteous and polite." "Oh, he was wonderful." I learned early on about fooling people. Only one woman ever said, "You're the same kid." So we'd hit them with, "You didn't win the grand prize, lady, but what you did win, no trip to Bermuda, but the next four years you get these four magazines free. All you've got to do is pay the postage which comes to ninety-two cents a week," and the magazines are monthly anyway, so by the time they're finished it's $191 and catch-you-later. It was a scam.

S: Do they get the magazines?

J: Oh, yeah, yeah. And if they don't pay, they get a six-foot, eight-inch black man coming out saying, "You owe me for the books." That led to a job selling circus tickets. Meanwhile, I'm just a punk. I don't really work. I sold Christmas cards and did all the chicken-shit stuff that eight- and twelve-year-olds did, but that was my first job. And the money was pretty good. So, the summer after my senior year in high school, I did it again. And got so good at it, I'd pick up the phone to impress friends at a party, dial a number at random, and sell them something: red roses; you name it. I took the Kuder Preference Test. It came back my two strongest areas were sales and criminal tendencies. Fine.

That led to selling circus tickets on the phone. The boss was running from the government, a fly-by-night hit-and-miss person. He sat down with my parents. "We'd like to take the boy to the Wisconsin State Fair. We want him to be a talker," which is a barker. The state fair provided me an opportunity to work a microphone in front of five or six thousand people walking down the midway. Any inhibitions were gone then.

I went to college to be either a radio producer or a disk jockey or a sportscaster. It was just filling four years, just something I had to do. Then I realized, "I could work in a radio station for $136 a week or work in the carny for $250 a week, cash. I think I'll go that route." So I did. I might have been about twenty-two when I made a thousand dollars in one week and thought, "Wow!" Yet I'm thinking this ain't right: the people saying, "Be an attorney." I was impressionable but could never be conned. So I decided I was going to walk my own path and suffer the consequences. The fact that I didn't do all these nice and wonderful things, I'm still haunted. But I get satisfaction by the line, "You never lived up to your potential. You're wasting your potential; you should be this, you should be that"—parents, neighbors, professors. The professor would say, "Hey, man. You have a 3.6 acumen, and you've let it slide to a 3.2. Don't you care?" "Well, what do you care?" I was flippant; I was snotty; I was cocky. Why am I being counseled by some guy who (a) doesn't give a shit; (b) is going to transfer to the University of Iowa next year? The great comeback line is, "I was not put on this Earth to live up to your expectations."

S: Does your family know what you're doing these days? If so, what do they make of it?

J: They're dead. My father died when I was in the carny full-time. You won't find any guilt trip or any remorse on this. I would check in every couple of weeks, then once every month. Meanwhile, I was bopping all over southern Indiana, wound up in Cincinnati, Ohio, happy as a hog in shit. Three weeks later I checked into my post office box and got these telegrams. I felt really bad, went home to my motel room, got drunk—only time ever in my life I consciously set out to get drunk—cried all night, and then forgot about it. There's nothing I can do. My mother died about eight months later. The carny creed: "No money, no friends, no relatives, no home." There's no one on this earth that is going to suffer for anything that I do, one way or the other, good, bad, or indifferent, and you're hearing me say it objectively without remorse. With awareness of when I felt guilt and how much. And, "Gee, I'm sorry I couldn't have been there, but what do you want from me?"

S: What did you do in the carny that you were so successful at?

J: Both talking on the phone and working microphones. You'd hit a town—

S: This is a circus?

J: It was any number of things. They worked big state fairs where there would just be a country western singing show, and I might be the barker. Or they'd have the two-headed woman show which was a couple of twins, nicely placed, optical illusion, and I might be the barker. ("Talker" is the preferred carny term.) The same outfit, the same California crooks. Finally the parting of the ways, late '72. I sold everything I owned, took $250 in cash, my brand new backpack, and went around to see the world. A right-wing hippie, ten years behind the left-wing kids that did it in the sixties, but at least I did it.

S: You're not so right-wing.

J: Yeah, I am.

S: And they're not so left-wing.

J: No, they're jerks. . . .

    After I finished with the carny, and been hitchhiking around the country, I went back and became a housemother, a proctor, at my fraternity. To rebuild it. I ran into my old college roommate, who was their adviser. I said, "What's happening? How are the boys?" Well, though we had a hundred-man limit, they were down to fifteen guys. I had nothing better to do. So I became the house proctor.

S: And *you* [that is, the rebel] made everything run properly and kept the rules?!

J: Yeah. [Shades of Bill Margold returning to proctor at juvenile hall.]

S: Jesus. For how long?

J: Four years.

S: Four years [astonished]!

J: I built them from fifteen men and a disaster area to a brand-new mansion where we painted "Home of the Yellow Snow" on our white front wall, outraged everybody. We became "the Yellow Snow." [Piss on Purity.] It's just an expression. People said, "It's a reference to exotic cocaine" or "Frank Zappa's song, right?" It was neither. Four years later I figured my job was done, we were the best fraternity on campus, they were happy, they were crazy.

S: But you were a parent!

J: Yeah, oh, yeah.

S: [You could be that way] as long as it was siblings [as with Margold]. They weren't really your children.

J: Though I was a few years older than them, I attended the parties and paraded through my fair share of pussy. They gave me my own apartment and they took care of my basic needs, but I was still hustling money on the side, managing bands, and doing various and sundry shit. I was just marking time. "Everybody retires when they're sixty and they can't do shit. I'm in my mid-twenties. I'm retiring for a few years because I want to enjoy life." So it was a four-year nonstop party. I spent the bicentennial month of July stoned out-of-my-mind. But, before I did it, everybody was away for the summer; the fra' rnity was locked up tight; I wasn't going to mess with anybody; nobody v .s going to mess with me; I was just going to sit in the basement and vegetate for a month. And I did.

S: After that you came to L.A.?

J: Yeah.

S: To be in the porn business?

J: No. No, no, no. I came to Los Angeles to be a writer. Finally the living-up-to-your-expectations caught up with me: "Man, you're crowding thirty and you're not dead yet, it's time to see if you can't do a little something." I figured I'd come to California to be a writer. Four months and four thousand dollars later, I suddenly realized I'd better do something. So I found another job on the phone where I could wear a sweatshirt and moccasins and survive. And that job led me to people who needed somebody who could sell video over the phone. I didn't have any intention of working for them. He said, "Do you know about prerecorded video?" "A little bit." "Do you know that they have these porn movies on tape and we can sell them to various stores all over the country?" I said, "Okay, fine." I look back now— we're talking about ten years ago—it never entered my mind that I was making a fatal jump. It was just "Hey" -

S: It found you and you found it.

J: Yeah, and I'm happy as a dog in shit.

S: Now, here you are, *the* historian, with a book coming out that you're proud of. Watch out. Don't accomplish too much!

J: I don't intend to. I'm just a porn guy.

S: That's all. You're just a little old farm boy.

J: The whole sandbag thing [to play someone for a sucker by acting innocent—softening them up—and then clobbering them]. There's no facade, there's no ulterior motives, just a commentary on the human condition. You can find a couple people that will tell you I'm totally devious, not to be trusted, that I don't care for anybody or anything. Not true. But there still is the commentary-on-the-human-condition satisfaction. When I got into porn I said, "I've been a con man all my life. I'm going to have to sell this stuff; and that's selling, that's not conning. I may have to white lie and fudge, but that's selling." I'm going to tell these people the truth. [If you asked them] the highest executives in this Industry would say, "Jim Holliday doesn't lie. If you ask him to lie, and he sees the reason for the lie, he'll do it. But if you say, 'Hey, Jim, what's the program?' he'll tell you the truth."

And that [an honest man] is what's most frightening of all [to other people]. Once you come clean. Margold is my cosmic brother. Two cosmic brothers who speak the truth. I offer a new perspective on people who think there is more deviousness in truth. I'm bemused and enjoy it and roll with it. All right. Are you ready for this? There was a time that I seriously considered—I don't like messing with religion, but there was times when people were pushing me into being a minister.

S: You and Margold are in a morality play.

J: When they [moralists] say to him, "Watch out. Christ is coming," he says, "Good. If Christ can come twice [orgasm], we'll put him to work."

S: Okay, let me end with this. You're in a supposedly amoral, immoral, disreputable industry. Yet the only thing you and Margold are interested in is morality [rebellion]. So you don't need to get paid a lot of money. Because you're into something else.

J: The minister for the porn world.

PART THREE

PROBLEMS
WITH MORAL
PROBLEMS

INTRODUCTION

I have decided—except for editing to make the conversations readable—to let us speakers stand before you mostly unadorned by commentary. I hope it is not naive to think that you can thereby judge our meanings, feelings, motives, and desires and that this method of presentation leaves you freer to form your judgments than the methods traditionally used by psychoanalysts, ethnographers, historians, biographers, theologians, philosophers, lawmakers, journalists, and artists.

I should know better. There is no objective route to morality, which, once the biology is in place, is a central feature of erotic excitement. And most moralities do not thrive on the kinds of ifs, buts, and ands that make my informants complicated, interesting, worth knowing.

Nonetheless, naïveté: that when these informants speak at length and in depth, you get a better sense of the nature of the porn industry (and of my more primary study—erotic excitement) than you get from propagandists' shortcuts. For they have given us too many answers; they have no questions left, only coercion.

Not that skepticism and uncertainty are not moral positions.

For this third part, then, let us slip into hot waters. First, listen to Merlin, who most people would say is bad, who asks that the rule of law established by our Constitution hold sway in his case. Then Ron, who brings a touch of grimness that can extend our sense of what porn is and does.

Chapter 9 **MERLIN: CONSTITUTIONAL ISSUES AND DOING BUSINESS**

Now, Merlin; referred by Bill. He neither looks nor acts like the famous S&M pornographer he is. Not once has he shown toward me even a flicker of either cruelty or submission. He loves to talk and does it well. He is always open, despite the risks: personal (might I embarrass him?) or social (might I reveal him publicly in a dangerous way?). Especially appealing to me is his honesty in letting me know when he is about to be discreet and withhold. He is wry, enthusiastic, intelligent, thoughtful, without artifice (except perhaps in being without artifice), enjoys teaching me about the S&M business. Like Bill and Jim, he prides himself on being a rebel. Like them, he is decidedly not a sharp dresser. He has—to put it mildly—an unathletic build and could pass for the manager of a Sears warehouse. He is relaxed about appointment times with me.

I would be shocked to see him seriously at work on a masochist partner. (Working in a space suit protects me from some aspects of my versions of reality.)

Here is our first interview.

Merlin: I edit and publish five adult newspapers. I produce films that deal with sadomasochism. Some of it is done erotically, and some of it is done sadomasochistically. My basic guidelines are that, whatever happens to anybody, it is always very clear in the film that it is consensual. It is also usually clear at some point in the film that the person has enjoyed it, although they might not have appeared to enjoy what was happening throughout the whole thing. One of my publications is called *Bizarre Erotic Fantasies*. Most of the fantasies that we receive revolve around sadomasochistic fetishes. But I think that when you talk about erotic behavior in general, a lot of it revolves around S&M, such as the old cliché costume of the lady in the high heels, garter belt, and black nylons. That is erotic to a large percentage of the male population of the United States, and it is based on sadomasochism. High heels shape the girl's legs. And she can't run away from the male. In that way she's rendered different than she would be in her track shoes and gym shorts. I'm surprised, in the age of pantyhose, that the garter belt and nylons have remained erotic symbols; many women dress that way to please or excite men.

So that's a brief description of what I do. We also publish writings that deal with this, obviously have a lot of fiction in our newspaper, publish art work that deals with this subject matter. What else can I tell you? My background. I was a schoolteacher for eighteen and a half years. I'm forty-five. Married. First and only. Twenty years.

S: Staying with her?

M: Oh, yes.

S: Children?

M: None.

S: A girlfriend?

M: Right. Or in our terms, "slave."

S: Oh.

M: That's why I [laugh]—

S: You've got to fill me in.

M: The wife was into it when we were first married, before we were even married, because I wouldn't marry somebody without telling them I had this drive and interest. I said to her, "If you really want children, you should divorce me and have children." I really do not want children. At one point I considered divorce because she was not sexually appealing. We are still very happily married but with certain undercurrents of unhappiness. She is still into sadomasochism, because, obviously, having another woman in the house is not what you call your normal pattern of behavior. It is probably somewhat masochistic on her side to have accepted such an arrangement, but that is one of the ways she has shown me how much she loves me and trusts me. I have a bad back, and both ladies keep hovering over me, telling me that I look a little bit tired, maybe I should go home early, which makes me feel very taken care of.

S: Okay. I interrupt you, and I want you to go on. You used to be a school-teacher.

M: I was a schoolteacher for eighteen and a half years. I got into the business world as a tax deduction. I ran a flying school, but the paperwork was taking an inordinate amount of time. So I bought a computer. I then became ill, had pneumonia twice in a row. So I got out of the business because I couldn't pay attention to it. Shortly after, Peggy, who is my girlfriend-slave . . . . She is an extremely masochistic lady. She has admitted that after she met me and knew she could experience pain in a controlled way—not because somebody was hating her but because somebody was loving her— she realized she had driven her husband on several occasions to a frenzy where he would hit her, because that's what she needed. She found it very distressing because she never liked to think of herself as doing something that bad [provoking a beating]. She was a severe masochist without an outlet. I digress, you'll have to forgive me.

S: You keep going, you're doing fine.

M: One of my first secretaries was shocked when she was typing our mailing list. She said, "There are priests and reverends and doctors on this list." I said, "Why not? Can't they have sex, too?" She said, "But, but, but."

   Further background, I was originally a speech therapist when I got out of college. [Laugh.] I was a speech-and- drama major in college. So produc-ing films came about naturally. Also I am able to talk because I was a winner of the public-speaking award in New York at my college, called the Ottinger Public Speaking Contest. In those years it held a big check of $150, which was a lot of money then. It even got in the *New York Times*. I've been in the *New York Times* twice in my life.

S: What was the other?

M: As the lighting designer for a Jewish off-Broadway theater group. I de-signed the lighting, and a *Times* reviewer went to the theater and said, "Lighting designed by Merlin M. added to the entire production."

S: Where did you go to college?

M: I went to Hunter College in the Bronx. It was a great school. I lived in Brooklyn, but Brooklyn College required an average of about eighty-five in order to get in. I had about a seventy-eight high school average, mainly because I kept failing things like math and French, which was another story. At any rate, I had my first talk with a professional—the school psychologist—about sadomasochism at that time because I'd confessed to a girl my desire to tie her hands behind her back while we were having sex. She told me I was sick and perverted and ought to seek help. So I went to see the school psychologist, a young lady about thirty-two. She said, "Why do you think you're sick?" And I said, "Because this girl said so." She said, "Did you force her?" I said, "No. If she didn't want to do it, I didn't want to do it either." And she said, "Well, do you desire to do this to strangers?" And I said, "Well, sometimes I fantasize, when I see a very pretty girl who would appeal, 'Boy, wouldn't it be nice,' but I would never do anything like that." She said, "Then you only want to do it with people that enjoy it and want to do the same thing you do?" I said, "Yes, but I can be fairly persuasive." She said, "That's okay. You're not sick, you're unusual, but you're definitely not ill, just if you ever find yourself wanting to do it with people who don't want it, then go get help, but right now you're okay."

When we were first married we were involved in "swinging," exchanging with other couples. We exchanged photographs with people of a sadomasochistic nature. Then it occurred to me that I could sell the photographs. I only had one model, my wife. So I got out a great blonde wig. And she said, "What the heck, I don't look like me anyway."

Now, getting back. At this point I also had a girlfriend. When Peggy and her daughter moved in with us, I dropped the other girlfriend, who was quite upset by this. Besides being masochistic, she was very vindictive, which I did not realize. I began getting calls from this girl and she would say things like, "You really should be careful." And I said, "What do you mean?" She said, "You've got that kid living with you and I know that you have sex with her." "Doris, you're crazy, you really fantasize an awful lot." Then one day Doris called and said, "You don't know how good I am to you." I said, "What do you mean?" She said, "Get rid of all your pornography, because the FBI is onto you and the child porno thing." I said, "Doris, you're sick." She said, "Well I'm going with an FBI agent, and I know what I'm talking about." Then one day there was a knock on the door. I went to the door, and there was a man standing there, "I'm from the FBI, and I have a warrant to search your house." I said, "For what?" He said, "It's all in the warrant." I said, "Can I read it first?" He said, "Sure," and I said, "Can I call my lawyer?" He said, "Of course." So I called my lawyer. He said, "It's a legal warrant; they have a right to search your house. Be as cooperative as you can and say as little as possible."

They came in. I can only say that it's profoundly upsetting to have seven or eight people go through everything in your house, cart out all your financial records, your videotape player, your computer, everything. Two of the men had a very deep interest in some photos I'd taken of Peggy, as I had of my wife, and some of them we had talked about selling. I don't believe we had sold any at that point. One of my fantasies is a little-girl fantasy, but only with Peggy dressing up like a little girl. And they saw some of those photos and they said, "Oh, look, little girl." I said, "No, that's no little girl, that's the little girl's mother. She's thirty-six years old." I said, "Come on." And they said, "Well, you do things with the little girl, right?" I said, "Absolutely not, why do you think all this stuff is locked away? Why do you think the FBI is up in my attic instead of in my bedroom? The little girl knows nothing." Evidently I impressed them . . . . What I didn't know was when the FBI comes, they come with the local police. It was the local police who were really interested if I was abusing the girl, not the FBI.

Then I called an attorney. He said, "I have to know if you did it; you have to tell me the truth." And I told him everything. I told him that I had sold photographs of my wife, that I had published a small newsletter dealing with bondage and discipline, which I sold by mail order only. I told him the post office was aware of the nature of my material and had never bothered me. He said, "How are they aware?" I said, and this is the truth, "I saw my mail was being opened. So I saw the superintendent. He said, 'What makes you think the post office is opening your mail? It just might come through opened.'" I said, "Only the post office uses that silly half-white scotch tape, and all the envelopes are re-sealed with that stuff. I don't really care if someone wants to read my mail. I have no real secrets, but people send me money."

S: Why did they pick you?

M: Evidently something got ripped open and somebody saw it. I said, "I sell adult photographs, and people send me cash, which is stupid. But if you get a postal complaint, and the man says he sent me cash and I said I didn't receive it, and I'd complained to you that you're opening my mail, we have a very big problem here, don't we?" And he said, "Yes, we do." He said, "Probably one of the clerks has become aware of the nature of the material and is just curious. Before you go to the postmaster, let me talk to the crews." And it stopped. I might add that none of my photos or movies show any type of sexual copulation. There is no oral sex, anal sex, vaginal sex. Rarely have I shown an erection. One or two times.

At any rate, on with the story. So this attorney said, "I am a former federal prosecutor. I know some people in the FBI. Let me call and see if I can't get a little information." And he called up the FBI. "I've spoken to my friend. The agent said the results of the search were extremely disappointing. That probably means that they haven't had a chance to look through everything. But I think I can take care of it and you won't be indicted. However, you ought to let me handle it myself." "What do you mean?" "Well, you're probably going to get very impatient with the way I handle it.

It may take a long time to get your stuff back. But if you try to make waves, the FBI will just indict you to get rid of you. It doesn't cost them anything to indict you." I said, "But I do need certain things back rather quickly." And he said, "What?" And I said, "My computer." He said, "What do you mean?" And I said, "Well, I use it to publish a newsletter. I also have another side business where I store mailing lists for companies. They're not my mailing lists, they belong to these other people. If they call me up and say to me, 'I need a copy of my mailing list,' I can't say to them, 'Oh, the FBI thinks I'm a child pornographer, they took my computer.'"

So he arranged—it took about two weeks—to get the computer back, but they wouldn't give me my data disks back. They insisted that I go to the FBI and under the supervision of one of their computer specialists recopy all my data. I'll never forget that. It took about a year to get everything back, and in the course of that year I learned some things about law and order that jaded me. Example number one. The FBI coming into your house on the say-so of a woman who if they had just investigated her a little bit they would have found out she was rather demented in my view. I'm not a diagnostician. Number two. They came to my house and wanted information about photos they had taken from me. My attorney came, and he said, "This is the way we're going to work it. They will show you a photograph. You and I will take the photograph, go into the next room, you will tell me everything you know about that photograph, then I will decide what I shall tell the FBI about it." I said, "Why are we going through this charade?" He said, "Because what you say can be used against you in a court. What I say is hearsay and can't be used against you." A very, very smart lawyer.

To make a long story short, they asked me about this one photograph. I said, "I bought it on Forty-second Street. You know, it's copyrighted by somebody, it's stamped on the back of it. I don't know anything else." The last thing they showed me was an eight-by-ten color photograph of a girl, naked, and it had been ripped up and scotch-taped back together. I had never seen it before, and we go into the next room. My attorney says, "I think you're in trouble." I said, "What do you mean?" He said, "This girl looks underage." I said, "I agree." He said, "You do? You told me you never had anything." I said, "I didn't. I have never seen that photograph before in my life. Why would I tear something up and leave it? I have a fireplace, I'm an intelligent person. If there was anything in my house I wanted to destroy, I would have burned it." And he said, "You're right." He said, "Sometimes they just put in a ringer to scare you." This was very upsetting.

When I got back all my videotapes—I have fifty or sixty—they told me that they watched every minute of every videotape. Sometimes you put two labels on top of a tape: you fill up one label. So you put on another one. They tore the one off to see if maybe underneath it, it said "Little Girls in Action," or something. And when I picked up my stuff—and this is the final, crowning indignity—I said to the FBI agent, "Now you've given me all my stuff back, are you now convinced that I'm not a child pornographer?" He said, "No. You don't think we searched your house without having good reason. Somehow you got rid of the stuff, but we know you for what you are."

And that just really—it can build a hatred in you—is the only thing I can say. On the other hand, my lawyer put it in perspective for me. He said, "This is still the greatest country in the world." But I was ranting and raving. He said, "You don't understand. If this was Russia, they would have come into your house, they would have searched your house, and then they would have taken you into the backyard and shot you. End of discussion. We still have due process, and you still are able to get your stuff back, and you're still able to do what you want."

Now this may sound very bizarre to you, but that single incident is what made me make my mind up to leave teaching and become a full-time pornographer, I guess I have to call myself. I just felt if I could be harassed so much for something I didn't do, I might as well do something. I have since found out that pornographers are not as wealthy and rich and it is not as easy a life as the newspapers would have you believe. I'm not associated with the Mafia. I've never . . . I deal with people: how would I know if they're connected to the Mafia? I know that they are very powerful people and that they can cut me off from my public because they own the distribution throughout the country, but whether that distribution is Mafia-controlled or not I have no idea. Nobody has ever come to me and said, "You will do it or else." That's how I decided.

S: They made you a rebel?

M: Yeah, I guess that's pretty much what I am. I am essentially a rebel: it never occurred to me before all this to look at our Constitution or question a court ruling or disbelieve a police officer. It never had occurred to me. Today I say to myself, "Where in the Constitution . . . . I know the Supreme Court has said so . . . . The Constitution does not say that you will have freedom of the press except for sexual matters. It says 'Freedom of the Press.'" I wouldn't mind it if they could tell me exactly what it is that is dangerous or threatening to society. If I were showing my stuff to little kids, I could understand it. If I made unsolicited mailings, I could understand it. I don't mail unsolicited to people. Some people in the Industry do that. I never have. I try to cooperate with the laws as I understand them.

For example, we had a case in New York my attorney brought to my attention. The Spectra Photo case. Spectra Photo was a photo processing lab. The same day they raided my house, by the way, I was part of a nationwide so-called clean-up; they raided twenty-two other locations. That same day they seized Spectra Photo, which was a swingers' photo-processing lab. They claimed that Spectra had sent obscene material through the mail. That Spectra had indeed processed photographs of naked children. Of course, when they got into the courtroom, it was children in bathtubs, things like that. Fifty percent of the material that they presented had the legend "Processed by Kodak." It had been sent to Spectra for reprints.

Probably people interested in child pornography were using Spectra to process photographs. I don't see any way that society is going to stop the father who is into photographing his daughter or his son from doing it. You can stop it after the fact, when you catch them. I hope the government doesn't intrude that far. I feel sorry that there are some kids who go through that type of thing. By the way, Peggy's daughter, it came out in therapy, had been molested by her father. I never found out the gory details, but she said her father had done nasty, nasty things to her. And when she told her mother about it, her mother had the typical reaction all mothers have, I guess, when the father is accused of doing something to the daughter. "Why are you telling me such a lie; you're just jealous of Daddy," or something like that.

I might add that she was later molested by a friend on a picnic outing. That time her mother believed it and took action. The end result was that the man received treatment, but that's another story. Where was I? Spectra. Spectra was acquitted on the child-pornography charge but was convicted on seven counts of having mailed obscene, sadomasochistic photos through the mail. So I said to my attorney, "Well, what can we find out?" So we got a transcript: the photographs allegedly showed genital mutilation. I said, "What is genital mutilation?" By the way, one of my attorneys was a woman. Her eyes were open wide during this. She said, "I don't really know." I said, "Well, I sell photographs. I have some photo sets, and there's a pin being pushed through a girl's nipple. Is that genital mutilation?" She said, "I think that that would probably qualify as genital mutilation." I said, "What about a clothespin on a nipple?" She said, "That's not really mutilation." I stopped selling them. I also had one videotape where we had a scene where a needle was pushed through a girl's nipple. I removed that.

S: Even I've seen that stuff.

M: But I don't produce it because there was a decision—

S: It seems to be legal enough [there is a regularly published, nonporno magazine emphasizing the cosmetic value of piercing and its progenitor, tattooing].

M: I guess I'll have to digress. The first two videotapes I made I sold to a porno distributor. After I sold them, I realized that he was continuing to make money from these things and I wasn't getting any further income. He had paid me quite well, because my work was good. With my background as a teacher, I'm used to controlling people. If you're directing people on a set, you have to control them. I'm pretty good at that. I'm a pretty nice person, and so I was able to get real people to be in the [B&D] videos. The distributors had never seen that before. So he snapped these things up. He paid me three times what he normally pays anybody for a first videotape.

He was caught up in what is called the Miporn operation, another cute one, perhaps another experience where I became rebellious against government. I don't know if you're familiar with it. Miporn occurred in Miami. The FBI set up two agents as millionaire porno kingpins. They proceeded to buy and cause to be shipped into Florida various allegedly obscene materials. The reason I lost respect for the government is that one of my friends had produced 8-millimeter bondage movies. He met these Miporn guys and said to them, "I'm having trouble finding someone to duplicate my 8-millimeter stuff." They said, "We can take care of that." He said, "Finc." He gave them the masters, couldn't get them back for about six or seven months. Obviously in that time they showed them to people and deemed them not to be obscene because they gave him his six or seven hundred copies.

Then they took him out to a racetrack. They said, "Your stuff is really good. But you should put some sucking and fucking in there." And he said, "But I don't do that." They said, "But just think of all the money we could make for you if you'd only do that." They paid for him to bet at the track, and they paid for his dinners. He said, "No." Two months later they called him up and again tried to convince him to include this stuff in his films. And he said, "No." Shortly thereafter he was picked up by the county sheriff, right before election. And there was a big play in the newspapers about this pornographer. Then they let him settle out of court: he agreed not to take or sell photographs for two years and they would retain all the allegedly obscene material that they had seized. They never put him on trial. Very interesting. But the point I'm making is that these FBI agents really were out there actively trying to convince people who didn't want to do this to go into the business so that they [FBI] could make better collars [arrests].

In this Miporn incident—you may have read about it—all the people they picked up were found guilty. And just before sentencing, the FBI agent who had been chief witness against all these people was convicted of shoplifting. Their attorneys went to the judge and said, "Your Honor, you're sentencing these people on the testimony of an FBI agent who has been arrested and found guilty of shoplifting. How can you believe all his testimony?" The judge said, "You're absolutely right. We'll order all new trials." [Laugh.] So, this guy told me, the FBI said they were going to retry him but without his [the convicted agent's] evidence. "We'll use other evidence." He said his first trial cost him $160,000. He said he was just about wiped out. He didn't have the money for another trial. So he made a deal: he would plead guilty of one count and would probably be sentenced to probation and probably serve no more than a year. So he did that. At the sentencing, the judge said, "Do you have anything to say before I pass sentence?" He said, "Your Honor, can I have some time? I need one day."

He went to all the porno bookstores in Miami and bought all the porno movies he could find. He went into court the next day and said, "Your Honor, I don't understand one thing. You asked me if I had anything to say. Yesterday after court, I went out and on the streets of Miami, I bought this and this. I don't mean to offend Your Honor or make you look at it. I'm just trying to demonstrate that material of the same nature that I am being sentenced for is readily available in the society. Why, then, am I being singled out?" And the judge said, "That's a good question. I don't have a good answer for you, but I will tomorrow." And the next day, the judge said, "I have your answer for you: they caught you. And second, you decided to plead guilty. So I'm sentencing you to six months in a federal penitentiary and five years' probation."

He comes back to New York, goes to the probation officer, he says, "Do I have to go out of business?" The probation officer says, "No. All you have to do is not send anything to Florida." Now that's insanity. It's ridiculous that the government spent so much time and money and effort, that this man spent so much time and money and had to spend six months of his life in jail, which destroyed his family. I almost understand terrorists. I can understand their feelings. I get so angry. Fortunately, I'm not that type of person.

S: Your sense of fairness was turned not to terrorism but to—

M: Publishing obscene material—no: pornographic material. That's probably why I haven't been arrested. I don't believe that what I produce is obscenity. Twice there have been government actions. I publish a newspaper. I had no problem for about a year and a half, and then one day I delivered my newspapers [to the post office]. The next day I got a phone call, a supervisor, who said, "Come and get your filthy material and mail it with 'sexually oriented material' on it." I said, "I don't have to do that." He said, "You certainly do. Nobody can mail this obscenity this way. It says in the postal regulations 'Sexually oriented material must be mailed saying sexually oriented material.'" "Is there a supervisor I could speak to?" He said, "You can speak to anybody you want, but it's not going to be mailed from this post office."

So I went to the Mail Classification Section and said, "I would like to see a supervisor." The girl said, "You don't have to see a supervisor; you can see anybody." I said, "I think I'd like to see a supervisor." She said, "You'll just have to take your turn." I said, "Look" (and I showed her the newspaper). She said, "I think I'll get you a supervisor." She got me a female supervisor. I said, "Look, I really feel very badly about having to expose you to this because it's not my intention." She said, "You're not exposing me to anything. It's my job to look at this type of material and rule on it." I said, "Fine. You should be aware of a few things before you rule. Number one, this is a First Amendment issue. This is a newspaper. It is printed on newspaper presses; it has advertising in it; it has news articles in it; it has editorial content, it has stories; it has letters to the editor; it has everything that makes a newspaper a newspaper. It only goes to subscribers who have requested that they should receive it. And they do not wish to have it say 'sexually oriented material' on it. Now I know what the regulation says, but *Screw* newspaper, which has pictures of people fornicating, which mine does not, is mailed second-class matter. Send mine third class."

She said, "That's entirely different." I said, "There's nothing in the regulation that says second class is exempt and they don't have to write 'sexually oriented material' on it. *Playboy* goes to many subscribers all over the country and they don't have to write 'sexually oriented material' on it. So before you rule against me, please be aware that if I have to, I'll have my attorney do whatever he has to do. Recent decisions found that if an employee of the federal government makes a ruling they should have known better than to make, they can be held liable for personal damages. I'm not threatening; I don't want you to get that impression. I just want you to maybe go that extra step for me and talk to legal counsel before you come down on top of me." She said, "Can we have some time?" I said, "How much time do you need?" She said, "Forty-eight hours." I said, "Absolutely. I have no argument with the Post Office."

I came back forty-eight hours later. She said, "Mr. M., we have no problems with your publication. For our files we would like a letter saying it goes to subscribers only and your assurance that you will do that." I said, "Absolutely, no problem. I must tell you one other place it goes. It does go to other people in the Industry. And it does go to my advertisers without their requesting it because I feel they are entitled to a copy to see if their advertising is placed." She said, "We have no trouble with that, either." And that was the end of it. Everything went fine. Then I asked her, "Can I have the copy that you pulled so I can make sure that the subscriber whose sample was pulled gets his issue?" "Sure." She goes and comes out about fifteen minutes later and says, "This is a bit embarrassing. When we saw your stuff, there was a lot of laughing, and I guess somebody was so amused by it that they took it home." And I said, "Well, I'm glad to know that there was a lot of laughing rather than a lot of being offended. That pleases me no end."

The second time was here in California. I mailed the newspaper without doing "double enveloping" or saying "sexually oriented material" on it. The Post Office called me in and said, "We've just examined this stuff. This is sexually oriented material." So I told them the whole story about New York. "That's New York. That doesn't hold true out here." "What would you like me to do?'" "Well, you either have to write 'sexually oriented material' on the front or you have to put the piece in a second envelope and write 'sexually oriented material' on the second envelope. I said to them, "But in New York I could do it. New York said newspapers are an exception." "I don't care what New York did," he said. I said, "But I thought we had one Post Office in this country and one federal government." He said, "I'm telling you what my ruling is." I said, "I'll tell you what. I'm not going to argue with you; I'm just going to cooperate." I cooperated. "Why make waves" has always been my philosophy, in certain ways. I guess when my back gets up against a wall, I do make a few waves. All right. So now you know a bit more.

People who are afraid of exposure, I say to them, "If I publish your photograph, I'm going to do it on the inside of my newspaper, which means that somebody who is looking at it is probably already interested. Your mother or your father is not going to pick up that newspaper and turn to the inside to look for pictures of their daughter or son. If your mother or father is interested and they find pictures of their daughter or son, they're going to say, 'My God, isn't that wonderful.' If you are worried about your boss seeing it, he's also going to have to be interested. He's not just going to pick it up." I assume you're aware of the Janus Society here in L.A.

S: I've heard of it. Into leather?

M: Into sadomasochism of a consensual nature. They act as a meeting place, and they have parties where people do things, exhibitionistic type things.

S: Heterosexual, homosexual?

M: Both. I would say that Janus itself is heterosexual. It has an offshoot called "Leather and Lace," which is the lesbian, and it has another that's homosexual [male], but I don't know what its name is.

S: That's where I've heard of Janus: through Leather and Lace.

M: The ladies in Leather and Lace make people like me look like we don't know what it is to torture a human being. Those ladies are downright cruel. [Laugh.]

S: That's where I got the pictures. It was a catalog for piercing.

M: In my car I have thirty-two issues of something called *Piercing Fans International Quarterly*. *Gauntlet*. He, too, has changed his publication policies. He used to carry fantasy stories about people with twenty-eight-pound weights hanging from their nipples, obviously fantasy stories, sometimes illustrated with drawings. He said he no longer publishes that because of fear of prosecution. The law that they're using reads "depictions." My lawyer said, when I asked if I should stop selling photo sets, "I don't think you will get into trouble for photo sets." I said, "What do you mean?" He said it was hard for a judge and a jury to believe that this one photograph is so exciting that it's got to be obscene. He said, "Your videotapes might get you in trouble. The photos, I don't think so, particularly since if you're ever arraigned, the D.A. is going to talk to your lawyer, and once I can show him that you have a pattern of removing from sale things that you think are obscene, he's on very weak grounds: the jury will sympathize with you. The last thing they want is the jury to have any sympathy."

S: Another place where I've seen such photographs is *Drummer*.

M: It's a homosexual publication.

S: Now they've got pictures of guys drawn and quartered, strung up—and they're publishing all the time.

M: [Big sigh.] Homosexuality has achieved something that, I keep on editorializing, sadomasochism doesn't. There were enough practicing homosexuals that they kind of went up front and said, "Hey, you said we're sick, but we're not. We know what we're doing, and we're not sick." And finally after enough years, and enough homosexuals in the country who came out of the closet, and enough gay liberation parades, the psychiatric community decided that you're only sick if you're unhappy being a homosexual. [Laugh.]

If I feel happy being a sadomasochist, and I find a happy partner, and we live a happy life, then we're not sick as long as we're not going out on the street and inducting people or something like that.

Getting back, gosh, there's so much to tell you about.

S: Tell me more of your progress into publishing your material. The first step was home pictures. And then a network developed—or you found one— and you mailed the photos around. You've been in the publishing business—

M: Three years full-time. It's about four years ago when the FBI came into my house. I had been publishing a small computer-generated newsletter dealing with the B&D/S&M to the people who I had accumulated on my mailing list for many years—photographs and stories and stuff like that. I was one of the first tabletop publishers; many people who own computers now are going into publishing in a small way. It's a new phenomenon and freedom of the press. Everybody now can have a press, essentially. I know one man who is into spanking fetishism and publishes a small newspaper about spanking. He had a dot matrix printer. If he needed one hundred copies, he just set the dot matrix printer to printing one hundred copies. That was how he published. And fascinating where he got his people. He put an ad in the *New York Review of Books,* discreetly coded, of course, and he got people who were interested.

It's really amazing. I'm into bondage and discipline, I enjoy seeing a person restrained and sometimes causing them pain, with the pain translated into pleasure. He's into spanking, where the person is not restrained. His spankings, unlike mine, are not designed to hurt but to be erotic, if you can figure out how a spanking can be erotic. I'll give you an example. A twenty-seven-year-old woman thinks of herself in terms of being a little girl who has to be punished. And somehow she associates spanking with sexuality, maybe because her father gave it to her. I'm not sure what her psychological modus operandi is, but she can enjoy a man paddling her and then sexually stimulating him with her hands or mouth. But with me, I like the restraint, that the person is straining to get loose even though they really don't want to get loose.

S: With or without paddling? Paddling is not the important part of it? Restraint?

M: No, they both are. I don't personally enjoy paddling, because I consider it brutal. I guess some people would consider it brutal that I use a whip. Paddling usually results in large areas of bruised flesh. A whipping usually results in a pattern of lines, although it can result in bruising, too.

Let's go further. You asked about the publishing. So I was into desktop publishing. A guy I know had been a swinger publication publisher for fifteen years. He was in deep financial trouble and did not know how to run his business. Maybe he could be my partner in publishing a B&D newspaper. But he said, "There's no market for B&D." I said, "Of course there is. Why don't we become partners, just in this newspaper. You don't have to do anything. I will put it together, but you will have to show me how physically to do it. I don't know anything about how to prepare a newspaper for publishing. I don't even know how you size a photograph. These are skills I don't have." There are no schools.

And he needed me because he was the worst business person I've ever seen. Like people would send in an order, he wouldn't fill it for a month or two or sometimes never, going on a theory that nobody would ever complain, because if you're from Oshkosh, you don't want your local postmaster to know that you ordered adult material. I couldn't tolerate that. He also had little scams going, like he would have photos of models and he'd place ads in his own paper as well as other papers saying, "Send me five dollars and I'll send you my phone number and everything." And guys would send five dollars cash, he'd take the cash out, he'd throw the letter away, he put their name on a mailing list and never answer them. Then he would send a mailing offering them ten swingers' magazines for thirty dollars and they would send him thirty dollars and he wouldn't send the magazines. I did not like that.

Or sometimes he would write a letter and he'd say, "Hi, I'm so glad to get your letter, your five dollars. Enclosed is my photograph. Unfortunately, my phone is being disconnected, but if you care to meet me, I can come to visit you but I do need gas money to visit you. Could you send me two hundred dollars?" Guys would send two hundred dollars. I mean this is patently illegal behavior. I would not be a party to that.

So when I started, I told him no way and he said okay. We put out the newspaper, and he was amazed that it sold. Not counting our labor, we made about seven hundred dollars initially, which wasn't bad for one lousy newspaper. Then he did come up with the one idea that was very good. He said, "Look, you live with two women, why don't we start a telephone sex service? Everybody is doing it." I said, "But we need Visa and Mastercard." He said, "You can get that. You were a businessman." So I went and got Visa and Mastercard, which is now almost impossible to do, because the minute they hear mail or phone order, they don't give anybody anything because the potentiality for fraud is so great it has to be unbelievable.

I give you one example of what I mean by that. I have a list in my computer at home of ten thousand customers with valid Visa and Mastercard numbers who've ordered from us. If I chose to put in a hundred-dollar charge for each of those ten thousand people, what's that, a million dollars, okay, a million dollars and before they get the bill, I could be out of the country. (I wouldn't get a million. The bank would discount it 5.5 percent.) Now I would not do that. I'm basically an honest person, but there are some unscrupulous people, particularly in the state of California—which seems to have every scam that was ever invented—who would go and do that. So we started the telephone sex business.

S: When Visa and Mastercard give you permission to be in business, do they know what your business is?

M: No. If they knew what my business was, they would cancel it.

S: How come they don't know? How come they don't ask? How come they don't want—I don't know what—a credit rating?

M: Okay. When I went to them the first time, I told them that I was in the computer software business and that I was operating out of my house, that I had a flying school before and have had Visa and Mastercard, which is true. And they said because I had been a client of the bank's for ten years—I was a Boston schoolteacher, which was true at that time—and they investigated that, and they said, "Hey, he's a reliable guy, give it to him."

Two things occurred. This partner and I split up. Before we split up I got enraged—you called it rebellious. I got angry at people who do what we call "charge-backs." You may not know it, but if you order something by phone and it comes to you and you charged it, you can keep the merchandise and never pay the bill, because all you have to do is say when you get your bill from the bank: "I do not know anything about this transaction. Can you provide me with a record which contains my signature?" And the bank can't do that; so what do they do? They credit your account, and they debit the merchant's account. There is nothing the merchant can do about it. It's one of the risks of doing business by telephone or mail order. Okay. So I said to myself, "These miserable so-and-so's." We verified that the phone is listed in their name, we verified their address. "I'll show them." So I made phone calls in an attempt to get them to send me the money.

S: Now I'm lost. Who were you calling?

M: I was calling the clients who had charged back against our Visa and Mastercard, who had done phone calls with the girls.

S: Oh, and then the clients denied any charge.

M: That is correct.

S: Oh, okay, so you're a merchant who has the same thing done that somebody could have who is selling I-don't-know-what—

M: I called the man. He said, "What is the nature of the business?"

S: What man?

M: The man [dirty phone caller] who I believe ultimately was responsible for us losing our Visa and Mastercard. I said I was called about the Visa or Mastercard charge that he denied ever making. He said, "What is the nature of your business?" I said, "I'd rather not discuss that with you on the phone." He said, "What do you mean? Is this one of those adult things?" I said, "What do you mean by that?" He said, "Look, I'm an executive, and I leave my credit cards in my desk. Somebody could very well have had access to it but I never did anything like that [make a dirty phone call]. I don't recognize your company name at all. And that's it."

The next night I got a phone call at home from this man, and again he was very indignant. The intriguing thing is that I don't see any way he could have gotten my home phone number unless the bank gave it to him. So he must have called the bank. He probably was an executive at the bank, because it happened so quickly. Banks don't usually give out people's home phone number unless it is to somebody who has access to it. Two days later, I received a phone call from Visa and Mastercard telling me that my account was canceled. I said, "Why?" And they said, "Because you're in the phone sex business." I said, "No, I'm not." He said, "What do you mean?" I said, "Well, I do factor for people."

S: You do what?

M: "Factor." That means that I accepted charges from them, deducted a percentage, usually 10 percent, and then gave them their money less 1C percent for the privilege of using my account. They said, "Who do you factor for?" I said, "I don't know if I should tell you." She said, "If you don't tell us, we're going to cancel you." But it was true that I had factored. I didn't add that I also factored for myself. They said, "We don't care what you do; you weren't authorized to do that, and therefore we're canceling your account." I called up my attorney. He said, "There's nothing you can do about it; there's no law that makes a bank do business with anyone." I said, "But can they harm my credit rating? If they put this in my credit report, I'll never get another Visa and Mastercard." He said, "I think the bank will keep it to themselves, because if they were to do that without absolute proof, it would be defaming your character and you could sue them." So that's how I lost my Visa and Mastercard.

S: How did you get it back?

M: I formed a new business. My partner and I had split up. I had an office. I called a different bank and said I would like to use their Mastercard. They said, "What business are you in?" I said, "Women's lingerie." They said, "Fine, a representative will be out to see you." She came in and sat down. I said, "Look, I have a bit of a problem here." She said, "What is it?" I said, "My problem quite honestly is that we sell a kind of racy lingerie, very sexy, and I don't know how the bank would feel about that. I don't want to cause any trouble." You have to understand these representatives get a percentage or commission whenever they sign up a new client. She said, "I appreciate your being so forward with me. Do you have a catalog?" I said, "As a matter of fact I do," because I had prepared myself with some printed lingerie catalogs I had gotten through my adult publisher, who also sells lingerie. She said, "This is rather sexy." (Because you could see bare breasts practically. You did. There were some that were bare-breasted.) The fascinating thing about the catalog was that it was shot mainly of transsexuals [males].

S: Oh, cut it out. [Laugh.]

M: No, I'm not kidding you, it's the truth. It's the truth. Two of the models in the catalog were transsexuals. I asked the guy who published it, "Why did you use transsexuals?" "They make themselves prettier than women. They know what a man wants to see and they provide it." So she said, "Do you carry inventory?" I said, "No, we don't." All right. So she said, "What do you mean?" I said, "I drop-ship."

S: What is that?

M: Drop-ship means that you get the order, you call up your supplier who has five thousand of these things, and he ships it to the address you give him. You pay for it with a big mark-off. I said, "I own a house; I'm a stable member of the community; I was a teacher for eighteen and a half years, if there's any difficulty, I don't want you to put yourself out." She said, "Your attitude is so nice. I'll tell you what: I'm really supposed to get a copy of your advertising material. What can be done about that?" I was prepared for these questions, because I had been through it once. I said, "The way we market this is, we get the names and addresses of men and sometimes women who are interested, and we have the computer generate a highly personal letter. We send the letter out, and if they want a catalog, they have to respond. So we have highly qualified leads."

That sounded very professional to her. I gave her a copy of the computer letter, that said at the bottom, "When you receive our catalog, you'll be happy to know that you can use Visa and Mastercard." I said, "Tell the bank that I don't have a catalog, because it's stupid to print up a catalog that says Visa and Mastercard if I don't have them yet. But the letter is how I intend to do business." She took the letter, and I got Visa and Mastercard.

A year later I got a second Visa and Mastercard from another bank, a back-up. To get it, I rented a one-room office, called the bank, and told them I was in business, and asked if I could get Visa and Mastercard for mail-ordering videotapes. They asked what type of videotapes. I said, "G and PG, of course" [ratings for wholesome movies]. They said, "What do you mean 'of course'?" I said, "I have a new marketing approach." They sent a salesperson out. He said, "What's your new marketing approach?" I showed him a letter that said, "We want to have only wholesome entertainment in your house, and we are going to be the specialists in wholesome entertainment. If you order your videotapes from us, you will be guaranteed of the lowest possible price, etc., etc., but please be aware that we only handle religious and G and PG tapes." The man was very impressed and gave me my Visa and Mastercard.

When we fill out a sales slip, we never write on it exactly what it is. We may write "subscription" or "videotape," and that's it. We've never had a problem. And we learned to confuse their computers: by telephoning our clients collect to their house. Today we add the telephone charges on to their bill. One way computer banks find out what business you're in is they see all these charges for exactly the same amount. So we no longer have charges for exactly the same amount. And through sophisticated techniques, as well as knowing what we're doing, our charge-back rate is under about 3 percent.

S: Stop again. What's charge-back?

M: Charge-back means that somebody says I didn't buy that, and the bank gives them their money back. That's called the charge-back. Our rate is about 3 percent. Your average department store runs about 4 or 5 percent. So we're pretty good, and we're a good client for the bank. We do about $250,000 a year on the telephone. Now that's not as good as it sounds because the bottom line is we make about $500 a week from the telephone service. That's 10 percent profit approximately.

All right. So my friend set me up in the phone sex business. It blossomed very quickly, once you find out how easy it is and how thrilling it is. I had this apartment in New York. So I put the girls in New York, and I put in a special phone line. And I would go into New York and sit in the apartment, answer the phone, and ask these gentlemen what they wanted, and quote them a figure for their fantasy. Most of them were very shocked to hear a male voice. I figured that that got rid of the phonies.

S: Why would phonies call?

M: Because so many men call just to hear a woman's voice, or they call because they can't believe that such a thing really exists, or they call because they're a religious fanatic and want to save the woman on the other end. "Find Jesus and repent, sinner." I had to make it clear to the people that there was going to be no sex [no arrangements for prostitution] but that they could live their fantasy out.

Let me interrupt here. Since this first interview, I have come to know Merlin better. He continues to balance on the razor's edge, experiencing both sides of the S&M equation in his relationship with society. (As this book goes to press, he has just been searched by the FBI, one of thirty-two pornographers nationwide who may soon be indicted [Barrett 1990].)

Chapter 10 **RON, PARTICIPANT-SKEPTIC**

Having read this far, you may wonder why I have not remarked on—but have only let Bill, Jim, Merlin, or Alex say a few words on—one or the other of two great issues: (1) where does the money that finances porn come from, and where do the profits go; (2) what about physical or psychologic harm, such as AIDS? So let us get another informant's descriptions of porn, less light-hearted and benign than the representations made by most of the others. Here is Ron.

R: I worked for a porno producer for a while, who I met through Janus [S&M society]. He recruited me to write some scripts for him, but otherwise he got no one from Janus. I mean he was unable to find anyone who was interested in being in any of his product through the S&M scene. I guess he thought he would find people who were extremely sexual, very uninhibited, wild, and ready to do anything in front of the camera. But if you know anything about S&M people, they're not that way at all. They're the exact opposite: measured, careful, and premeditated, the last people to be up for just anything: they're up for what they're up for.

S: Tell me about the porn business. You're experienced—I don't know whether a lot or a little—in the ordinary porn business.

R: A fair amount. My first adventure in it was a result of my work in the commercial S&M scene. [He once managed a B&D establishment.] There's a lot of overlap there: a lot of the women who do commercial S&M do other forms of commercial sex. Some of them strip; some do prostitution; some do porno films. They are women in the sex business. The sex industry is their industry, and many of them are utility hitters within that industry. I met one of those when I was working at Club Kincaid. She and her husband were producing a porn film. She had been in porn films, in addition to stripping, in addition to her work at Club Kincaid. And she hired me. She's hardly representative of anything. She's representative of her. That's it. A unique example.

As with prostitution, it is a complicated question whether or not they have any interest in sex in [deciding] what they do for work. I think they do, by the way. In the same way you would choose to be a psychiatrist: you choose a field of endeavor for a living because you have some interest in it. People who make a living off of their sexuality must have some interest in sex or they would have chosen some other means of making a living. So I don't buy the view that some of them espouse, that it's purely for the money and they would never do it under other circumstances. To some extent, the money makes it all right for them to do it, that it's something they like to do but have guilt feelings about. Being handed money to do it settles the conflict for them. There are some who are compelled to this by wretched economic circumstances, but they, for the most part, don't end up in porno films but working the street, because they're junkies, because they're run-aways.

Most men and women in porno flicks seem to be people who have been around and make a conscious decision to seek this out or are perfectly prepared for it when an opportunity comes along. Pan and Pandora, the first people who hired me, had both been performers and then decided there was more money and more fun in making their own. So they womped up some cash and made their own first production. That was where I was hired. Pandora was working at the club as a commercial dominant.

S: How did she get to that? From what sexual route?

R: She was already a porn performer and a stripper prior to that. I think she went into commercial B&D largely to supplement her income. But once she got into it, I think she discovered that she had a liking for it. It created stresses in her marriage, because her husband just has no interest in it. His ridiculing attitude discouraged her from pursuing it in a private context, but she continues to do it commercially. In any case, they had both had plenty of experience in the porn business before I met them. They were not virgins in this area. I was. So when they got the idea to produce this first film, an S&M-oriented, hard-core porno film, a rare item, Pandora asked if I would be interested in writing a script. And I wrote a script for them. Not great but a beginning. It's in distribution! *Bizarre Encounters*.

S: Are you the writer listed?

R: Not by my own name. I then met another producer, the guy who came to Janus hoping to recruit on-camera talent. He failed to do so, but he recruited me as a writer. I did six or eight pictures for him, scripts ranging from fifteen to twenty-five pages, all for a seventy-minute final product with six commercial scenes in it, with the classic breakdown of three boy-girl scenes, a boy-boy-girl, a girl-girl-boy, and a girl-girl, according to a strict formula. You can arrange them in any order, but they've all got to be in there: there's got to be six of them; they've got to fit into seventy minutes; and they have to be composed in that way.

I was able to churn these things out in two days and was paid five hundred dollars apiece, cash. If I could have done it more steadily, I would be living very well indeed. Unfortunately, that sort of work is sketchy. These guys keep getting busted and having to flee, and all kinds of other things happen.

S: Do you get any whiff of the more criminal element from where you're working? I would presume not, if you're sitting at a typewriter writing scripts.

R: No, I've always made it a scrupulous practice to avoid contact with the bosses of any people I work for.

S: But you know they're there?

R: Oh, yeah, sure.

S: That's the part I've never heard about. Everybody knows it. "Everybody knows it." But the people I've talked to [Bill and Jim], not a word.

R: The employers keep their distance from the performers. That benefits both; the people that run this business know that performers are not hardened criminals who subscribe to the harsh codes of the criminal subculture. They therefore could not be relied upon to go to jail to protect the identity of an employer. So those employers protect their identities by insulating themselves with a layer of guys who are essentially bag men [money transporters].

People who produce independently have found that it is best to sell their product outright rather than trying to distribute it and get gate money back from it.

S: What's "gate money"?

R: Money that people put out to either buy the cassette or rent the cassette, because recovering the money from those in the distribution arm of this industry is very difficult: if they don't want to pay you, you cannot make them. So most of the independents—people like Pan and Pandora—simply make the product, take it to a distributor, sell it outright for a flat fee, and go make another.

At the creative level you're not. Most of the producers are former performers who developed the contacts, the skills, the credits, and the experience necessary to make their own product, to get out from in front of the camera. That is the ambition of most porno people: to transcend the necessity of fucking in front of the camera and get behind the camera. An interesting business, but more business than sex.

It's a haunting fact that performing in porn in the current environment could have lethal health consequences, and the people who operate this business have no moral qualms about that at all. Margold was quoted in an article in the *L.A. Times* on this subject recently as saying that people aren't interested in safe sex in porno films. They're paying, as he put it, "to see people working without a net," to see these people taking these risks. Well, whatever the public may be paying, the people who are hiring aren't paying them very much to take those kinds of risks. It would take an awful lot more than a thousand dollars a day to get me to take that kind of a risk, I'll tell you. There's not enough money in Fort Knox to get me to take that kind of a risk.

One girl I know, Betty; this is her situation: she's older than most of them, in her middle thirties, attractive but not stunningly beautiful. There's a great premium on youth in this industry. So it's very rare for a woman this woman's age to work steadily. How is it that she works steadily? Her willingness to do things that even other porno stars won't do. Her specialty is anal intercourse. She's willing to do double penetrations, multiple anal penetrations, things of that kind, with lots of different performers. All the things that other people won't do. When I confront her about this, her answer is, "I take very good care of myself. I think my immune system is in good shape. I just don't think I'm very likely to get anything."

The people who hire her know that they are hiring her precisely to do high-risk behavior. And they obviously have no problems about it. Doesn't this say something about the people who run this industry? They are just not concerned with the moral issues. It doesn't bother them. However glib and slick they may be, there's something chilly about the personality that says, "I'm going to take this intimate aspect of human nature and turn a buck off it by any means. I don't care what damage it does to the people I hire, and I don't care in what light it portrays them, or portrays human sexuality, or anything else. I don't care what anybody thinks about anything. I'm in this strictly for the money." That's the mentality that makes porno films. They're not all stupid, by no means. They're intelligent people who ought to know better.

I'm not in favor of active legal efforts to suppress it. Freedom of expression is more important than occupational health. It's not a form of expression I want to see prohibited. So we have to count on the judgment of the individuals [performers, directors, producers] involved. We have to say, "It's up to them to protect themselves from this danger. They've got to not do it." If porno performers as a group started refusing, it could bring reform in the Industry.

S: Take the woman you just mentioned who said she's got a good immune system. It seems to me that you can't blame the producers. She's as informed as anybody. She's willing to take the risk; she's not the victim of a conspiracy to make porn. She has victimized herself.

R: Yeah. She's a thirty-seven-year-old consenting adult who has been around plenty in this world and who reads.

S: Aren't all performers? Are there any who don't know about AIDS? Or any who are being exploited?

R: They may know something about it, but they've been told other things about it that are not really true. Some people have encouraged their rationalizations in an exploitative way. The senior performers in the Industry, the ones who have been in the business a long time, the ones who command high day rates, the ones who are in a position to have some influence, are the ones who should be carrying the banner for this. Now the Mitchell Brothers, in San Francisco, are trying to produce safe-sex porno films. Margold encouraged them to do that. But performers have such low consciousness about this that they don't like to do it because it's hard for them. Safe sex is complicated and clumsy and these guys are pretty insecure. They don't want on-camera failures; it throws off their normal M.O. [modus operandi]. So they don't want to do it, the producers don't like it, and the audiences don't like it.

So there's not much momentum for doing safe-sex porno. The performers are probably where it has to start. If the big names in the Industry say, "I'm just not going to do unsafe stuff in films anymore," I know what I'd do. I'd make safe sex more interesting, non-fluid-exchanging, arousing sexual behavior; place more emphasis on other erotic elements besides conventional hydraulics so that when the time came to do that, the safe-sex precautions would not seem clumsy and out-of-context. If there was a hot, steamy build-up to the use of latex gloves and lubrication, when it came time for the woman to put the rubber on the man in a sexy, seductive way, the audience wouldn't be deprived of the sexual sensation of what they were seeing. That's the service the porno industry could do for humanity, but service to humanity is not a primary priority of the porno industry.

I will tell you this little thing that sums up everything about the porno industry that I dislike: there is now more emphasis on anal penetration than ever in the history of the medium. In fact, in the next year or so, a couple of videos will be released that are all anal penetration, precisely because this has become the forbidden fruit of the moment. There are various sorts of voodoo going around in the porno community about what can be done. For instance, almost all the girls use spermicidal sponges to reduce the risk.

Even people who can be ruthless and unethical in business recognize that there is a quantum leap from being tough and marginal in business to being a guy who sells drugs to kids. I see that difference clearly. I see very clearly what's crooked and what isn't. My definition may be more liberal than Ed Meese's, but I have my own ideas about this. For instance, Merlin, not a nice man in a lot of ways, but not a crook, not one of those guys. Max [B&D club proprietor] is a crook. He would say or do anything to anyone for his immediate economic benefit. There is no law, no morality, no ethical limit that would stop him from saying or doing anything to secure his own ends. That makes him a crook.

Now Merlin, he's a slave driver and a skinflint in some ways, but I don't think he'd hurt anybody. If he thought he was doing something that was hurting people, he wouldn't do it. He just couldn't do it. He used to be a schoolteacher, and though he's come a long distance from there, something in him would stop him from doing a really bad thing. In his dealings with me, he has been honorable. I saw nothing indecent in his behavior toward any of us. And he's concerned about how his behavior is perceived in a moral context, not just because he's afraid of the legal consequences. He doesn't see himself as a bad person and doesn't want other people to see him that way either.

What we're talking about with the sex business: big cash business where there's a lot of fiddle, a lot of latitude. Obviously, these kinds of companies are not known for their enlightened labor relations. They're run by people who have a nasty view of human beings and who exploit people. There *is* something that feminists are right about about pornography. There is something they are very wrong about, but there's something they're right about. They are wrong about the content of the material, which, for the most part, pictures a gentle and idealized human sexuality that is surprisingly mutual and democratic. Indeed, if the way sex is portrayed in pornography were the way it existed in society, society would be more to the liking of many feminists. It would be a kinder society if people's sexual lives were as carefree, hassle free, mutual, and pleasurable as they are depicted in porno. A rather utopian world. But where feminists are dead right is their perception that female porn performers represent a class of oppressed female workers. Male performers represent a class of oppressed male workers. Workers in the sex industry overall are underpaid for the work they do and the risks they take. They enjoy few protections or benefits and no long-term security. It's a hard life, though one chosen as freely as any other hard life.

S: I haven't read their material adequately, but I think they're really into a rage against men, and they are not into a rage against the criminals.

R: Right. They object to its depicting a sexuality they don't like. The feminists who object to pornography are the women who feel pressured by society's sexual expectations of women. They don't look like the people in those movies; they don't want to be like the people in those movies. In no sense do they want to do those things. They feel that this material creates unfair expectations of them on the part of men. I really think that's what it's about. Pornography is mainly an expression of male sexuality that they find threatening because of the demands that it implies. That's what they're pissed off about. In the same way that if men read women's romance novels, they'd find much to be annoyed about: in the idealized portrayal of men, because most of us are not handsome, swashbuckling guys. Most of us are not physical men of action. Most of us are not enormously wealthy or broodingly handsome and would find it difficult to live up to the standards of romance novel heroes. The pressure on men to perform up to the heroic standards in our society has plenty of bad effects on men. But they don't recognize that in the political way that feminists do.

If I were starting a masculist party, I'd address the unfair and discriminatory expectations placed on men. It's easy to be a successful man if you look like Burt Reynolds, have a few million in the bank, and an eighteen-inch cock that always stays hard. But little consciousness-raising has yet occurred among men on this subject. So I agree: feminists are addressing their own psychological reaction to this material. If instead they cared to examine the porno industry itself [they have; there is a literature—published and on film], they would see that it is an industry that exploits women [they have]. It also exploits men. I think it exploits women a little worse. I could give them a couple of other industries that they could go after. I think the food service industry exploits women.

S: Which industry doesn't, I ask rhetorically. The feminists are absolutely right: there are not equal rights.

R: But pornography is a weak target. By their obsessive focusing upon it—this is what Betty Friedan says, and she's so right—they have undercut their case in other more important matters. They've made too big a flap over something unimportant. Not to mention that their charges are clearly wildly off the mark. They ought to look at the material [films] and see if the way pornography portrays women is really exploitative. It rarely is. It rarely is. Women in pornography are much more empowered about their sexuality than women are in feminist literature. Women in feminist literature are frequently depicted as victims whose sexuality is brutalized by men, and so on and so forth, whereas women in pornography are usually depicted as sexual aggressors. It [sex] is usually their idea. In the classic porno movie setup, the guy comes—the plumber comes over to fix the sink, and the bored housewife starts casually undoing her blouse while the poor guy is under the sink with his monkey wrench. The classic porno setup is with the woman as aggressor. That may be the very thing that feminists find so threatening: it raises the possibility that this is something they could do, a responsibility they don't want to assume. So.

You'd have to go a long way to find an industry with worse labor practices. They work people very hard; they pay them very little, really, for what they do. The profit-to-investment ratio is incredible for the people making these things. They spend nothing, they make a fortune. In the sense that you [employee] are a very exploited form of labor: the thing you got paid five hundred dollars for is going to make fifty thousand for somebody else. I've heard these same complaints made about the mainstream film industry, but the scale here is different. As a porno performer, you're putting up with a couple of days of hard, even abusive behavior that compromises your ability to do anything else in your life ever again, because the piece of evidence of your past misbehavior continues to exist. You're doing this for six, seven, eight hundred bucks a day. It seems like big money. Yet when you realize what the stakes are, it's very small money. That other people who have insulated themselves from these risks are making tremendous profits from your hardships creates a nasty atmosphere.

The days and days and days of eighteen-hour shooting schedules, of physically abusive practices, of heavy drug use on the set in order to keep people up and motivated for long periods of time: it's like working in a coal mine. A tough goddamn job. These people get into it thinking it's going to be easy money. It doesn't turn out to be easy money. It turns out to be very hard money, and after you've done this, you're poisoned for anything else. Most people who get into this business out here originally intended to enter the entertainment business in some other capacity.

But after you've done porn films, you can't do anything else. You can't even do commercials. It's even very hard to get work as an extra. If the word gets around that you've shot X, that's it! So the best thing you can hope for is to body-double for a star if you happen to have a similar body. So I see these women, twenty, twenty-two years old, throwing away their future plans, to make what will probably be lifetime earnings in this career of under fifty thousand dollars. Another thing. There's an endless appetite for new faces and new bodies, which means they work them to death for about six months or a year, put out twenty to thirty videos with them. And then they can't get work any more. New ones have come along. The audience is sick of looking at the old ones and wants to see new ones.

S: What about the men?

R: Well, very few men can do that job. So their situation is in some ways better. They [only the fittest few] enjoy much greater longevity and they're paid more, because what they do is a much more specialized thing that very few men can do. So if they can do it, they have a long working life. Basically, the major headliner porn stars of today are the ones from ten years ago: John Leslie, Ron Jeremy, those guys, they've been around a long time, because they can do it. It doesn't matter whether they're physically unattractive. It doesn't matter whether—as many of them get to be—they're temperamental and difficult. It doesn't matter that their day rates have gone up. Because they can do this particular trick.

Ron comes in for another conversation.

S: You were saying you had more to tell me about pornography.

Ron: Yeah. I am coming to know more and more people in that world, drifting toward that world for economic reasons. The better I know it the less I like it and the more I realize that there's a pathological interaction between the people who perform in these pictures and people who run this business. The lives of many of the people in the porno business are extraordinarily distorted and dysfunctional. Much more than people in the S&M scene, whose energy is diverted into S&M, which drains off their aggressions.

Some, but by no means all, of the people in the porno business seem to lead uncontained lives. They appear to have difficulty regulating their internal and external aggressions and do self-destructive things, of which their participation in porno may very well be the most spectacular example. Some have drug problems. Others have difficulty sustaining any relationship that isn't destructive. Of course, these same observations could be made of people in many other fields. And it makes me want to take these sons of bitches who are making huge livings off of them and do things that Ed Meese wouldn't even do to them. I want to send these guys away for about a hundred thousand years. I'm not an alarmist about AIDS. But a lot of the guys in porno films do both hetero- and homosexual porn films. So they're in the infection pool. Also there's a lot of intravenous drug use in the porno community. These people are at super high risk. They have to know this is dangerous, but they tell themselves things about it that are untrue.

Then there's a girl I worked with recently. A similar history: IV drug use, boyfriends who were drug dealers, freebasing, big drug problems through the years, generally disorganized life, makes five thousand dollars a month cash and still drives an old beat-up car and lives in a funky little apartment because most of the money goes for drugs and to pay old debts and to support boyfriends. People who, for one reason or another, are casualties of their era, people who got derailed during the social experimentation of the sixties and seventies and never found their way back to more productive life—these people have become meat for this industry. The people who came out here to act and really never stood a chance, who haven't got the talent or aren't special enough. "Hey, go home. You can't do this. One of these days you're going to wake up one way or another; you'd really be better off waking up in Lincoln, Nebraska, than here. Go back." That's what somebody needs to say to these people. Instead, somebody says, "While you're waiting to make it as a big star, here's a way that you can earn seven hundred dollars a day." As I get more involved, it stirs up feelings of social consciousness I haven't had for years about anything.

I see the porno industry as being able to exist mainly because there are so many fragile, vulnerable people out there who get into trouble and see this as the only way out of it. No one much gets into it because they want to at the performing level but because they don't know what else to do to solve their personal problems, which center on their economic problems, often related to drugs. Those girls who work where Norma [his wife] works, it's the same goddamn thing: a bunch of nice girls, scarcely a girl there who doesn't have something to her, not as dumb as you might expect. Not all airheads; some are pretty bright, and some may have other talents. But no one will ever know, because they have to make two hundred dollars a day. You won't get to explore your talents if you have to have two hundred a day cash all the time.

Why are these girls always broke? They make more money than most straight people I know. God, if I were twenty-four years old and making eight hundred a week in cash! If I were making eight hundred a week in cash *now*, I'd consider myself to be doing great! Yet they live in motels, they drive beat-up old cars, and they live terrible, impoverished lives. Where is all that money going? I look at these girls' boyfriends, and I know where that money is going. Even with Betty, who no longer has an active drug problem, it was like that. She has a different problem: she's a compulsive spender. She used to be an obsessive-compulsive cocaine user. Now she's an obsessive-compulsive consumer of other things so that her lifestyle always runs ahead of her ability to pay for it. She's always scrambling. The last big expenditure will be for a funeral.

S: Drugs are like atom bombs in that we are totally evolutionarily unequipped to deal with them.

R: Yeah. It really nukes people's lives. It nuked mine. You know what I really am? I'm a victim of post-traumatic stress disorder from the sixties.

S: Post-traumatic sixties disorder.

R: Yeah. Post-traumatic sixties disorder. I've got it. A lot of my friends have got it, too. We got off the rails early and never found them again. I don't think we were led astray by evil people. The people we looked to for leadership—the Timothy Learys and people like that—were misguided themselves. I was there in the early days of the psychedelic revolution. We thought we were on to something. And we were. We didn't know what. We had good ideas and bad ideas. And the bad ideas proved more powerful than the good ideas. The good ideas remain.

We're seeing the consequences of this now in the failed social experiments that people I knew, myself included, embarked upon. It's a terrible fucking shame. I dropped out of high school in the eleventh grade though I had a 3.8 grade average, ranked number fifty-seven or so in a class of about nine hundred. I could have gone on to college and had a wonderful career. But I believed that the world was going to be a completely different place, in which academic qualifications and careers would have no roles. We were going to remake everything from the ground up. So now I'm a thirty-five-year-old high school dropout with almost no qualifications. Wiser heads would have said, "You always bet the favorite": continuity is more likely than radical change. Change is gradual. No one could tell me this then. People were telling you the opposite in a very seductive, dramatic way: "We're going to throw all that away. We're starting from scratch." So now here we are. It was Bambi meets Godzilla, a short, brutal encounter that left us all about a millimeter thick when it was over.

How am I supposed to go out now and get an office job in a PR firm? Personnel managers have learned to spot guys like me. I can take out my earring, and I can let my hair grow for three weeks, and somewhere buried in the closet I've probably got a fairly acceptable suit I could put on. I'd go in there and act perky and bright and enthusiastic, and that personnel manager sitting across the desk from me, looking at my résumé with these four- and five-year gaps in it, would be thinking, "Ah, another one of those guys. This guy is trying to get back on the boat even though the boat has left." [Laugh.]

S: You can write porn scripts and write books.

R: That's what I'm doing, but five hundred dollars a script and being able to sell only one or two once in a while and knowing that writing the kind of novel I want to write could take three years, God, I don't know! When I try to visualize where I might be in three years, I can't. I look out there; I see nothing.

But for the porn thing, there's no question that porn has become the refuge of an awful lot of casualties: the walking wounded.

Chapter 11 **CONCLUSIONS**

What have I wanted to say? Neither my perspective—the psychoanalyst listening—nor my observations—what the informants said—argues for or against pornography as being good or bad. Anyway, that is not the main purpose of the book (though I think about the issue a lot and am preoccupied with it, here at the end). I am interested, rather, in preventing a complex subject from being simplified, in arguing that all of us who have opinions should recognize that our opinions are not facts, and in exemplifying how a belief that people and their behavior are complex can lead to a search for fuller data. My observations, though gathered in a sort of ethnographic way and in more depth than those of other writers, do not answer the moral and political questions. (No one else does any better, I think.) You may see, however—I've tried to be quiet yet visible—that I try to influence you in my direction.

Is mine the immoral stunt of being amoral? No, but I guess I have been too benign for those for whom pornography is bad and too sour for those who believe it is just good, dirty fun.

Somewhere in his smiles, Bill rages at his parents: anarchy is not just political behavior. If this study can be believed, then we have an idea why Bill is a pornographer, why porn is a carnival for Jim, why Merlin yearns for justice, why Ron is a good observer of the porn business, and how intricate are the performances of Happy, Kay, and Nina. (A political act is also a private act. An erotic act is the point of a pyramid made up of the nonerotic. A nonerotic act has erotic harmonics. An adult act has infantile primordia. At bottom—at least before we get to the hardware, biology—the boundaries are fluid.)

A few thoughts to round out this exercise. (Remember: I do not use *porn* and *pornography* as synonyms. *Porn* is the X-rated Industry and its depictions, the product—films and videotapes—produced primarily for men who identify themselves, by means of what gives them an erection, as erotically interested in women. It is a subcategory of pornography, which I define as a product—a depiction—made for the purpose of stimulating someone's mind to create erotic excitement.)

1. By now you have fathomed my opinions: pornography seems more the result of our changing society than a cause of change; pornography (with a few exceptions, such as using children) does little good and little harm, if by "good" we mean that something promotes health or the general welfare and by "harm" that it leads to the evil use of others in the real world; if we are to ban pornography because it can harm, then (a familiar argument) we must also ban alcohol, automobiles, non-X-rated movies, law, politics, vitamins, high heeled shoes, computers, money, skiing, animal experimentation, someone else's religion, and sunshine.

But, putting aside whether pornography is harmful to us, should it be banned because someone says it harms the performers? So far, there is nothing but anecdotal evidence—individual cases not examined closely—that the performers are at higher psychic or social risk or more unhappy (undefinable, unmeasurable word) than if they had gone into another trade, such as Olympic volleyball or politics. (AIDS is a new factor but not an essential of pornography; no one catches AIDS from looking at a piece of pornography. Ron illuminated that dark subject.) Implied in my discussion is the idea that the performers choose their work out of free will: no gun at their heads. But that great philosophic question—what is free will?—is as difficult to answer here as it is for the rest of the population, those who are more victimized by society and even those who are less so. At any rate, my interviews brought me people who, by common standards, were not coerced into the trade as were, say, galley slaves.

Pornography is also a fine place to study sin that consists in willfully harming oneself. Bill dramatizes that, as he knows, when he calls porn "the playpen of the damned." But he also shows us that, because we act under the compulsion of our past, our choices—free will—are limited. He and Happy, for instance, during the interviews you have read, were into self-destructiveness as a way of life, as a way of salvaging a life. They may not choose to forego that salvation no matter how hard you thrash them. (And the righteous in our society are still restrained from chopping off hands or heads to improve sinners.)

The bottom line in morality is the question of free will, intention. Those who feel pornography harms also feel that the pornographers know what they are doing, know the harmful contents of their work, know the consequences, and nonetheless persist for their own selfish reasons. Of course they do, but who shall say who has more free will, people like Bill or the people he employs? At what bend of an impulse does fate end and moral law begin? Are the women performers more coerced than the men? (Answer: yes, no, and it depends.) Are the women who work in porn more coerced than those who perform in the nonporn movie world? Is Bill more of a brute than the brutes who in earlier years, without there being public outcry, ran Hollywood studios?

These hard moral issues have not been resolved, not even by philosophers or theologians. Nor presidential commissions. Nor radical reformers.

2. So, you can see I am not incensed about most of pornography's evils. As when I studied perversion (Stoller 1975, 1985a), the more I learn, the less bizarre the subject seems. This reflects my personality and the political beliefs that arise therefrom. My viewpoint is also defended by more thinly constructed outposts, such as my never having seen these informants at work but only in the sterilized environment of my office (plus one visit to Bill's home/office and three XRCO Awards events). That spacesuit, I have noted, protects me from the true environment of porn. And seeing Bill's videos is also no way to sense the full raunchiness of the process of making the films. (Nothing in them except the erections and ejaculations is real; the rest, by his design, is pubescent, naughty-boy foolishness that hides serious-minded civil disobedience.)

There are moments, nonetheless, when another side of me wonders, with pain and self-directed anger, what am I doing treating these to me strange behaviors as if they were as inconsequential as autumn leaves. I felt that, for instance, when Bill would dismiss the problem of spreading disease throughout the X-rated Industry. And also whenever we avoided talking about porn's financial relation to crime. And I am upset when an informant reports on the many perversions available for viewing on tape. (Such intimations have made me prefer the word *porn* to their benign phrase "X-rated Industry." I doubt if my equanimity would be intact if Bill, Jim, Merlin, and Nina were my children.)

But Bill and Jim and Merlin would not disagree. For if they, too, did not sense clearly porn's awfulness—awful tastelessness, audience, production technology, place in society, business connections with crime, shit-slinging, piddling, and playing in poo-poo—they would need another locus than porn for unloading their oedipal rage. I suspect that, except for the most dim-witted bimbo, everyone at work on a porn production—from the gentlest (such as Kay) to the noisiest (such as Bill and Jim)—is, with different degrees of visibility, thumbing his and her nose (perineum) at society. For at—in, on— porn's bottom is anger: rebellion against mores, institutions, laws, parents, females, males. Those radical feminists simplify who ignore that all porn—not only Bill's—makes fun of men as well as women.

Some lesbians rub out maleness with the thought that our species needs only sperm, not males. (A feminist Marxist cure: bank sperm, not money.) They hate knowing what we all know—build into our psyches—from infancy on and what is hidden deep in the structure of porn: "'What is the function of the father? . . . but of course, to fuck the mother'" (Kohon 1987, quoting a woman colleague; Ephesians 5:22–23 puts that more delicately). Mother is *the* primeval. (The Bible and the psychology of men make that pun a double entendre.) But—the child learns—father has *his* power, even over mother, the creator of life and death.

Let us pause for a few paragraphs here and pay our respects to history, since it resides in the nucleus of each cell that makes up porn's body. For the desires that energize the porn industry are ancient (as ancient, Freud would say, as the family as a manifestation/origin of culture). Take the next as an example. It is a quotation from those "seemingly inexhaustible wells of wisdom," Kremer and Sprenger, who created the *Malleus Maleficarum* (published circa 1487–1489). "From the point of psychology, from the point of jurisprudence, from the point of history . . . [it] is supreme" (translator Montague Summers's introduction, 1946):

> Wherefore in many vituperations that we read against women, the word woman is used to mean the lust of the flesh. As it is said: I have found a woman more bitter than death, and a good woman subject to carnal lust.
>
> Others again have propounded other reasons why there are more superstitious women found than men. And the first is, that they are more credulous; and since the chief aim of the devil is to corrupt faith, therefore he rather attacks them. See *Ecclesiasticus xix:* He that is quick to believe is light-minded, and shall be diminished. The second reason is, that women are naturally more impressionable, and more ready to receive the influence of a disembodied spirit; and that when they use this quality well they are very good, but when they use it ill they are very evil.
>
> The third reason is that they have slippery tongues, and are unable to conceal from their fellow-women those things which by evil arts they know; and, since they are weak, they find an easy and secret manner of vindicating themselves by witchcraft. See *Ecclesiasticus* as quoted above: I had rather dwell with a lion and a dragon than to keep house with a wicked woman. All wickedness is but little to the wickedness of a woman. And to this may be added that, as they are very impressionable, they act accordingly.
>
> There are also others who bring forward yet other reasons, of which preachers should be very careful how they make use. For it is true that in the Old Testament the Scriptures have much that is evil to say about women, and this because of the first temptress, Eve, and her imitators; yet afterwards in the New Testament we find a change of name, as from Eva to Ave (as S. Jerome says), and the whole sin of Eve taken away by the benediction of MARY. Therefore preachers should always say as much praise of them as possible.
>
> But because in these times this perfidy is more often found in women than in men, as we learn by actual experience, if anyone is curious as to the reason, we may add to what has already been said the following: that since they are feebler both in mind and body, it is not surprising that they should come more under the spell of witchcraft.

For as regards intellect, or the understanding of spiritual things, they seem to be of a different nature from men; a fact which is vouched for by the logic of the authorities, backed by various examples from the Scriptures. Terence says: Women are intellectually like children. And Lactantius (*Institutiones,* III): No woman understood philosophy except Temeste. And *Proverbs* xi, as it were describing a woman, says: As a jewel of gold in a swine's snout, so is a fair woman which is without discretion.

But the natural reason is that she is more carnal than a man, as is clear from her many carnal abominations. And it should be noted that there was a defect in the formation of the first woman, since she was formed from a bent rib, that is, a rib of the breast, which is bent as it were in a contrary direction to a man. And since through this defect she is an imperfect animal, she always deceives. For Cato says: When a woman weeps she weaves snares. And again: When a woman weeps, she labours to deceive a man. And this is shown by Samson's wife, who coaxed him to tell her the riddle he had propounded to the Philistines, and told them the answer, and so deceived him. And it is clear in the case of the first woman that she had little faith; for when the serpent asked why they did not eat of every tree in Paradise, she answered: Of every tree, etc.—lest perchance we die. Thereby she showed that she doubted, and had little faith in the word of God. And all this is indicated by the etymology of the word; for *Femina* comes from *Fe* and *Minus,* since she is ever weaker to hold and preserve the faith. And this as regards faith is of her very nature. [pp. 43–44]

So we see that men's fear and therefore hatred of women is very old, as old as God (to judge from the religions of the Old Testament).

Yet porn is not so uncomplicated. Though its manifest content—the storyline—is occasionally antifemale, it is false to say that all or most porn scripts are simply antifemale. Both in their contents and in their effects on society, these stories are often full of freedom—women depicted having a marvelous time far beyond what the laws, mores, and elasticity of anatomy seem to allow.

A woman complains that when a woman's genitals are shown in pornography, all women are—she is—humiliated. I agree, though in a better world where everyone knew you cannot humiliate women that way, the picture would fail as a pornographic device: only those who can be humiliated can be humiliated. That is, if we are not, in some way, in agreement with our humiliators, then the barbs do not stick. (Before upright women feel that their sex is singled out for anatomy humiliating, they should note that—at least in the films Bill showed me—men display plenty of the nonheroic droopsy-noodle, bareass nakedness inherent in our species' males. By no means are most pornmen of museum quality. The only essential attribute is their odd trick: they can muster a genuine erection in a false setting.)

A further complication: women "subvert" women, conspire with men. Many heterosexual women exemplify this in being turned on by "male" pornography that shows female genitals. Such a woman (the women tell me) is excited when she reads into the photo her identification with a woman who, in revealing herself, excites a man to want her: his excitement about her excites her. And to hell, she feels, with the subtleties of humiliation and revenge: if his excitement grows because of her shame, so be it. (At least in her fantasies or pornography, though less so with a real man, where tenderness is prized.) If her nakedness shames her, then, via the idea that her shame excites him, her shame excites her.

Bill knows all this. So he brings an additional dimension—parody—to his work. Inside his pornography is his hatred of pornography: of pornographers (including himself), performers, customers, as well as the forces arrayed against pornography. He loves the idea that the left—the reformers—join the right—the enforcers—to kill porn, for he reads their behavior as proving that they are fools for not seeing the foolishness of porn, and for seeing it as more vicious than he does. To him, they overrate the tumescent cock. (Though in his enjoying his victimhood from childhood on, he understates men's fantasizing and practicing brutality to women.) There is a nasty dilemma here, one played out endlessly as The Battle of the Sexes: when females are enraged at males, then will they express it to their sons, even and especially when, in infancy and childhood, the boys cannot yet defend themselves? The males do, in time, grow up and retaliate, closing the circle. We shall never know who started it, what is the chicken and what the egg. The result, at any rate, is more fertilized eggs and thus more chickens.

3. I do not trust the motives, logic of argument, or findings of those who say that pornography is essentially a man's game, that its only purpose is to degrade women, that it increases the frequency of rape. Not only do these people deny that there is women's pornography, but, I bet, they do not believe that men and women can (much less should) love each other, support each other, and be fully intimate with each other in a relationship. If they see men only through eyes that hate, they can see only hatred: how, if you are color-blind, will you comprehend green?

Here is Andrea Dworkin (1989) in a BBC broadcast. I agree with her premise. The problem is hyperbole. A little goes a long way; we should not equate our exaggerations with reality and then treat people—with laws, for instance, that criminalize porn—on the basis of our rhetoric.

Her premise is that men fetishize women and need "aggression for their excitement": would men "ever be able to perform the act of intercourse if they [men and women] were in fact equals? The interlocutor asks, "Do you think sexuality without penetration is more genuinely reciprocal?" She says, "I think it is more reciprocal in many ways on many levels, certainly as an act of trust and friendship and recognition by a man, as a way of recognizing a woman as an individual. . . . So I think so. . . . And it also would allow men to experience multiple orgasms." True respect will come only with mutual masturbation? There cannot be mutual gratitude in intercourse?

She and her colleagues cannot imagine sexual intercourse—not porn, not Bill's cartoons—where partners mutually, nonfetishistically consent. They can only argue that such consent is nothing more than coerced—determined by historicisms that unconsciously enslave women, making them collaborators in a country occupied by fascists.

And in defining all pornography as male wickedness to women, they deny that there are gay pornographies exclusively for men and lesbian pornographies primarily for women and heterosexual pornographies by and primarily for women.

4. Is pornography prostitution? This is the present legal tactic, a trick for catching a slippery fish. Words, of course, can mean what one chooses; yet the performers (except Bill) do not feel that their sex acts are prostitution, even though they are paid. First, there is no customer; one's partner is just another performer. Second, the performer is not hired by his or her partner. Third, both performers are hired and by a third, nonparticipating party. Fourth, both actors know that they are acting and respect, more or less, the problems their partner has in doing this peculiar act.*

Another way some women performers distinguish what they do from prostitution—not a strong test—is that those who have been prostitutes prefer the porn business, feeling that it is distinctly different from and easier, safer from assault, friendlier, and less degrading than their previous trade. They and the men are as Bill wants it: family.

Are people like Bill, who hire women into the business, pimps? With poetic license, one could say so, as has been said, with poetic license, of Hollywood agents. But again there are distinctions. The Hollywood agent lives off his client's earnings, whereas those like Bill do not. On the other hand, the agent does not hire people for full-fledged sex acts, whereas Bill does. But Bill does

---

*Here, however, is an example of an act of prostitution in pornography, the only one I have heard of, where the participants knew its true nature. Another director, not Bill, tells me a man and his wife are doing a film. The filming is highly improvised. As it proceeds—with his wife, as part of the story, in a different room—the man decides (a new salary demand) that another woman in the film, who has been a prostitute in real life, should perform fellatio on him. This woman despises the man but, offered a few hundred dollars more, complies. Both participants in *that* act feel that it is prostitution, that he is trying to degrade her (his revenge against women).

not keep women in his thrall, does not frighteningly dominate them, does not have the pimp's identity and pride in being that sort of criminal.

5. Let these truisms serve, then, to underline my position that the work embodied in this book cannot resolve the moral or political problems raised by porn. But I have a further belief to state, that those who present us with no better data than mine should not pretend to certainty—scientific, moral, or political. I think that, because they know this, they have no recourse but rhetoric: gimmicks and tub-thumping. Only with those techniques can they erase uncertainty, theirs and ours.

The proper way for me to deal with this issue of what others have published on pornography is not to throw it away in a few lines as I have done. I might review at least the recent literature and quote, rebut, untangle, dissect, confront. My sense is, however, that I should not take the time but simply accept the condemnation of poor scholarship, letting others with greater commitment do that tedious but useful job. (I can, however, recommend a chapter by Jarvie [1985], who takes on, at length, the main antiporn advocates worthy of attention. I especially enjoy his leaning on the rhetorical device of using logic to counter rhetoric.)

I shall let the problem of scholarly argument go now with the thought that in my nonscientific, naturalistic ("ethnographic") approach are clues useful in arguing against the methods, findings, and conclusions of those who are certain that they can measure porn's effect on our society. (Political passion reaches for higher truths than those to which I can publicly aspire.)

6. I would remove the quotation marks around "ethnographic" if I had done the following:

a. studied the product—films and videotapes
b. watched the process of getting financing
c. listened to the writers and director develop the story and title
d. observed how the performers were chosen and hired
e. watched a filming to see how the director worked, what film techniques were used and why (for example, type of film, cameras, lighting)
f. understood for what the funds were used
g. watched and understood the editing process
h. ditto advertising
i. ditto distribution
j. studied who are the customers and why
k. studied how porn film critics are created, what are their criteria, what they are thinking
l. ditto the antiporn commentators

m. sought out the past histories of all the types of participants
n. followed up on the later lives of participants
o. understood the legal issues
p. studied the courts and legislatures as they deal with pornography.

Now *that* would be a piece of ethnography.

7. In spite of these weaknesses and those that come from my not being a trained, competent ethnographer, I have, from competence as a physician, psychiatrist, and psychoanalyst, ways of working and viewpoints few ethnographers have at hand. The bottom line is—I brag with certainty—uncertainty, a state conducive to curiosity and skepticism.

The advantage of transcripts is that they bring you closer to the event. Then you are freer to make your own judgments, especially when you know that the tapes do exist, making possible a check on my editing. Many—perhaps all—of my beliefs about porn and its people are there in the transcripts and so do not need repeating now. But you are still allowed your independent conclusions. How much of Bill's provocative talk is braggadocio and how much villainy? How severe is Happy's moral lapse, and what price should she pay *in urbi et orbi* if her hand plays on a stranger's genitals?

I have not deleted anything I have said so as to hide an opinion, improve my grammar or vocabulary, or look different from the way I act with informants and patients. The only artifact is that, by cutting away some of my remarks, I seem less active than I was.

How often, in a case report, do we get a physical description of the patient-informant, much less the author? How we dress and comport ourselves within our clothes, our postures, movements—an unending mass of communication—are mostly or entirely removed from reports. (And not always to preserve confidentiality.) How often, when you meet someone you have only heard about, are you surprised into shifting your sense of his or her presence? Though I have done a bit of that via narrative and in the transcripts, the product here is meager. When psychoanalysts and ethnographers come to care about such information, our work will improve.

Even so, this naturalistic kind of study—a beginning wherein we observe and describe on the way to finding classes (that is, clusters of individuals with salient common features)—cries out for scientific method: controls, adequate-sized populations, statistics. Bill, Jim, Merlin, Ron, Happy, Kay, and Nina are rebels; is their kind of rebellion typical of pornographers; what kind of rebels; what kind of rebellion? What does "typical" mean? Elsewhere in the world, we break problems into pieces and invent experiments that get closer to the nature of a piece. But so far, with pornography, the experiments—one hundred undergraduates fill out forms before and after viewing movies—produce conclusions too untrustworthy for examining human behavior as complexly motivated as erotics. For I know, if I could study each of those who do make porn a career, that each is as distinctive as the next. Who is not? (How much n=1 weight can a study bear and still be science?)

8. As I said at the start, this book is a piece of an effort to understand dynamics—conscious and unconscious—underlying the scripts and other forms of fantasy (such as habitual behaviors) that start up and maintain erotic excitement. Perhaps the conversations herein confirm for you that there is no essence: erotic excitement. Just as there is no essence: art but, rather, as many arts as there are products labeled art. In both art and erotics, *each episode feels different and is done differently from every other episode,* even in the same person. The dynamics of erotic excitement should be studied as matters of aesthetics, just as we do with other excitements such as art.

9. I have often written my belief that in the center of most erotic excitement is a desire to harm, to degrade, to be harmed, to be degraded, ranging from the smallest trace to a massive presence. But I dislike the logic that says that if an element is present, the matter of degree makes no difference, as if telling a joke is no different from seeing the same event in the real world, as if any act that degrades a woman or a man is a rape (Jarvie 1985). With no difference between theater and reality, the audience would storm the stage, not just weep in their seats. And porn is theater (as well as secret agit-prop for an erotic proletariat to which even a Rockefeller could belong). Everything but the erection and ejaculation is simulated in porn, and even that display is surrounded by hokum. Though porn might incite to masturbation, the argument that it incites to bodily harm is propaganda; for without pornography, most societies in the world's history have nonetheless promoted rape. If you want to create a raping society, you need more than porn. A smart dictator might better use legitimate movies, theater, television, books, news broadcasts, product advertisements, methods and contents of teaching children, religious vehicles, the political extremities of right or left, kissing blond babies, presidential commissions, and on and on: mobilize for war.

I suspect that most men are incapable of rape. It is one thing to fantasize an act but another to get oneself up to do it. The idea that all men would rape, given the chance, is, I think, a delicious paranoia for some folks (delicious not because they secretly want to be raped but because high righteousness feels so good). We know, nonetheless, that the record of history shows how brutal men can be to women. And porn certainly has elements of those impulses. But porn is such a pathetic mark. And if it is suppressed, do you expect that women will be treated better than they were before porn was cheap and easy?

10. Perhaps women can come to understand (without the need to accept) the strange version of women's erotic desires that male pornographers, reflecting most men—certainly pornographers' male customers—have. I believe that most men, not knowing better, think that women and men are fundamentally the same in what they want, how to get it, how to express it, and how it expresses itself in our bodies.* But, whatever overlap there may be in the bell curves that describe male and female erotic impulses, the two sexes have many differences. This can be seen in heterosexuals but becomes even clearer in homosexuals (Tripp 1975).

The need for orgasm is more peremptory in most males, the need for intimacy in most females: different androgen intensities?† Anatomy is the male's big focus; the psychic is female's. Erotic looking is more powerful and convincing in males, other sense modalities in females. As a result, heterosexual men more seriously fetishize a woman's (and gay men a man's) anatomy, judging the whole personality by, for example, the size and shape of breasts (in the case of male homosexuals, penile size and shape, for example), whereas heterosexual women more seriously look at and palpate a man's (and lesbian women a woman's) personality.

Fetishizing in this way, men mistake how women want to be treated, including how they are to be looked at and palpated. I suspect that many men see women's bodies as having only the external anatomy of femaleness; women's erotic desires, these men think—you can see it in heterosexual pornography for men—are the same as men's (in some depictions, insatiably so): as if real-life females, though crazily unpredictable, are erotically male in the soul. So, for instance, breasts are, sensually speaking, phalluses-on-another-place, and if a woman does not cooperate or is slow to respond, she is teasing, frigid, or snotty, not erotically different. (Women's pornography dreams of the opposite: men who are male women. The tough cowboy-soldier-sheik ends up, by the power of tenderness in a good woman [schoolmarm, nurse, fair-skinned slave], amenable to giving up or forced to give up that withdrawn homosocial irascibility known in myth as masculinity.)

---

*To what extent the different viewpoints are biologically driven and to what extent culturally-psychologically-psychodynamically driven cannot be parceled out yet. Radical feminists say biology plays no part; that strikes me as a poor horse to bet on.

†Maybe if the need for orgasm, once excitement is instilled, were always as driven in females as in males or as bearable in males as in females, the two sexes would understand each other better. Then some of the meaning of porn would be clearer to women, and some of the meaning of Harlequin Romances would be clearer to men.

11. These differences in how each sex perceives the other allow too much room for hostility. Yet, the tension produced—the trace of hostility (sometimes not just a trace)—increases intensity (just as, for too many people, a drop-off of the chance to be hostile yields boredom). In a new relationship, misunderstandings between the sexes may heighten excitement, but when the same issues remain unresolved, they lead to withdrawal: anger, despair, undoing by means of daydreams—for example, turning to pornography—the search for new partners. (In this regard, it is said that porn has improved the erotic lives of many more heterosexual couples than it has driven men to brutal acts.)

At any rate, the problems that energize men's and women's pornography look insoluble to me. Political solutions, such as wiping out pornography or wiping out males, seem utopian.

12. When thinking about pornography, critics should separate two factors in the arithmetic of good and bad: how much is it *in the nature* of pornography to do—not just depict—evil, and how much is evil *coincidental*?

Examples of questions on the first issue are these: How often does pornography, by its power to excite, incite assault? How often, instead, does it soften the hard soul by inducing masturbation? How much does it teach hatred and treachery, and how much does it teach anatomy, amatory behavior, and lighthearted but firm pleasure? Which is more likely to contain the verisimilitude of attack and degradation and thereby promote them: novels and non-X films or porn? Does pornography bring out the natural rapist said to exist in men? Is pornography more conducive to felonious assaults than, say, alcohol, other drugs, gang membership, white supremacy, war, and certain other patriotic terrors?

Examples of the second factor—evil extrinsic to the nature of pornography but generated by it—are the threat of AIDS spreading among performers and the Industry's control at the top by criminals.

13. The above items are mostly about pop politics: interested parties manipulating society, using pornography—an almost defenseless target of opportunity—as if *it* were the place for a showdown between good and evil. (It can be cowardly to be brave about the wrong things.) But, we know, the real world of hatred, not the theater of pornography, should be our concern. Still, in the precise details of erotic life—fantasies and action—I have found a safe way to look at some of the dynamics of rage, useful as long as I do not do as pornhaters do: equate fantasizing with realizing.

Here at the end I turn back to my focus on the power of humiliation, rage, and revenge to shape erotics (Stoller 1975, 1979, 1985a) and its implication that these linked forces—humiliation, rage, and revenge—can poison any human endeavor. And to psychoanalysts' belief that we sometimes get below the surface of behavior and catch glimpses of its invisible structure of desire that can enlarge and modify the ideas of other critics, such as anthropologists, economists, historians, psychologists, and similar philosophers.

With more hope that human behavior will become less malignant if we all get insight—where id was, there shall ego be?—I could enthuse that the search to understand is wonderful, and, piling on one last cliché, to agree: yes, Virginia, there is a Santa Claus.

No such luck. Logic is an idiot's delight.

REFERENCES

Barrett, P. M. 1990. "Multiple Jeopardy? Porn Defendants Face Indictments in Courts Far from Their Bases." *Wall Street Journal,* February 27, 1990, pp. A1, A12.

Bennett, J. W. 1946. "The Interpretation of Pueblo Culture: A Question of Values." *Southwestern Journal of Anthropology* 2:361-374.

Braginski, V. B., Y. I. Vorontsov, and K. S. Thorne. 1981. "Quantum Nondemolition Measurements." *Science* 209:547–558.

Colby, K. M., and R. J. Stoller. 1988. *Cognitive Science and Psychoanalysis.* Hillsdale, N.J.: Analytic Press.

Devereux, G. 1980. *Basic Problems in Ethno-Psychiatry.* Trans. B. M. Gulati and G. Devereux. Chicago: University of Chicago Press.

Dworkin, A. 1989. Trading with the Enemy. Programme 2. BBC, March 4, 1989.

Ellis, H. [1910] 1936. *Studies in the Psychology of Sex.* New York: Random House.

Encyclopedia Britannica, 14th ed. 1929. Vol. 3.

Evans-Pritchard, E. E. 1968. *The Nuer.* New York: Oxford University Press.

Herdt, G., and R. J. Stoller. 1990. *Intimate Communications.* New York: Columbia University Press.

Jarvie, I. C. 1985. *Thinking about Society: Theory and Practice.* Boston: Reidel, chap. 25.

Kohon, G. 1987. "Fetishism Revisited." *International Journal of Psycho-analysis* 68:213–228.

Kremer, H., and J. Sprenger. [c. 1487–1489] 1928. *Malleus Maleficarum.* London: Pushkin Press.

La Barre, W. 1978. "The Clinic and the Field." In *The Making of Psychological Anthropology.* Ed. G. D. Spindler. Berkeley: University of California Press, pp. 259–299.

LeVine, R. A. 1973. *Culture, Behavior, and Personality.* Chicago: Aldine, pp. 215–220, 291–293.

Los Angeles Times. Part I, p. 24, July 23, 1987.

Malcolm, J. 1990. *The Journalist and the Murderer*. New York, Alfred A. Knopf.

Malinowski, B. 1929. *The Sexual Life of Savages in North-Western Melanesia*. New York: Harcourt, Brace, and World.

Rainwater, L. 1970. *Behind Ghetto Walls*. Chicago: Aldine.

Stoller, R. J. 1975. *Perversion*. New York: Pantheon.

———. 1979. *Sexual Excitement*. New York: Pantheon.

———. 1985a. *Observing the Erotic Imagination*. New Haven and London: Yale University Press.

———. 1985b. *Presentations of Gender*. New Haven and London: Yale University Press.

———. 1988. "Patients' Responses to Their Own Case Reports." *Journal of the American Psychoanalytic Association* 26:371–391.

Tolstoy, L. n.d. *War and Peace*. Trans. C. Garnett. New York: Modern Library.

Tripp, C. A. 1975. *The Homosexual Matrix*. New York: McGraw-Hill.

Turner, V. 1975. "Symbolic Studies." In *Annual Review of Anthropology*. Ed. B. J. Siegel. Palo Alto, Calif.: Annual Review, pp. 145–161.

———. 1978. "Encounter with Freud: The Making of a Comparative Symbologist." In *The Making of Psychological Anthropology*. Ed. G. D. Spindler. Berkeley: University of California Press, pp. 558–583.

Williams, W. 1987. *Hard Core*. Berkeley: University of California Press.